What the Printer Should Know about Paper

What the Printer Should Know about Paper

Third Edition

by
Lawrence A. Wilson

GATFPress
PITTSBURGH

Printed on Williamsburg 60-lb. Offset from Union Camp

GATF*Press*
Graphic Arts Technical Foundation
200 Deer Run Road
Sewickley, PA 15143-2600
Phone: 412/741-6860
Fax: 412/741-2311
Email: info@gatf.org
Internet: http://www.gatf.org

Orders to:
GATF Orders
P.O. Box 1020
Sewickley, PA 15143-1020
Phone (U.S. and Canada only): 800/662-3916
Phone (all other countries): 412/741-5733
Fax: 412/741-0609
Email: gatforders@abdintl.com

GATF*Press* books are widely used by companies, associations, and schools
for training, marketing, and resale. Quantity discounts are available
by contacting Peter Oresick at 800/910-GATF.

Contents

Publisher's Foreword

The origin of paper can be traced to China in 105 AD, when the eunuch Ts'ai Lun reported its invention to the Emperor Yuan Ch'u. A millennium passed before the secrets of paper-making reached Europe. By the fifteenth century it was common and inexpensive enough to permit the technological breakthrough of Gutenberg: printing with moveable type on paper.

Paper remains the central material of today's printer, and knowledge of paper is essential for efficient, quality printing. The purpose of this book is to provide printers this fundamental information and to enable them to avoid or solve paper problems in the pressroom.

Since 1957 when the first version of this book, written by Robert F. Reed, was published by the Foundation, numerous changes in papers and in printing technologies have occurred. This new edition by Larry Wilson has been completely rewritten and reorganized to reflect these changes.

Please feel free to contact me with comments and suggestions about this book. We will continue to revise it to keep it up-to-date.

Peter M. Oresick
Director, Technical Information and Education Programs
GATF

Preface

As an offset plant manager in the 1960s, I can recall running trials for paper companies that were attempting to correlate paper properties with pressroom performance. Over the years, trials such as these have generated data and information that have led to significant improvements in print quality and pressroom production. Blistering in the web dryer, for example, is no longer a major problem. Misregister due to poor roll shape has been significantly reduced, and the number of impressions between blanket washes has significantly increased.

Experience has convinced me that the printing industry has the knowledge and information necessary for operating productive pressrooms while meeting customer expectations. It remains only for printers to take full advantage of the available resources. *What the Printer Should Know about Paper* is an excellent source of information about paper in the pressroom. Now in its third edition, this book offers guidance for improving pressroom operation and can serve as a source of material for staff and operator training.

In this edition, I have incorporated information based on my own experience in solving pressroom problems and helping papermakers understand the role paper plays in producing a printed job. For example, in the critical area of paper complaints, my experience suggests that most printers do not collect enough evidence or generate appropriate data to support a complaint. In the book's section discussing the printer's role in handling complaints, readers will find procedures for collecting complaint information and data that, if implemented, will improve chances that a complaint will receive a fair and timely response.

This edition of *What the Printer Should Know about Paper* focuses more sharply than past editions on the impact of paper properties on print quality and pressroom production, information that can put printers in a better position to meet customer expectations. With a thorough knowledge of paper, printers can help customers select papers that meet production requirements and deliver the desired printing quality. The book also describes numerous procedures and techniques for reducing waste, increasing production, and meeting quality demands that can help printers achieve a more efficient and competitive operation.

Larry Wilson
Arrowsic, Maine
July 1998

1 Receiving, Storing, and Protecting Paper

Receiving Paper

Before accepting paper shipments, printers should inspect all paper for transit damage. They should also enter all damages and shortages on the carrier's delivery receipt and have the damage acknowledged by the carrier's agent. In addition, the printer should retain a signed copy of the inspection report and inform the paper manufacturer and shipper of any transit damage, such as that caused by improper loading or inadequate packaging.

Before settling a damage complaint, the shipper or papermaker must have supporting evidence that damage occurred during shipment, not after being received by the printer. Photographs showing the conditions of paper before and after unloading are therefore helpful in substantiating damage claims and in reporting the damage. To be certain that photos of the damage are taken before the paper is moved, the Graphic Arts Technical Foundation (GATF) recommends that an instant-photography camera be used.

Before the paper is placed in storage, all damaged wrapping should be repaired, taped, or, if necessary, replaced. In addition, broken skid bands should be replaced to maintain compactness and protect the paper.

Handling and Storing

Handlers should use proper procedures to minimize damage to rolls, skids, and cartons during unloading and storage. Rolls are particularly susceptible to costly handling damage. Bumping, tipping, or dropping a roll only a few inches can flatten it or cause it to become starred or bruised at its edges.

The floors on which rolls are stored and moved about should be clean and free of sharp objects like nails, stones, and splintered wood. Rolling paper rolls over rough floors or sharp objects can damage the outside layers. Resting the end

Rolls should never be rolled over floors that are rough or strewn with debris.

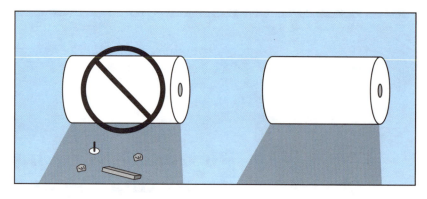

of a roll on sharp objects or protruding surfaces can cause even greater harm.

Nicks, gouges, and other results of improper roll handling may render large portions of the roll unusable. Correcting this damage may require the removal of large slabs of paper. Since the weight of paper in a roll varies as the square of its diameter, reduction of its full diameter represents maximum

Forklift truck equipment with a roll clamp that has a split arm, allowing the operator to handle rolls of different diameters simultaneously. *Courtesy Cascade Corporation.*

weight loss. A 1-in. (25-mm) thickness removed from a 40-in. (1,000-mm) roll represents close to a 10% weight loss. To calculate the weight loss of a roll for any given diameter and slab thickness, see "Paper Computation Formulas" in the appendix.

Since moving paper to locate specific items increases the likelihood of handling damage, paper should be warehoused and stored in a manner that minimizes its movement and handling. A good roll storage system provides for inventory rotation to insure that paper is used in the order in which it is received. This type of inventory system also prevents the accumulation of old paper stock.

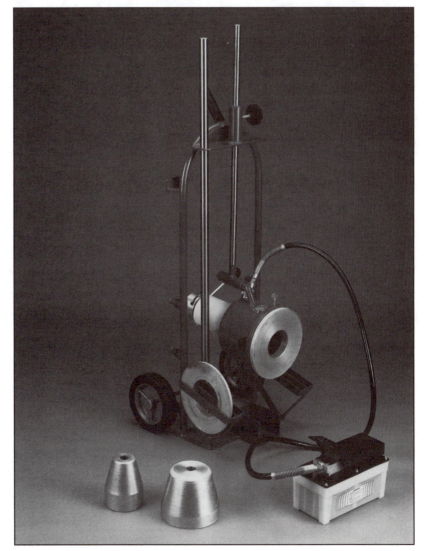

The Nim-Cor portable roll restorer is designed to salvage crushed rolls. It has a tapered expander head that is pulled through the crushed core by a hydraulic ram, thereby restoring the core to its original roundness. *Courtesy of Nim-Cor, Inc.*

To avoid flattening or starring the rolls, printers should take measures to avoid excessive roll clamp pressure. GATF recommends that clamps on clamp trucks have 1 in. (25 mm) of rubber vulcanized on them and that the truck be equipped with limit switches to prevent excess squeeze that could crush the core or flatten the roll. If a core becomes crushed, an inflatable device can be used to expand and straighten the core.

Rolls should be stored on their ends, because rolls stored on their sides will become flat and out of round. If rolls are

Rolls should be stored on their ends. They will become flat if stored on their sides.

Storing rolls of paper on their sides can cause them to become out-of-round.

Paper roll

Floor

stored on their ends in too many tiers, however, the excessive weight can flare the ends of the rolls at the bottom.

Paper should never be stored in direct contact with concrete or damp basement floors because the moisture absorbed from damp floors will distort or otherwise damage the paper. Platforms or racks should be used to keep the paper from contacting damp floors. In addition, paper should never be stored next to cold walls, radiators or other heated objects, or areas subject to sudden and drastic changes in temperature.

Roll-Numbering Systems

Paper manufacturers have created roll-numbering systems that provide detailed information on individual rolls. These roll-numbering systems show the month and day of manufacture, the mill, the mill run number, the paper machine on which the roll was made, the position on the parent roll from which it was taken, and the manufacturing sequence.

Printers who understand and use the manufacturer's roll-numbering system can warehouse rolls more efficiently by storing them according to their origin, time, and sequence of manufacturing. GATF recommends that, if possible, rolls be stored so that all rolls from each position on the papermaking machine, which is indicated on a roll card, are kept together. Using this information, printers can schedule rolls for printing in the sequence of their manufacture and reel position—e.g., all rolls from position one. The greatest variation of paper is across the width of the paper machine. The stresses and moisture content will vary according to the reel position. This variation in moisture and built-in stresses causes the paper to respond differently to press tension. If all the rolls are from the same reel position, however, there will be very little variation between rolls, resulting in a more stable running condition. This increases press running efficiency by minimizing the effect of paper-machine-induced variables. If a sequence of rolls from a particular reel position is causing trouble, that set of rolls can be set aside for later testing and inspection and can be replaced by rolls from another reel position.

Complete information that identifies the roll in accordance with the manufacturer's numbering system normally appears on a core card supplied with each roll. This card may be used for reporting performance and paper defects, allowing the paper manufacturer to take whatever corrective action is required.

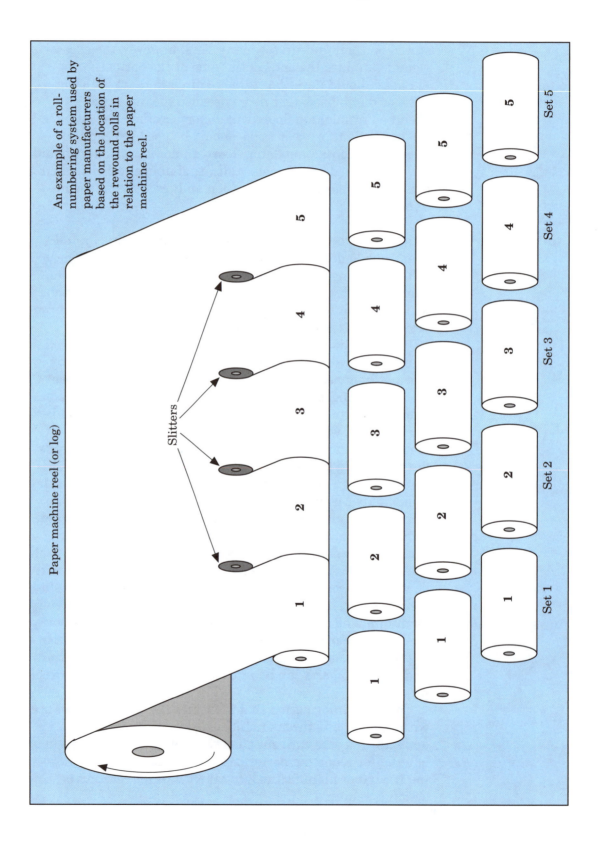

Paper machine reel (or log)

Slitters

An example of a roll-numbering system used by paper manufacturers based on the location of the rewound rolls in relation to the paper machine reel.

Set 1   Set 2   Set 3   Set 4   Set 5

Using a bar code scanner to electronically collect data from a roll label.

Bar Coding and Computers

Bar coding and computers make it possible to track each roll, skid, carton, or pallet of paper from its papermaking origin to finished product. A mill code, preceding the bar code on the label or packaging, identifies the name and specific roll-numbering system of the paper manufacturer. The bar code that follows identifies the manufacturing history of the paper, including the year, month, and date of manufacture. The bar code also includes mill location, paper machine number, machine reel number, and the position across the reel from which the roll originated.

Each unit of paper, when received, is identified and checked in by reading its bar code with a portable, wand-type scanner. This identifying bar code was generated by the mill's computer and logged into an electronic manifest when the shipment left the mill. This manifest contains information describing the paper in each unit and the information that appears on the label. The electronic manifest also provides prompt shipping notices and eliminates the inconveniences and extra clerical work involved when the printed manifest is delayed.

Identifying each unit of paper by its bar code eliminates manual checking, key punch entries of received paper, and the errors associated with these operations. Discrepancies between units of paper received and those indicated in the electronic manifest can be immediately detected. Each unit of paper can be tracked as it is electronically transferred

Bar-coded roll inventory control system
with rolls bar-coded by the mill.
Courtesy emTech Corporation.

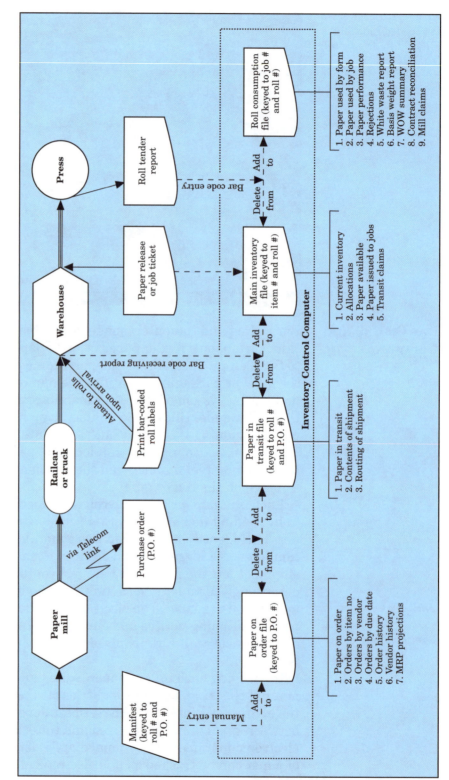

from transport to receiving, inventory, and warehousing. Using bar codes for identification can quickly update paper inventories and track each unit of paper as it progresses to its final state. Bar codes can also be used to tag paper used by a specific shift, job, or press; trace rejected or poorly performing paper to its manufacturing origin; and locate "lost" paper.

Protecting Paper from Moisture

Paper that contains too much or too little moisture may cause press runnability and register problems, as well as difficulty in folding and binding. It is essential, therefore, that paper be protected from the time it leaves the mill until it serves its intended purpose. Paper mills use wrappers and cartons to prevent moisture from entering or leaving the paper. Paper handlers should keep these original wrappers intact until the paper is needed. (See chapters 2 and 8 for additional information on moisture.)

2 Sheetfed Offset Paper Runnability

Paper Grain

Paper grain, a function of fiber orientation and drying stresses, runs in the direction that paper travels through the paper machine. Papermakers refer to fiber orientation as being either in the **machine direction** (grain direction) or **cross-machine direction.** Printers, on the other hand, refer to grain direction as being **grain-short** (or cross grain) and **grain-long** (or with the grain). Paper is referred to as being grain-long if the grain runs parallel to the press cylinders. This usually means the grain runs in the long dimensional direction of the paper. For example, grain that runs parallel to the 38-in. (965-mm) dimension of a 25×38-in. (635×965-mm) sheet would be grain-long. It would be grain-short paper if the grain ran in the 25-in. (635-mm), or short, direction.

On a papermaking machine the fibers are aligned with the direction that the machine travels. Hence papermakers refer to the fiber orientation, or grain, as being in the machine direction.

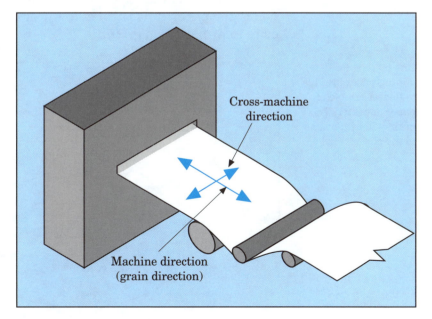

Cross-machine direction

Machine direction (grain direction)

Printers refer to paper
grain as being long if
it runs parallel with
the face of the printing
cylinders.

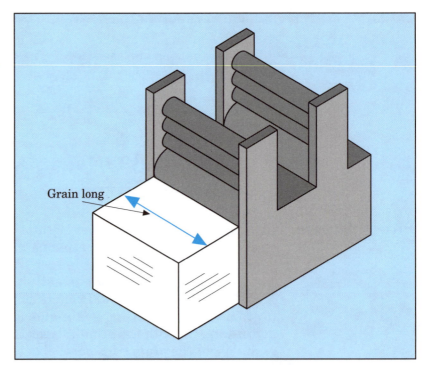

One way to determine the grain direction of paper is to
gently place a piece of paper on the surface of water (it is
important to keep the top side of the paper dry). As the paper
floats on the water, the side in contact with the water will
begin to wet and the paper will start to curl. The grain direction of the paper runs parallel to the curl. (See chapter 8 for
more information on grain.)

One method for deter-
mining paper grain is
to float a sample of
paper on water. The
grain will be parallel
to the curl.

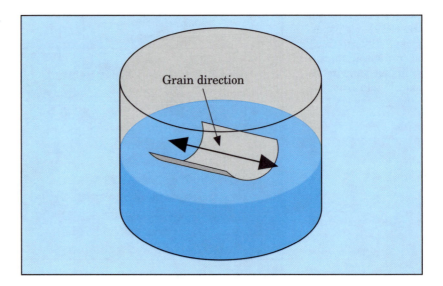

Effect of Humidity and Temperature on Paper

The ability of paper fibers to easily gain or lose moisture can result in runnability and register problems and has the greatest impact on sheetfed papers. Printers therefore should know how moisture behaves and how to measure and control it.

Moisture is always present in the atmosphere and is usually referred to as water vapor or humidity. **Absolute humidity** is the total weight of water contained in a given volume of air. It is expressed as pounds of water per pound of dry air. The atmosphere is said to be saturated when its air contains the maximum amount of water it can hold. When

Effect that a change in temperature has on relative humidity when absolute humidity remains constant.

Temperature		Relative Humidity
100°F	38°C	24%
95	35	28
90	32	32
85	29	38
80	27	45
75	24	52
70	21	62
65	18	74
60	16	88
56	13	100

Example: A pressroom environment is maintained at 45% RH and 80°F (27°C). At the end of the day, the air conditioning and heat are turned off and the room is closed. The next morning the pressroom temperature is 65°F (18°C). The total amount of moisture vapor in the air remains the same, but the relative humidity has risen to 74%. This increase in relative humidity would have caused any exposed paper to develop wavy edges.

saturated air is cooled, its capacity to hold water vapor is decreased, forcing some of the water to condense or change back into a liquid. Likewise, when air temperature is raised, its capacity to hold moisture is increased. The temperature at which air becomes saturated is referred to as its **dew point**. The ratio between what moisture the air has and the amount it could contain is called its relative humidity (RH). **Relative humidity** is the ratio of the quantity of vapor present in the air to the maximum amount the air could hold at a given temperature. When the relative humidity is 50%, the air contains only 50% of the moisture it could contain at that specific temperature.

Paper reaches what is referred to as **equilibrium relative humidity** when its moisture is in balance with the relative humidity of the air. When paper reaches equilibrium relative humidity, it will neither gain nor lose moisture. To accurately measure the equilibrium relative humidity of paper at a specified temperature, the printer should precisely perform the following test, which is conducted by measuring the relative humidity and temperature immediately surrounding sheets of paper while excluding the influence of the external atmosphere. For skids or stacks of paper, insert a probe or sword-shaped blade between sheets so that its humidity- and temperature-sensing elements are isolated from the external atmosphere and will measure just the atmosphere surrounding the paper. To measure relative humidity and temperature of roll paper, cut through four or five layers of paper with a sharp blade extending 7–10 in. (178–254 mm) inward from one roll edge. Lay the probe flat against the exposed paper and quickly cover it by taping the outer layers back into place.

Humidity, or water vapor, in the air can be measured with such instruments as hygrometers or sling psychrometers. Mechanical **hygrometers** use hair, nylon, paper, or membranes whose dimensions change when exposed to different humidities. Because mechanical hygrometers are dependent on these types of materials, they are not very sensitive or accurate. A **sling psychrometer** uses wet- and dry-bulb thermometers, and tables, to measure relative humidity. A properly used sling psychrometer gives accurate readings.

The Rotronic PS1 sword probe, which measures temperature and relative humidity when inserted into a stack or roll of paper. *Courtesy Rotronic Instrument Corp.*

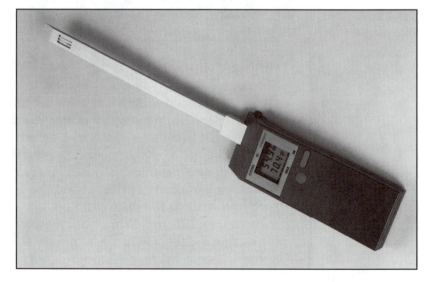

Without careful maintenance and the use of proper procedures, however, wet- and dry-bulb psychrometers can give misleading results.

At 50% relative humidity and 75°F (24°C), a 1,000-lb. (450-kg) load of sheets will contain as much as 8.4 gal. (31.8 l) of water, depending upon the composition of the paper.

At 10% relative humidity and 75°F (24°C), a 1,000-lb. (450-kg) load of sheets will contain only 3.6 gal. (13.6 l) of water.

Electronic hygrometers, because of their high sensitivity, accuracy, and dependability, are widely used for indicating and recording relative humidity and temperature, making them highly desirable for pressrooms. An accurate electronic hygrometer is especially useful in recording atmospheric changes and performance of air-conditioning equipment. Its dependable data can also be used to diagnose moisture-related paper problems.

Because paper has its best dimensional stability in the range of 35–50% RH, good sheetfed printing is best accomplished with a pressroom temperature of 70–85°F (21–29°C) and an RH between 35% and 50%. An RH in the 40–45% range has been found optimum for many sheetfed offset plants. Paper that is in relative balance with the atmosphere will usually remain stable throughout the printing operation.

Paper not in balance with the surrounding atmosphere should be kept in a moisture-barrier wrapper at all times. Pressrooms that are kept at an RH of 40–50% and a temperature of 70–85°F are more conducive to inks that dry by oxidation and polymerization because such inks dry faster at higher temperatures and a lower RH. (See chapter 8 for additional technical discussion about the effects of moisture on paper. TAPPI Official Test Method T 502 also gives the detailed individual steps for measuring the relative humidity and temperature for both sheet and roll paper.)

Temperature-Conditioning Paper

Cold paper brought into a warm pressroom cools the surrounding air and changes the relative humidity of that air. For example, a paper at 56°F (13°C) brought into a press room with a temperature of 75°F (24°C) changes the relative humidity of the surrounding air from 52% to 100%. This change in relative humidity causes the surrounding air to become saturated, resulting in condensation. If the paper is unwrapped and unprotected it will become damp and the condensation will cause wavy edges that cannot be removed completely by ordinary paper conditioning methods. Keeping the cold paper wrapped until it reaches the pressroom temperature will prevent condensation.

A reverse situation occurs when warmer paper is brought into a cooler pressroom. The higher paper temperature warms the surrounding air and lowers its relative humidity. Instead of moisture condensing on the edges and surface of the paper, moisture moves from the paper into the surrounding air. This loss of moisture causes the paper to shrink, which, in turn, creates tight edges. Tight edges, however, are more easily removed than wavy edges.

Paper with a temperature that is warmer or cooler than the pressroom should be given time to reach pressroom temperature. The length of time required to **temperature-condition** paper depends on the difference between paper and pressroom temperature and the size or volume of the skid, roll, or carton. The following chart indicates the time required for various volumes and temperature differentials between paper and pressroom. The time required for paper to become conditioned to pressroom temperature can be read from the chart when the following information is known: the difference in paper and pressroom temperature and the volume of the paper. To find the approximate temperature of paper on skids or in cartons, make a small hole in the wrapper and insert a steel-jacketed thermometer into the pile. Read the temperature after it becomes constant, remove the thermometer, and seal the hole with tape. For rolls, place the thermometer between the wrapper and roll end, since it is not possible to insert it between roll layers without damaging the paper. The volume of skids, cartons, and rolls of paper can be determined using the equations shown below.

The equation at the right can be used to determine the volume of paper in a skid or carton.

Skid or Carton Volume

$$\text{Volume (ft.}^3\text{)} = \frac{\text{Length} \times \text{Width} \times \text{Height (in inches)}}{1{,}728}$$

$$\text{Volume (m}^3\text{)} = \frac{\text{Length} \times \text{Width} \times \text{Height (in centimeters)}}{1{,}000{,}000}$$

The equation at the right can be used to determine the volume of paper in a roll.

Roll Volume

$$\text{Volume (ft.}^3\text{)} = \frac{\text{Diameter} \times \text{Diameter} \times \text{Length (in inches)}}{2{,}200}$$

$$\text{Volume (m}^3\text{)} = \frac{\text{Diameter} \times \text{Diameter} \times \text{Length (in centimeters)}}{1{,}273{,}326}$$

Example: A 48-in.-high (1,220-mm) skid of 25×38-in. (635×965-mm) paper is at 45°F, and the pressroom temperature is 75°F. The first step is to determine the volume of paper on the skid:

$$\text{Cubic Feet} = \frac{25 \text{ in.} \times 38 \text{ in.} \times 48 \text{ in.}}{1,728} = 26 \text{ ft.}^3$$

$$\text{Cubic Meters} = \frac{63.5 \text{ cm} \times 96.5 \text{ cm} \times 121.9 \text{ cm}}{1,000,000} = 0.75 \text{ m}^3$$

The temperature difference between the paper and the pressroom is:

$$75° - 45° = 30°F$$
$$24° - 7° = 17°C$$

To find the required time for temperature-conditioning, locate 30°F on the baseline of the chart for American units (17°C on the chart for metric units) and follow the vertical line to the curve for the volume closest to 26 ft.^{3} (0.75 m^3), and then follow the horizontal line to the time axis on the left. For this example, the minimum time for temperature-conditioning before unwrapping the skid is 35 hr. Printers

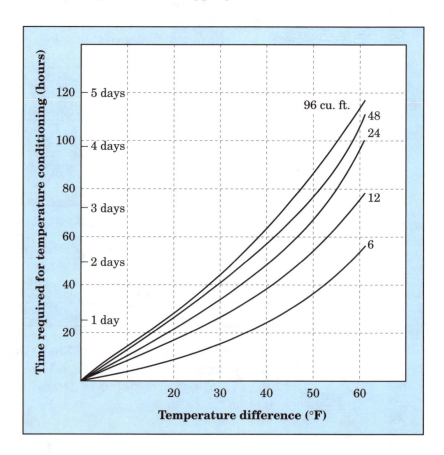

A temperature-conditioning chart for paper, expressed in United States units.

A temperature-conditioning chart for paper, expressed in metric units.

unable to store paper in a heated warehouse should set aside space in the pressroom for temperature-conditioning. Paper should be ordered far enough in advance to allow it to be temperature-conditioned.

To minimize edge distortion and problems in the bindery due to changes in moisture, printed loads should be rewrapped immediately after each pass through the press and after printing. Sometimes it is necessary to run smaller loads and rewrap them immediately after printing. Between printings, reusable plastic moisture-proof covers that fit tightly around printed loads can provide convenient and excellent protection

Rewrap paper with plastic skid covers immediately after each printing pass to reduce edge distortion and bindery problems.

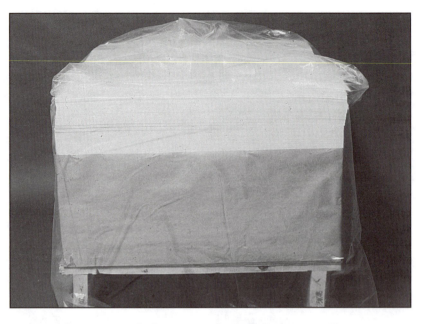

against dimensional change and edge distortion. Paper should not be cut any further in advance of going to press than necessary and should be protected with moisture-proof wrapping immediately after cutting. Skids opened for make-ready paper, as well as leftover paper, should be promptly rewrapped before being returned to storage.

Pressroom relative humidity should be maintained between 35–50% because most paper made in the United States and Canada is manufactured within this range. For high-quality, close-register printing requiring more than one pass through the press per side, the relative humidity of paper should be 5–8% above the pressroom relative humidity. Paper at this somewhat higher RH will lose moisture to the pressroom atmosphere at about the same rate that it picks up moisture from the press. This tends to minimize moisture change during successive printings and makes it possible to hold tighter register from one pass to the next. In order to maintain the proper balance between paper and pressroom relative humidity, paper should have an RH of 45±5%, and the press-room should be maintained at 40±5%. Check the paper RH to determine if and to what extent it is out of balance with the pressroom's relative humidity. This check is necessary to judge whether the paper will meet register requirements for the job and to determine the manner in which it will be printed.

Fewer register and paper edge problems will occur because of differences in the paper and pressroom RH if the job is printed on a multicolor press that requires only one pass per side. Jobs that require multiple passes through a press may have register problems if the difference in paper and pressroom RH is too great. Several alternatives exist for maintaining register under the above conditions.

- Avoid delays, such as holidays or weekends, between successive printings.
- Postpone printing until a weather change brings the pressroom RH more closely in balance with that of the paper.
- If the pressroom RH is too high, turn on heat up to a reasonable level to raise pressroom temperature and lower the RH.
- If the pressroom RH is too low, add moisture by introducing steam or using humidifiers. Close all pressroom entrances to prevent loss of added moisture and reduce pressroom temperature to a reasonable level.
- Press-condition the paper so that it will be in closer balance with the pressroom RH. One way to do this is to run the sheets slowly through a press, without printing, and rewrap the paper immediately afterward.
- If the sheets have developed wavy edges, install strip heaters or banks of infrared lamps above the feedboard.

The decision to print paper that is not in balance with pressroom RH should be based on the following factors:

- Sheet size: the larger the sheet, the worse the misregister for a given percentage of moisture change.
- Number of printing passes through the press: the more printings there are, the greater will be the accumulated expansion or contraction, depending on whether the pressroom relative humidity is higher or lower than that of the paper.

Paper that is sheeted in-plant, as well as paper that is cut in-line, should be protected from atmospheric exposure by moisture-barrier wrappers or plastic covers.

Pressroom Air Conditioning

Pressrooms and paper storage areas should have air conditioners that can maintain both relative humidity and temperature close to desired values. The air-conditioning system must heat and humidify the atmosphere during cold months and cool and dehumidify the atmosphere during the warm months. Printers should also provide for good ventilation, filtration, and uniform air circulation throughout the air-conditioned space.

Air conditioning, by maintaining a set temperature and RH, reduces the amount of moisture that the paper exchanges with the atmosphere. This magnitude of moisture exchange can be illustrated by the following example. Assume that a 2,000-lb. (909-kg) skid of paper with a moisture content of 6% is in balance with a 50% relative humidity atmosphere. Taking into account that for every 10% reduction in equilibrium relative humidity there is a 1% loss in moisture, this skid, when conditioned to an atmosphere of 10%, will lose 4% of its moisture. The total moisture loss to the atmosphere will be 0.04 × 2,000, or 80 lb. (9.6 gal.) of water (0.04 × 909, or 36.4 kg [36.4 l]).

Rapid changes in air temperature can cause problems even if RH remains constant. Because paper in piles changes temperature very slowly, it remains cool with a rapid rise in air temperature. This creates a situation where cooler paper is surrounded by warmer air. The warmer air, containing more moisture, will cause the paper edges to absorb moisture and become wavy.

The following example illustrates why constant temperature as well as constant RH is important for exposed paper. At the beginning of a shift, skids of paper are in equilibrium with a pressroom atmosphere of 45% RH at 75°F (24°C). Halfway through the shift the pressroom temperature rises to 85°F (29°C), with the paper temperature rising only to 77°F (25°C). The humidifier must add moisture to the warmer air to maintain a 45% relative humidity. Psychrometric tables show that when the pressroom air of 85°F with 45% RH is cooled to 77°F by the paper, the relative humidity next to the paper's edge rises to 59%. Moisture absorption from air with 59% RH is enough to make the paper wavy-edged. (The subject of paper performance and relative humidity is also discussed in GATF SecondSight 11, *Changes in Temperature and Relative Humidity Directly Affect Paper.*)

Air chilling should not be confused with air conditioning. Chilling the air without controlling the humidity will increase the relative humidity of the atmosphere and cause paper problems associated with excessively high relative humidity.

Air-conditioning design must take into account the extreme variations in temperature and humidity in different geographical areas. Without humidity control, the relative humidity will be 10% or lower when the outdoor temperature is below 0°F (−18°C) and the inside temperature is 70–80°F (21–27°C). When the outside temperature is around 100°F (38°C), the relative humidity in a building that has a temperature of 70–80°F will be 90% or more.

While 40–45% RH is desirable, weather extremes, building construction, and the cost of air conditioning may require that relative humidity be maintained close to 50% in summer and close to 40% in winter. This change from one level of humidity to another in adjustment to the seasons must be made gradually, over a period of one or two months. In southern regions where the temperature range is not as great and the average relative humidity is higher, economy may dictate a relative humidity of 55% or higher. Any increase over 50%, however, means sacrificing some dimensional stability of the paper and drying properties of ink. Moreover, at this higher range, paper manufacturers may not be able to supply paper that will be in balance.

The cost and efficiency of air conditioning depends to a great extent upon the type of building. Older buildings having no insulation, many windows, open doorways, elevators, and sawtooth roofs with skylights are difficult to air-condition. Humidifying such buildings in winter results in moisture condensation on ceilings, sidewalls, and windows. It also may be impossible to maintain constant temperature and humidity in all areas. For these reasons, many printers have been able to justify the cost of air-conditioning only in connection with the building of new plants. New air-conditioning design includes efficient roof and sidewall insulation and a minimum number of windows, which are double-glass and condensation-proof. For maximum air-conditioning efficiency, some buildings are designed with no windows. Generally, air-conditioning equipment for printing plants must perform the following:
- Supply heat during cold weather
- Add moisture (humidify) when the RH is low
- Remove heat during hot weather
- Remove moisture (dehumidify) when the RH is high
- Provide adequate air circulation
- Provide adequate ventilation and fresh air intake
- Provide air cleaning to reduce dust and lint

Various types of humidifiers add moisture to the atmosphere by using steam jets or water sprays. These are used primarily

Effect of changing relative humidity at constant temperature on amount of moisture in paper, and new relative humidity when outdoor air of specified relative humidity and temperature is heated to an indoor temperature of 72°F (22°C) without the addition of moisture.

Example: Outdoor air having 70% RH and 10°F (−12°C) temperature has only 6% RH after being heated to 72°F.

Outdoor relative humidity

	2%	3%	4%	6%	7%	9%	11%	14%	17%	21%	26%	31%	38%	46%
100%	2	3	4	6	7	9	11	14	17	21	26	31	38	46
95	2	3	4	5	7	8	10	13	16	20	24	30	36	44
90	2	2	4	5	6	8	10	12	15	19	23	28	34	41
85	2	2	4	5	6	8	9	12	15	18	22	27	32	39
80	2	2	4	5	6	7	9	11	14	17	20	25	30	37
75	1	2	3	4	5	7	8	10	13	16	19	23	28	36
70	1	2	3	4	5	6	8	10	12	15	18	22	26	32
65	1	2	3	4	5	6	7	8	11	14	17	20	25	30
60	1	2	3	3	4	5	7	8	10	13	15	19	23	28
55	1	1	2	3	4	5	6	8	9	12	14	17	21	25
50	1	1	2	3	4	4	6	7	9	10	13	16	19	23
45	1	1	2	3	3	4	5	6	8	9	12	14	17	21
40	1	1	2	2	3	4	4	6	7	8	10	12	15	18
35	1	1	2	2	3	3	4	5	6	7	9	11	13	16
30	1	1	1	2	2	3	3	4	5	6	8	9	11	14
25	1	1	1	1	2	2	3	3	4	5	6	8	10	12
20	+	1	1	1	1	2	2	3	3	4	5	6	8	10
15	+	+	1	1	1	1	2	2	3	3	4	5	6	7
10	+	+	+	1	1	1	1	1	2	2	3	3	4	5
5	+	+	+	+	+	+	1	1	1	1	1	1	2	2
0	0	0	0	0	0	0	0	0	0	0	0	0	0	0
°F	−20	−10	−5	0	+5	+10	+15	+20	+25	+30	+35	+40	+45	+50
°C	−29	−23	−21	−18	−15	−12	−9	−7	−4	−1	+2	+4	+7	+10

in plants that are not air-conditioned and to increase the RH during winter. Dehumidification requires air-conditioning equipment and is accomplished by cooling air to its dew point to extract moisture. For example, when a relative humidity of 45% at 80°F (27°C) is maintained, the dew point is 50°F (10°C). This condition requires either a plentiful supply of water at 45°F (7°C) or colder, or artificial refrigeration. Air-conditioning systems heat, cool, humidify, or dehumidify the air, as needed, and usually represent a good investment for the sheetfed printer.

Feeding

Paper Curl

A significant cause of poor feeding and delivery is paper curl. A sheet will curl if one side gains or loses more moisture than the other side. This difference in moisture pickup or loss is caused by differences in fiber orientation and sheet structure. Curl that is close to the core is called **roll-set,** wrap, or reel curl and can be easily identified since it always occurs across the grain and to the side facing the core. This type of curl may not show in every sheet; rather it tends to show at intervals in the pile. Roll-set causes curled edges to catch on the guides and trip the press. The only remedy is to sort the curled sheets from the pile or replace the paper.

Curl that is close to the core is called roll-set, wrap, or reel curl.

Another type of curl, known as **permanent curl,** is caused by the application of press moisture and can be severe enough to prevent proper delivery and jogging of the printed sheets. It is usually more pronounced in thinner and denser papers. Very tightly formed, highly refined papers like high-grade bonds and ledgers also exhibit this type of curl. The paper immediately reacts to moisture by curling away from its moistened and printed side. As the printed sheet dries out, however, its moistened side shrinks and produces a permanent curl toward the printed side.

Curl is not normally encountered when paper is printed on both sides. The permanent curl, discussed above, however, can seriously affect the application of products printed on one side, such as labels and box wraps, calendar pads, calendars, and letterheads. Press sheets printed on one side can be checked for this type of curl by cutting them to the size at which they ultimately will be used because the tendency to curl, if it exists, will be more evident as paper is cut to a smaller size. Curl can be reduced or even counteracted by passing the press sheets that have been printed on one side through the press again, and applying moisture with a blank plate to the unprinted side. Curl that results from printing on one side only can be minimized or even avoided by using the least possible amount of water on the press. This procedure works especially well with lightweight papers having light ink coverage.

Downward curl is less troublesome in most cases than upward curl. For first-side printing, it is usually preferable to have the curl, if it exists, downward. As the paper is printed and moistened, the sheet will follow its inherent tendency to curl permanently toward its moistened side. This moistening tends to bring the sheet closer to flatness. In certain cases, printed one-side curl can be eliminated only by having the papermaker deliberately make paper with a downward curl. Obviously, this requires close cooperation between the printer and the papermaker and an order large enough for a special run. It should be noted that there are decurling devices that can be very helpful in minimizing or eliminating curl.

Sheet Distortions and Defects

Sheet distortions such as buckles, puckers, holes, wrinkles, ridges, and welts interfere with press runnability. Scrap, torn sheets, turned-over corners, and sheets stuck together within the load are press stoppers and can cause blanket damage. Feeding problems that occur when the suction mechanism picks up more than one sheet are usually caused by edges that are blocked or crimped together by dull knives, edges that have been wetted, and high-porosity paper. If any of these problems are present when the paper is opened, the papermaker or merchant should be asked to replace it.

Static Electricity

During printing, static electricity may interfere with the sheet pickup and forwarding mechanism of the feeder and prevent sheets from advancing in proper alignment. This, in turn, jams and trips the press, causing variations in positioning at the grippers and side guide. After printing, static electricity can cause poor jogging, ink smearing, and sheet damage. It can also create problems in the bindery and other converting operations.

The basic cause of static electricity is a lack of moisture needed for static dissipation. If the moisture content of paper is in equilibrium with a relative humidity of about 35% or more, it will dissipate its static charges and prevent charge buildup. It is not surprising that problems resulting from the high buildup of static charges can become acute when a low relative humidity prevails in unhumidified pressrooms during extremely cold weather. The most effective means of preventing static electricity is to maintain a relative humidity in the 40–50% range.

Reducing the friction between paper and parts of the press also helps to minimize static generation. Silicone, antistatic sprays, and special tapes can be applied to reduce friction and increase slip at static-generating locations such as feed tables and hold-down rollers.

Static eliminators, or neutralizers, which use radioactive isotopes or a high-voltage corona discharge to ionize the surrounding air and enable it to conduct charges from the paper, are helpful. These devices may have to be located at various points throughout the press in order to neutralize static that is generated between the paper and press components. All printing presses, along with folding and converting equipment, should be properly grounded to help dissipate static.

Delivery

The printed sheet, after being delivered to the feeder, can experience ink chalking, ink setoff, blocking, poor drying, reduced ink gloss, and ghosting. Some of the causes are paper and fountain solution acidity, ink formulation, oxygen starvation, and static electricity.

Ink Chalking

Ink chalking is a condition where the ink can easily be rubbed off after it has set. This condition usually occurs with coated papers. For many years, chalking was assumed to be caused by excessive absorption of the ink vehicle by the paper coating, which left the pigment without sufficient binder. Since chalking is most prevalent with conventional inks that dry by absorption, oxidation, and polymerization, printers thought that any delay in oxidation and polymerization allowed ink pigment to be robbed of its binder through absorption into the paper coating. Such delay could be caused by several factors, such as too little drier, high humidity, excessive dampening solution, paper with a high moisture content, paper coating with a low pH value, or too much acid in the fountain water.

GATF research has shown that chalking is a paper and ink problem that can develop when the ink is not properly formulated for the paper. Chalking is simply retarded drying, caused by the inactivation of the ink drier. After testing several inks and coated papers, GATF found that, in every case, the ink eventually stopped chalking. Even in cases where chalking persisted for several days to several weeks, all of the samples eventually dried and stopped chalking. For samples that were still chalking after several days or weeks, the application of a little drying stimulator solved the problem.

To avoid chalking of inks, the following precautions are recommended:
• Be sure to select an ink that is suited for the paper.
• Be sure there is enough drier in the ink.
• Avoid adding nondrying compounds to the ink.
• Run as little fountain solution as possible.
• Use a minimum of fountain etch (the pH should be 4.5 or higher).
• Avoid printing a thin film of ink.
• Maintain a reasonable level of relative humidity (not too high) in the plant.

If a job has been printed and the ink chalks, trying these remedies on the following day may help:
• Wind the sheets a couple of times. If the trouble is not too serious, chalking may stop in a day or two.
• Overprint the sheets with a transparent size containing drier.
• Run the sheets through the press using a blank plate and apply a solution of drying stimulator via the dampening system.

Ink Setoff and Blocking

Ink setoff (sometimes called "offsetting") refers to the transfer of wet ink from the surface of a freshly printed sheet to the back of the following sheet in the delivery pile. **Blocking** occurs when the sheets become stuck together by wet ink and remain so as the ink dries. Later, upon sheet separation, the surface of the paper is picked, or disrupted. Careful examination may be required to distinguish between blocking in the delivery pile and picking caused by the ink-splitting forces.

Sheetfed offset inks dry in two stages. In the first stage (setting phase), the ink sets within seconds by partial drainage of its solvents into the paper. This drainage causes an increase in the viscosity and pigment packing of the printed ink film, creating an ink film surface that is no longer fluid enough to set off onto other sheets. In the second stage (drying phase), the ink dries by oxidation and polymerization, which gradually solidify and harden the ink vehicle.

Whether a sheet sets off or blocks depends on the absorbency of the paper and the setting rate of the ink. Paper absorbency is a property that is controlled by the papermaker. The absorbency of the paper involves a fine balance between high absorbency, which is desired to prevent setoff and ink blocking, and low absorbency, which is necessary for high ink holdout and gloss. For good runnability and productivity, printers want a highly absorbent paper that quickly sets the ink so presses can run at higher speeds without setoff or blocking in the delivery. For high ink gloss, density, and print contrast, however, a paper with low absorbency is preferred.

Ink setting is a function of both ink and paper. The mechanism for the setting of quickset inks consists of a gel varnish diluted with a low-viscosity oil. When the low-viscosity oil is absorbed by the paper or paper coating, the ink gels, or sets. The drying phase occurs by oxidation and polymerization, which usually takes two or more hours. To ensure uniform drying, paper should be uniformly absorbent from sheet to sheet within a given lot and from lot to lot. Inks can be formulated to set at different rates, and different papers are able to absorb ink oils at different rates. Printers, therefore, should match ink and paper to achieve the best runnability, production, and print quality. If a paper does not set the ink properly another ink can be formulated to correct the situation.

To prevent setoff in the delivery, the ink must set on the paper before the next delivered sheet contacts it. Controlling setoff also requires taking into account the following factors:
- Type of ink used
- Press speed
- Distance between the printing unit and delivery pile
- Rate at which the air cushion between the delivered sheets is squeezed out as pressure builds up on the pile
- Absorbency of the paper
- Type of spray powder used

Lighter-weight paper builds up less pressure in the delivery pile than heavyweight paper or paperboard. Thus, the weight and ink absorbency of the paper have an important influence on setoff and blocking. The best way to assure proper ink setting is to give the inkmaker samples of the paper to be used. In commercial work, this submission of samples may be impractical because of the variety of papers used. In such cases, printers can use inks that can be adjusted with compounds, according to instructions provided by the inkmaker. Any tendency to setoff should be noted at the beginning of a run and as the job is being adjusted for final approval.

Setoff is aggravated by static electricity generated in the paper during printing. It causes the sheets to cling together

An ink film setting on coated paper. Directly after printing *(top),* pigment is still dispersed throughout ink vehicle. Ink sets when the vehicle is absorbed by the coating *(bottom).*

Ink setting is greatly influenced by paper surface absorbency. Because papers vary widely in absorbency, samples should be submitted to the inkmaker in order to insure proper ink setting.

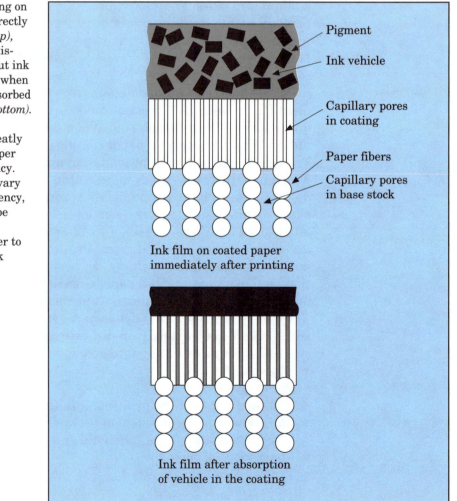

Pigment

Ink vehicle

Capillary pores in coating

Paper fibers

Capillary pores in base stock

Ink film on coated paper immediately after printing

Ink film after absorption of vehicle in the coating

An ink setting on uncoated paper. Directly after printing *(top)*, pigment is still dispersed throughout the vehicle. Ink sets when the vehicle is absorbed by the paper *(left)*.

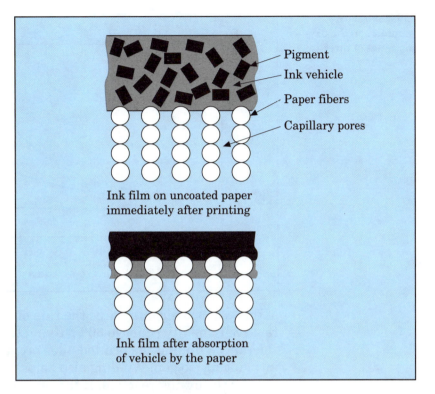

Pigment

Ink vehicle

Paper fibers

Capillary pores

Ink film on uncoated paper immediately after printing

Ink film after absorption of vehicle by the paper

in the delivery pile, quickly squeezing out the air cushion that keeps them temporarily separated. Static electricity becomes a problem when the pressroom's relative humidity falls below 35%. Humidification and static neutralizers on the press help to alleviate static problems. If sheets are to go through the press more than once, however, printers should use an absolute minimum of antisetoff spray. Otherwise, spray particles on previously printed sheets will transfer to the offset blanket and interfere with ink transfer.

Ink Drying

Ink drying occurs while printed sheets are in the pile. Quick-set inks, which are used almost exclusively for sheetfed offset printing, dry by solvent penetration followed by an oxidation and polymerization reaction. Their drying-oil vehicles require oxygen and the right amount of metallic driers for normal drying. Insufficient amounts of drier will slow down drying or even fail to dry the ink. Too much drier may prevent the ink from drying hard enough, causing it to rub off easily. The correct amount of drier, however, does not automatically assure proper drying. The air that is trapped between the sheets and the pores of the paper provides the oxygen needed for the drying process. The relative humidity

Effect of relative humidity on the drying times of three inks.

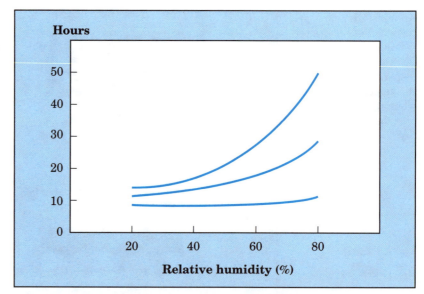

of this trapped air influences the rate of drying. When the relative humidity is above 60%, drying time is increased considerably. Winding the printed piles promotes drying by introducing oxygen. Winding also helps dissipate heat generated by the drying reaction. If the temperature becomes too high, it can cause ink blocking. Ink drying can be retarded by excessive paper moisture and high relative humidity. If the paper's moisture level is high and the paper's surface is very dense, or if there is excessive plate moisture during printing, ink drying can be significantly slowed.

Temperature has a marked effect on the drying rate of the ink, as it does with respect to all chemical reactions. At 75–80°F (24–27°C), drying will occur almost twice as fast as it does at 60–65°F (16–18°C). The best drying conditions exist when the pressroom temperature is 75–80°F and when the paper or paperboard is at pressroom temperature.

The pH of paper and fountain solution greatly affect the drying rate. There are generally no drying problems for uncoated paper with a pH of 4.5 or higher and a relative humidity of 50% or less. Uncoated papers generally have a pH well above 4.5. Some may have a pH close to or slightly above 7.0.

GATF research indicates that:
• Drying becomes very slow when the fountain solution has a pH lower than 3.0, and the pressroom relative humidity rises to 75% or above.

Effect of constant relative humidity (RH) and changing pH on drying time.

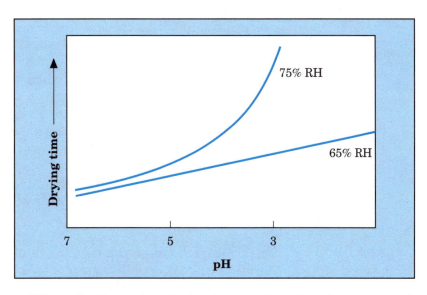

- When the fountain solution is transferred to the paper and evaporates, the pH inside the printed load diminishes and the relative humidity rises.

Running a fountain solution with a pH of 3.5–4.0 and an excessive amount of water on the plates can result in a combination of acidity and moisture that inhibits drying.

For coated papers, the pH of the coating is usually on the alkaline side, i.e., above 6.0, and generally between 7.0 and 8.5. As a rule, the higher the pH of the coating, the faster the ink's drying rate.

When ink-drying problems occur with sheetfed inks, the lithographer can look for one or more of the following causes:
- Insufficient or too much drier in the ink
- Fountain solution that is too acidic (too low a pH)
- Too much water emulsified in the ink
- Excessive moisture in the paper, in the atmosphere, or applied to inks and paper during printing
- Below-normal temperature
- Insufficient access to air and oxygen
- High relative humidity

If the ink's failure to dry is not discovered until the job has been printed, the problem is then how to save the job. If drying is delayed due to oxygen starvation, winding the sheets can supply the needed oxygen and accelerate drying. If the trouble is due to insufficient drier, or the drier being "killed" by acid in the fountain solution, the job may be saved by overprinting it with a transparent size containing a drier or with an overprint varnish.

Whenever possible, inks should be ordered to match the paper to be printed, particularly when a new and different type of paper will be used. Providing a sample of the paper before printing gives the inkmaker an opportunity to formulate inks and match them to the paper for an optimum drying rate. It is also advisable, several days in advance of the press date, to check the rate at which the ink dries on the paper. If modifying the ink is required to improve the drying rate, enough time remains to consult with the inkmaker and to make necessary changes.

Printed Ink Gloss

GATF research has shown that the final printed ink gloss of the oil-drying types of lithographic inks is related to the thickness of the ink film, the ink absorbency of paper, ink formulation, and paper gloss. **Dryback** refers to the decrease in the gloss of an ink film during the drying period of sheetfed offset inks. Excessive dryback can result if the ink's drying rate and the capillary absorbency of the paper combine to allow excessive vehicle drainage from the ink film. This excessive drainage can be avoided, or at least minimized, by formulating the ink so that it matches the absorbency of the paper.

Ghosting

Ghosting refers to the appearance of unplanned and undesired images in printing. It should not be confused with ink setoff or printing show-through. The two kinds of ghosting are mechanical and chemical, differentiated by their cause and the manner in which they appear.

Mechanical ghosting, quickly evident during sheet delivery, is caused by form layout, ink starvation, or a swollen or depressed area of an offset blanket resulting from a previous print job. Mechanical ghosting always occurs on the same side of the sheet as the ghosting image.

Chemical ghosting, also known as fuming or gloss ghosting, is a ghost of an image that is printed on the opposite side of the sheet. The print image and the ghosting image are back to back. Much more troublesome than mechanical ghosting, chemical ghosting occurs during the critical drying phases of inks and is not evident until some time after the job is off the press. It occurs with oil-drying inks during sheetfed letterpress or offset printing, but rarely occurs with heatset inks. Chemical ghosting is unpredictable, may occur sporadically, and may appear in some areas of a printed

GATF Mechanical
Ghosting Form show-
ing mechanical
ghosting (simulated).

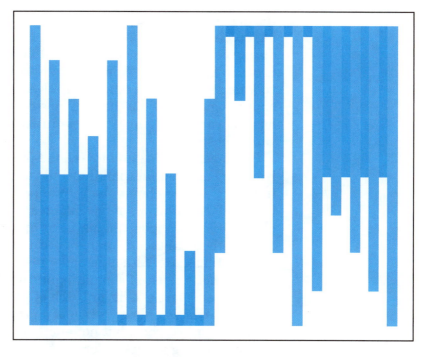

sheet but not in others. The outline of the ghost image will
be a replica of, and appear immediately opposite from,
another image on the other side of the printed sheet.

Chemical ghosts may appear as images having a higher or a
lower gloss than their surrounding printed background. It was
once thought that chemical ghosting was caused by the ink
vehicle penetrating the paper to produce a ghost of the image
on the other side. Research at various laboratories has
disproved this theory. It is now believed that chemical ghosting is due to differentials in ink drying times, which cause an
ink film to dry with varying degrees of gloss. If one area of a
printed image is made to dry faster than other areas, there
will be less vehicle drainage from the ink film into the paper
and a greater amount of vehicle retained to cover the ink pigments in this area. This area will have a higher gloss than the
slower drying area and will appear as a gloss-ink ghost. Con-
versely, if a specific area is made to dry more slowly because of
the retarding influence of another nearby ink also undergoing
drying, it will have a lower gloss than its surrounding, faster-
drying areas and will appear as a dull-ink ghost.

Gloss ghosting on the backup side of the paper is believed
to be caused by gaseous by-products emitted by ink still drying on the first-printed side. The printed images on the front
and back sides face each other for any two adjacent sheets in

the delivery pile. The gaseous emissions act as powerful drying accelerators for the ink on the backup side, especially during certain phases of drying. A dull-ink ghost is believed to occur when the ink from the first-printed side emits volatile products that retard the ink drying of images appearing opposite (on the backup side). Research at GATF has shown that adding large quantities of cobalt drier aggravates ghosting.

Chemical ghosting and its related problems of differential trapping, differential chalking, and yellow-staining result from a critical combination of circumstances in the drying of inks and the influence of one ink on another during drying phases. Chemical ghosting patterns appear more distinctly on smooth, glossy coated papers because of greater reflection and ink film gloss. Although paper may be involved in ghosting, it is not a cause of chemical ghosting. Ghosting often occurs in one part of a lift or batch of printed paper but not in other parts, in only a portion of a printed job, or in one area of the press sheet but not another.

The following suggestions may help to prevent chemical ghosting:
- Print the side having heavier ink coverage first.
- Wait at least a day to back up piles that have been printed on the first side. This additional time permits inks on the first-printed side to dry to a stage where they will have little influence on the drying rate of their backed-up images.
- Wind printed piles more frequently to get air into the drying prints and to dissipate the gaseous by-products of the drying inks.
- Keep loads in their proper sequence for backing-up and printing successive colors.
- Do not expose printed loads to uneven conditions of heat or cold.
- Run smaller lifts.

If chemical ghosting does occur, its undesirable effects can be minimized in the following ways:
- Overprint the job with a gloss or dull varnish to equalize image gloss. Since this often increases the amount of ghosting, try five or more different varnishes on different samples of the ghost overprinting.
- Overprint with the same color as a solid or heavy-toned screen if the ghosting occurs in a printed solid of one color.

Back-Edge Curl and Waffling

Back-edge curl, sometime called tail hook, occurs when a heavy solid area is printed across the back edge of a sheet. Back-edge curl results when the force and angle required to pull the sheet from the blanket exceeds the paper's elastic limits. Printers can reduce this type of curl by using lower tack inks or by creating a saw-toothed edge in the tail edge of the solid and in the trim area. Another way to reduce the risk of tail hook is to lay out the job so that the solid area will be along the lead edge.

Paper following blanket in image area with heavy ink coverage.

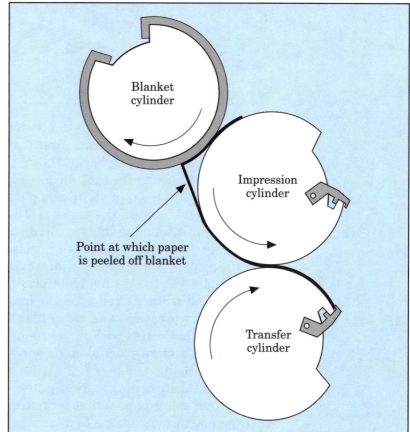

Sheets having solid bands of printed labels from front to back are vulnerable to a condition know as **waffling,** which is most likely to occur with coated papers with lower basis weight (lower grammage). The solid printed bands running from front to back are stretched by the printing separation forces. These printed stretched areas rise above the normal plane of the paper and may cause setoff problems in the delivery. Since these areas are actually stretched (some

A saw-toothed solid placed at the tail edge of the sheet to reduce tail hook.

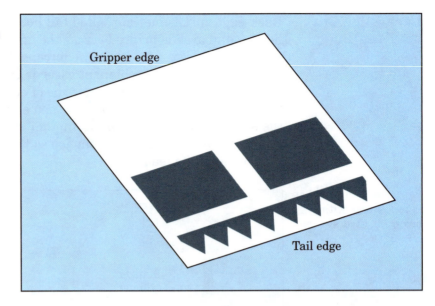

Gripper edge

Tail edge

sheets may be stretched more than others), register is also affected. Printing the wire side first may help to minimize register problems during backup since the wire side can offer greater resistance to the tack forces of the blanket and ink. Printing the paper grain-short would make embossing a lesser problem because the paper is stiffer and has greater resistance to stretching in its grain direction. Running paper short-grain, however, may result in register problems.

Waffling can be avoided or minimized by using a paper with a basis weight (grammage) that provides sufficient strength and stiffness, reducing the ink tack, reducing the back-cylinder pressure, and using blankets that allow easier paper release. Presses with large-diameter blanket cylinders that provide a more gradual angle of release may also alleviate this problem.

Mechanical stretching is most prevalent in thin, soft, light-weight, and softer papers that lack strength and rigidity in their cross-grain direction. To minimize sheet stretching:
• Keep back-cylinder pressure at the minimum for acceptable printing.
• If extensive solids are being printed, reduce the tack of inks as much as possible.
• Use blankets that provide as easy a release as possible to avoid overstretching the paper.
• Avoid positioning large solids on one side or near the back edge of the press sheet, as this can subject the press sheet to uneven tension.

Register

To maintain register, paper must remain flat and retain its dimensions during printing. Moisture imbalance between the paper and the pressroom can change paper dimensions. The moisture content of paper at the time of printing should therefore be in balance with the relative humidity of the pressroom. Since paper may not be flat when received, check for flatness when skids or cartons are opened. Then document any flatness problems, preferably with pictures, and notify the merchant and mill of the paper's condition. Be sure to rewrap the paper in a moisture-vapor barrier so there will be no gain or loss of moisture prior to its inspection by the mill or merchant representative.

Sheet paper for offset printing is almost always specified to run grain-long — the grain will be in the long dimension of the sheets and parallel to the face of the press cylinders. Grain-long paper is specified because offset printing plates and their images can be lengthened or shortened from gripper edge to tail but not from side to side or across the press direction. Running grain-long paper (grain parallel to the face of the blanket cylinder) permits the dimensional change to occur from front to back, where compensation can be made by shifting the cylinder packing from plate to blanket or vice versa. Running grain-short paper (grain perpendicular to the printing nip), however, allows the dimensional expansion to occur from side to side with no way to compensate for the change.

Another advantage of running paper grain-long is the ability to run paper with wavy edges. When wavy edges develop due to moisture absorption at the outer edges of a pile, grain-long paper will cause greater waviness to be in the running, or around-the-cylinder, direction, where it will have a better chance of being ironed out from the gripper to the trailing edge without causing misregister or wrinkling.

Grain-short paper (grain running perpendicular to the printing nip) may be used for black-and-white and single-color printing, for certain bindery considerations (for example, when there is a need to have the fold run parallel to the grain and for feeding lightweight papers where stiffness helps in the feeding of such papers), and when register and wrinkling are not potential problems. Grain-short paper, because it is stiffer and stretches less, is sometimes specified for multicolor work on multicolor presses where there are heavy, printed solids. This added stiffness and reduction in stretch also makes grain-short paper a good choice when printing lightweight papers. In addition, grain-short sheets have less tendency to tail hook, curl, emboss, or waffle during the printing of large solids.

Paper for duplicator presses is usually cut grain-long but printed with grain direction perpendicular to printing cylinders because register is of no consequence in one-color work, and the paper is stiffer and therefore feeds better.

Moisture

A change in moisture content that causes paper to change dimension is unlikely to be a problem for one pass through a multicolor press. Where two or more passes per side are involved, however, dimensional change due to moisture gain or loss between successive printings can be serious. Unlike mechanical stretching, these dimensional changes occur while the sheets are standing in the pile between printings. The following precautions help to minimize this problem for multipass printing:

- Have the paper at a relative humidity slightly higher (about 5%) than the relative humidity of the pressroom.
- Run as little dampening water as possible. Adding alcohol or an alcohol substitute to the fountain solution reduces the amount of water required to keep the plate clean.
- Be certain that the paper is grain-long. Grain-short paper should never be used for color work requiring more than one pass through the press per side. Grain-short paper can sometimes be run on multicolor presses if it is perfectly flat, although this too is a hazardous practice.

Mechanical Stretching

Sidewise misregister, which occurs all along the off-guide edge and in the around-the-cylinder direction, can result from a mechanical stretching of the press sheet. In offset printing, the uniform impression squeeze and separation of paper from the blanket tends to stretch the paper in the direction of its travel. For grain-long paper, the effect is an "ironing out" of the sheet. This effect may be increased when large areas of solids are printed. Press sheets will closely regain their original dimensions as long as the paper is not stretched beyond its elastic limit. If this occurs, however, some of the stretch may be permanent, which can cause a shortening of sheet dimension in the cross-press direction.

Most of the stretch occurs in the first printing unit of a multicolor press. When this happens, succeeding colors will print wider, and it will be difficult to compensate for register. Stretching in the around-the-cylinder, or running, direction

When paper is stretched beyond its elastic limit, the cross-press dimension is shortened causing next-down images to print wide.

Cross-press direction

First image printed

Second image printed

Grippers

will cause colors succeeding the first one to print short. Printers can overcome this problem by packing the plate and blanket to print short on the first unit and longer on subsequent units.

Random Misregister

Random misregister is a situation where colors fail to register on the press sheet on certain subjects while registering on others, and where areas of misregister vary in location on different sheets. It usually occurs when printing heavily embossed papers or papers with a puckered or cockle surface. Although reducing back-cylinder pressure to a minimum may help, such papers often require high back-cylinder pressure in order to have the ink transfer evenly from blanket to paper. The problem can be reduced somewhat by first running the sheets through the press without printing. Close-register work on large sheets of paper with such highly uneven surfaces should not be attempted.

The following are other causes of random misregister:
- Incipient shrunken edges, too slight to be readily observed
- Slippage at the grippers
- Improper packing
- Distorted blankets
- Improper plate mounting
- Excessive back-cylinder pressure
- Sheets that are not square

Sheet-to-Sheet Misregister

Sheet-to-sheet misregister is register that varies in degree from sheet to sheet and is most prevalent with lighter-weight papers. Misregister occurs primarily in the around-the-cylinder direction, but it is worst along the back edges of the sheets. This type of misregister can be caused by an ironing out of the sheet during printing, by differences in sheets due to multiple-roll sheeting, and by lack of sheet flatness. To minimize the problem, printers can run with a minimum of back-cylinder pressure, use a lower-tack blanket, use the lowest tack ink possible, and run the paper through the press without printing (prior to the actual pressrun).

Tight Edges

Moisture loss from a pile of paper causes the paper edges to shrink and leaves the inner area unaffected. This results in a paper with tight edges and a center area that is full and baggy. As a tight-edged sheet passes through the nip of an offset press, the fullness of its center is forced forward and outward, causing the sheet to fan out toward its back edges. After printing, the press sheet returns to its original condition, resulting in the image getting progressively narrower toward the back edge and consequently shorter than the plate image. If a tight-edged condition is severe enough, the ironing out of the fullness of the center of the press sheet will form wrinkles near the center, but not extend to the back edge.

Wavy-edged paper *(left)* and tight-edged paper *(right)*.

Since misregister often can start with the first printing, it is important to measure the print length along the back edge to be sure it is the same as that of the plate image. Printers can use a precision calibrated metal rule — the best instrument for precise measurement and control of register — to compare the distance between the plate register marks and the distance between the same register marks on the printed sheet. The direction of the difference between the lengths of register marks on the plate and paper shows whether the

Tight-edged sheets will cause images to get progressively narrower toward the back edge of the sheet.

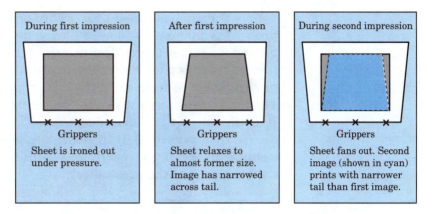

During first impression	After first impression	During second impression
Grippers	Grippers	Grippers
Sheet is ironed out under pressure.	Sheet relaxes to almost former size. Image has narrowed across tail.	Sheet fans out. Second image (shown in cyan) prints with narrower tail than first image.

cause is wavy-edged or tight-edged paper. For tight-edged paper, the distance between the printed register marks will measure less than the distance between the plate register marks. The opposite is true for wavy-edged paper: the distance between the printed register marks will be greater than the distance between the plate register marks.

To help determine if misregister is occurring with the first color down and if register problems can be expected on successive passes or colors, a small number of sheets printed with the first color should immediately be reprinted to see if the two passes of this color fall in register. If the two passes fail to register, appropriate actions should be taken.

In the case of single-color printing on tight-edged paper, wrinkling can sometimes be prevented by cutting the blanket packing along the side edges to relieve the pressure or by trimming off the side edges of the sheets. Tight-edged paper can sometimes be brought to a usable condition by running blank sheets slowly through the press using light impression or by placing the paper in an area of higher relative humidity so that its edges may regain some of the moisture lost to a drier atmosphere. When doing multicolor work or printing that requires two or more passes per side, it is better to replace tight-edged paper, a practice less costly than conditioning the paper to the pressroom atmosphere.

Wavy Edges

When a pile of paper absorbs moisture at its exposed edges, the edges expand and become wavy. The greater degree of waviness for grain-long paper will occur along the short dimension of the paper or parallel to the direction of travel through the press. These edges are referred to as the cross-grain edges.

As a wavy-edged sheet passes through the nip of an offset press, its waviness is ironed out, causing a compression toward its center area. After printing, the sheet moves back toward its edges, which results in a printed image that gets progressively wider toward the back edge of the press sheet. The image fans out and is now longer than the plate image. It is difficult, if not impossible, to compensate for misregister caused by wavy edges. If the waviness is severe enough, its ironing out will produce wrinkles running from the center to the back edge of the press sheet.

Images printed on wavy-edged paper will be wider than the plate image, toward the tail edge of the sheet. It is nearly impossible to compensate for misregister caused by wavy-edged paper.

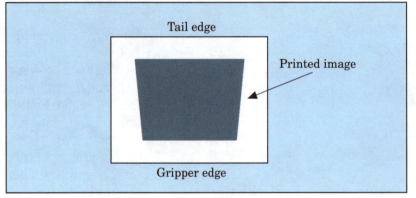

If, as a result of wavy edges, the print is found to be longer than the plate image, one or more of the following steps can be taken to minimize the effect:

- Place the paper in a hot, dry area or use heat lamps or heaters to reduce moisture and waviness at the cross-grain edges.
- Cut notches in the packing along the side edges of the blanket to relieve pressure on the wavy edges of the sheets as they go through the printing nip.
- If possible, take a narrow trim off the paper's side edges.
- Use a bustle wheel to put a slight kink in the gripper edge of the sheets as they feed into the gripper.
- Run blank wavy-edged sheets slowly through the press with a very light impression. This can sometimes return the paper to a usable condition.

Sheet Squareness Normal tolerances for trimmed paper are generally adequate when paper is printed using the same gripper edge. These tolerances, however, may not be tight enough for "work-and-flop" or "work-and-tumble" jobs that use a different gripper edge during back up. Work-and-flop printing requires accurate dimensions and squareness of all corners for back-to-back register. The paper manufacturer should always be advised when paper is to be used for work-and-flop printing and when it is used on perfecting presses, which also flip the paper for reverse-side printing. During makeready for a work-and-flop form, a few sheets should be backed up to check register. If the register is found to vary excessively because of variability in sheet-to-sheet size, the paper should be trimmed before proceeding.

Sheets that are out of square can cause problems during or after printing. With corners, a departure of just a few degrees from 90° can be troublesome. If an out-of-square condition is not discovered until after printing, it can present serious problems in the bindery, in cutting, or in diecutting. Many forms can be run with some variation in sheet size, as long as the sheets are square and the same gripper and side-guide corner are used for all printing and subsequent operations. For this reason, the gripper and side-guide edges are sometimes indicated on skids.

A sheet may be checked for squareness on a printer's layout table or by the following procedure:

1. Turn the sheet over on itself so that its longer dimension will be folded in half.
2. Match two of its corners exactly and staple them together so that they coincide in subsequent steps.
3. Line up the two sides exactly, extending from the stapled corner to the fold line.
4. By using a straightedge or ruler, work the paper back from the stapled corner across the lined-up edges toward and across the fold line.

An out-of-square sheet can cause problems in the bindery, in trimming, or in diecutting. Paper should be checked for an out-of-square condition before printing.

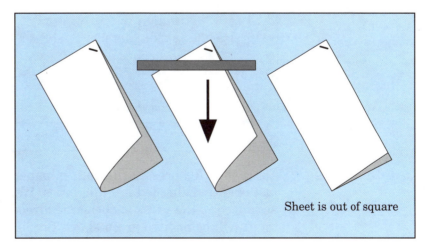

Sheet is out of square

5. Work the straightedge across the sheet to form a sharp fold. Let the two free corners and edges move freely and seek their own position during folding.
6. If the opposite corners and edges do not coincide exactly after folding, the sheet is out of square.

Bowed edges can create problems when the printer is trying to maintain hairline register or print a job that demands hairline cutting tolerances of printed borders, such as a label job. Like out-of-square sheets, bowed edges can cause register problems in binding or diecutting operations. The following steps can be taken to check each of the four edges for bowing:

1. Place two consecutive sheets from the pile on a flat area large enough to accommodate at least the two sheets.
2. Turn the top sheet over along one of its edges in the same manner as turning the page of a book, so that opposite sides of the paper are now facing forward.
3. Bring together the two edges of the sheets along which the turn was made.
4. If they butt together and touch equally throughout their length, there is no bowing.
5. If their corners touch but there is an open space between their middle portions, they have a concave bow.
6. If their middle portions touch but there is an open space at their corners, they have a convex bow.

A bowed edge makes hairline register difficult. Paper should be checked for bowed edges before printing.

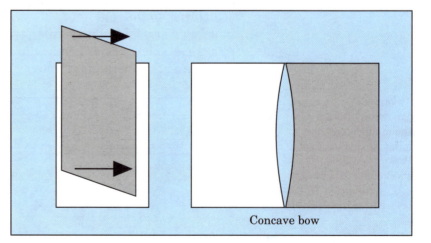

Concave bow

Roll-to-Sheets   Some sheetfed presses run rolls of paper that are sheeted just prior to being fed into the press. If the cut sheet is advanced to the press in the same direction it leaves the cutter, it will be printed grain-short. Because of the problems of printing grain-short paper, roll-to-sheet equipment has been designed with the roll and sheeter at right angles to the movement of paper through the press. The paper is unwound and sheeted at right angles to the press, so that it enters the press as grain-long paper.

Contamination Problems

The complete contact of rubber blanket and paper in offset lithography, along with the inherent tendency of the blanket to lift all loosely bound material from the paper, makes heavier demands on the paper than do other printing processes. The paper's surface must be clean and strongly bonded and must not release any materials that will react unfavorably with the chemistry of the plate, ink, and dampening system.

Paper used for sheetfed offset lithography must have high surface and internal bonding strength to withstand tackier inks. It should also have a degree of moisture resistance to prevent weakening of the paper surface. Excessive water resistance, however, can cause water retained on the surface to interfere with the transfer of ink from the blanket to the paper. Blanket contamination occurs when any type of material becomes attached to the blanket or plate and interferes with print quality. Contamination from paper may be classified as that which produces hickeys or voids in the printed images.

Doughnut and Void Hickeys

A doughnut hickey consists of a small, solid printed area surrounded by a white halo, or nonprinted area. A void hickey is a white, unprinted spot surrounded by printing. Either type can vary in size and configuration, depending upon the material that is producing it. A magnifying glass (preferably a 10×) is needed to analyze hickeys and their sources.

Doughnut hickeys are caused by ink-receptive material adhering to the plate. Void hickeys are caused by water-receptive material adhering to the plate. In this example, a solid particle on the blanket is producing a doughnut hickey on the printed sheet.

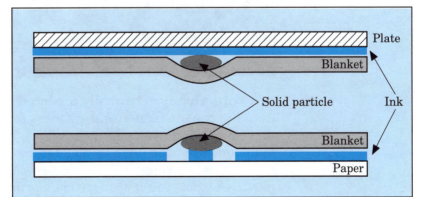

Doughnut hickeys, or ink hickeys, are caused by solid particles that adhere to the plate or blanket and are ink-receptive in the presence of dampening moisture. As a raised surface, they print an image of themselves but prevent their immediate surrounding area from printing. Ink hickeys can usually be identified by their characteristic shape and sharp edges and by the white halo surrounding them. Under a microscope, their edges often appear darker than their center. Sources of doughnut hickeys are ink skin particles, greasy dirt from the press, particles of press rollers that are breaking down, and chips of paint from ceilings. Once ink skin becomes attached to a blanket or plate, it remains there until removed. Ink skin particles come from several sources:

- Dried ink on the ends of press rollers or particles from deteriorating rollers
- Accumulation of ink on press tie bars
- Drying of ink in the press fountain
- Ink skin from the ink can
- Poorly ground ink

Once the skin has become mixed with the ink, there is no way to remove it. Such ink should be discarded. The only remedy for ink-skin hickeys is to wash up the printing unit, including the ink fountain, and start with fresh, clean ink.

A typical ink-skin hickey, enlarged.

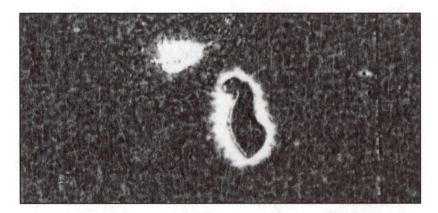

A **void hickey** is normally produced by contamination from the paper that prevents printing from occurring because it is water-receptive and ink-repellent. These hickeys can be found on either the plate or blanket. Paper-oriented contamination rarely accepts ink or produces doughnut hickeys. If a particle accepts ink initially, it may print as a doughnut hickey and then gradually change to a void hickey as it accepts water and refuses the ink. Although paper particles normally accept water and produce void hickeys, coating lumps or scale occasionally may accept ink and produce doughnut hickeys. With repeated dampening these may become water-receptive, refuse to accept ink, and after a number of impressions change from a doughnut hickey to a void hickey. Paper-produced doughnut hickeys are generally less sharply defined than ink hickeys, and their centers have less printing intensity.

Paper cutter and trimmer debris generally produce void hickeys that are elongated and irregular in shape and size, and may have fibrous, fuzzy edges. Paper slitter debris usually creates splinter-shaped voids. Vessel segment picking produces a small void hickey that is usually trapezoidal in shape.

Lint

Lint, also called fuzz or fluff, which comes from loosely bonded surface fibers, can cause fiber buildup in the image areas when it mixes with the ink. A white sliver-shaped void is produced in the inked impression as the fibers absorb water and repel ink. These paper fiber voids should not be confused with voids caused by the longer fibers originating from the fabric covers of dampening system rollers, washup rags, or papermaking felts. These fibers produce voids averaging ⅛ in. (3 mm) or more in length.

A solid printed on linty paper, enlarged.

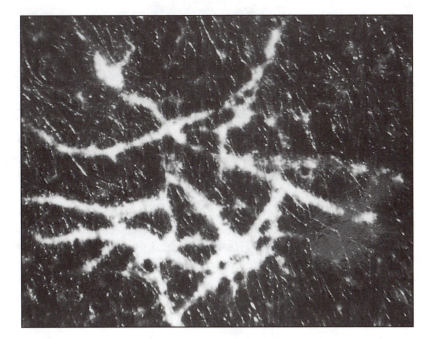

Coating Lumps, Slime Spots, and Foreign Particles

Other sources of paper contamination that normally produce void hickeys include coating particles, coating scale, starch surface-sizing lumps, slime spots, and pickouts of foreign particles. Such particles may change not only their ink- and water-receptivity, but also their shape as they are broken or crushed under the pressure of repeated impressions.

To distinguish between loose paper debris and particles that have picked out of the paper's surface, it is necessary to fan down through the printed load to the sheet where a spot first appeared. If the spot was caused by cutter, slitter, or other loose surface debris, the paper surface will show no damage. If picking or disruption of the paper's surface occurred, the surface will show a rupture or crater where the particle was lifted out.

A pickout on uncoated paper, enlarged.

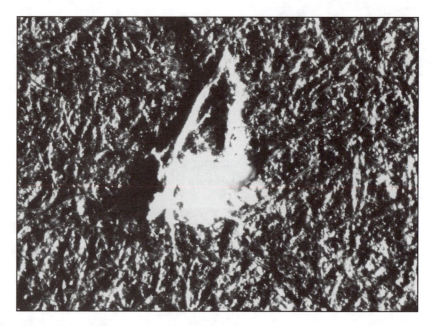

Particles originating from paper will normally be found on the blanket. With continuing press operation, however, they may work back to the plate and inking system. If particles are found on the plate only, and not on the blanket, it is most likely that they originated from sources other than paper. Nonpaper sources of particles that can produce hickeys are airborne contaminants and antisetoff spray. Antisetoff spray particles are water-receptive and reproduce as small void hickeys.

Particles on the plate or blanket that are believed to be causing either type of hickey should be removed with a clear adhesive tape and mounted on a heavy, clear plastic film. Sandwiched between the two layers of plastic, the particles can be retrieved for identification. Folding the tape over so that it adheres to itself makes it impossible to retrieve the particles without destroying them. When it is difficult to remove the contamination, removing the unwashed blanket may be necessary.

Piling

Piling is the accumulation of small, evenly distributed and continuous areas of material on the blanket in such quantity that they interfere with printing. Piling can originate from inks, paper coatings, fillers, or dusting. Factors contributing to piling include the dampening system, blankets, paper, inks, stresses or friction applied to the paper during its passage through the printing system, and slippage between the blanket and the paper's surface as the rubber flows, or

Paper coating piling: an enlargement of a print taken at the start of the run *(top)* and the same subject after 2,300 impressions, showing the effects of coating piling in the halftone printing areas.

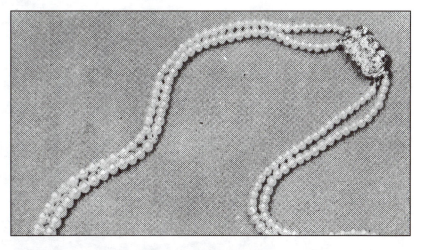

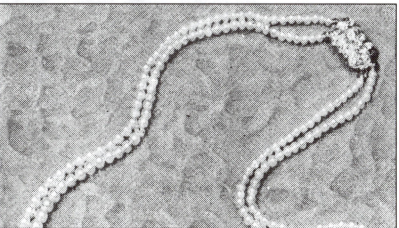

Effect on print of piling on blanket: slight piling *(top),* moderate piling *(middle),* and severe piling *(bottom).*

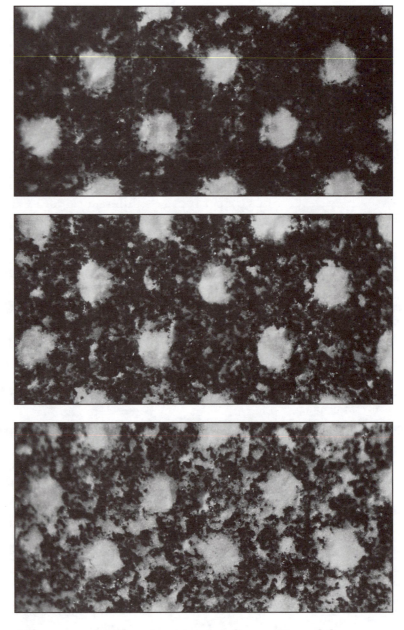

deforms, under the nip pressure. Separation of the paper from the blanket surface places tensile and bending stresses on the paper that tend to remove any material not firmly anchored to its surface.

Superimposed on these mechanical interactions of blanket and paper are the interactions between water, alcohol, ink, and paper, as well as changes in the blanket's tack that occur when the rubber blanket reacts to cleaning solvents. The numerous combinations possible among these various factors involved in piling account for its complexity and help explain why a single lot of paper may cause piling in one printing situation, but not in another.

Piling in the nonimage areas of a blanket may result from the deposit of loosely bonded fillers in uncoated papers or poorly bonded coating pigments in coated papers. Nonimage area piling can result from improper ink and water balance. Coatings that lack moisture resistance may be softened by moisture on nonimage areas of the blanket and be transferred to the blanket with each impression. This buildup in non-image areas is sometimes called **milking.** It usually becomes more severe as paper progresses through a multicolor press and as the coating continues to be softened from repeated moistening. **Dusting,** or powdering, originates from slitter and cutter dust and is usually concentrated most heavily in those areas of the blanket that contact the outer edges of the sheet or web. Dusting is most readily evident on the first printing unit and decreases in intensity on succeeding units. Dusting and milking are normally opposite reactions to the amount of water on the blanket. Less water on the blanket will most likely aggravate dusting but will tend to minimize the milking effect by moving the coating material into the ink train.

The accumulation of a fine, white material on the nonimage areas of the blanket is sometimes described as **whitening.** If nonimage area piling becomes thick enough on the blanket, it can interfere with ink transfer from the plate to the blanket at the image area boundaries. It can also cause plate scumming and wear.

Image area piling is a puttylike buildup of material from paper and ink, or a combination of both, and takes on the color of the ink. This type of piling, if it occurs predominantly in screened areas, will be seen as mottle and will result in a loss of detail in halftone images. Image area piling may also occur at the trailing edges of solid images, where it is sometimes referred to as tail-pick.

Image area piling can result from paper that has a low resistance to wet or dry pick, linting, excessive ink tack, poor ink stability, or a combination thereof. It is usually more prevalent on the later printing units because of the paper surface having been softened by applied moisture in the earlier printing units. Excessive paper dust, however, can cause image area piling on earlier printing units. Image area piling can also be caused by unstable inks or highly absorbent papers that cause the ink to develop excessive tack during printing. (See carryover piling in chapter 3). Other possible causes of image area piling are inks that are improperly ground, overpigmented, or improperly formulated, as well as blankets that have become excessively tacky.

Surface Cleanliness

Lack of surface cleanliness can interfere with print quality in the form of unwanted voids, specks, and hickeys. This lack of cleanliness should not be confused with similar problems caused by picking of the paper's surface due to inadequate surface strength or by inks that are too tacky for the paper. There are two types of contaminating materials that originate during paper manufacturing and can subsequently degrade the surface cleanliness of paper. The first type of contaminant is superficial and is caused by loosely attached particles existing on the paper's surface. Typical sources for this type include lint, loosely bonded surface fibers, dirt falling from overhead, textile fibers from paper machine felts, and fibers or coating debris created by slitting, cutting, or trimming. Paper suspected of having surface debris can be checked by wiping the edges of the pile with a black piece of velvet or other cloth. Visible elongated or sliver-shaped particles are usually characteristic of cutter or slitter debris, which normally exists at the outer extremities of the sheet area. Debris existing within the pile can be similarly detected by wiping the inner area of the sheets. Shaking a dozen or so sheets from a pile over a clean black surface permits the loose debris that falls from the paper to be seen and collected. Illuminating the top sheets of a pile with a beam from a low-angle light in a darkened room also reveals the presence of surface debris.

For determining the presence of surface fibers that are too small to be easily seen with the naked eye, bend the sheet of paper sharply and use a magnifier, at a grazing angle, to examine its surface. Surface debris and the extent of its presence are often difficult to determine by examining a limited area of the paper. The best method for detecting surface debris is to run several hundred sheets of each side of the paper through an offset press with at least normal printing pressure, using a freshly cleaned black blanket and without inking or dampening. Surface debris will be picked up by the dry blanket and can be removed for identification.

The following technique is helpful for analyzing surface debris.

1. Use a black blanket and clean it thoroughly by alternately washing it with water and naphtha.
2. Run 200 test sheets. Use the same squeeze pressure for all papers being tested.
3. Place a strip of transparent tape on the blanket and roll it on with one press revolution.
4. Strip off the tape. This removes the dust and leaves a clean area on the blanket.
5. Measure the reflection densities of both the dusty and cleaned areas of the blanket with a densitometer. The difference is a measure of the amount of paper dust accumulated during the test.
6. Repeat the test for each paper being compared.

The second type of paper contaminating material originates from various foreign material that is embedded in the paper's surface and can be lifted out of the paper by image and nonimage areas of the rubber blanket. These lifted-out particles, called **pickouts,** can originate from scale, rust, slime spots, filler agglomerates, starch spots, scale from surface sizing, coating lumps, and particles that build up on paper machine rollers, felt, or dryers. The amount of threat that they pose to print quality depends on the frequency of their occurrence, the extent to which they can be lifted from the paper during printing, ink coverage involved, and the size of solid printed areas.

Printing papers can be checked for cleanliness by sampling sheets from a given lot of paper and printing with heavily inked solids. This procedure will reveal both surface debris and pickouts. Examining the prints and any contaminating material transferred to the offset blankets provides a quick prediction of the paper's cleanliness.

Picking and Tearing

Picking and tearing occur when the internal bonding of paper fibers or the bonding of coating to the base paper is not strong enough to withstand the forces required to split the ink film. Picking and tearing can result from either insufficient bonding strength in the paper or excessive ink tack.

Picking occurs when areas larger than single fibers are pulled from the paper surface and stick to the blanket or plate, causing spots in the printing. Tearing, on the other hand, is a continuous removal of the paper surface, which delaminates an area of the press sheet. (The term "delamination" is reserved for a phenomenon that occurs on blanket-to-blanket web presses.) If a large delaminated area of the paper surface sticks to the offset blanket, the result is known as **splitting.** Splitting usually starts in a solid printed area and continues to the trailing edge of the sheet, sometimes developing into a V-shaped tear. Picking, splitting, or tearing may be minimized or overcome by following these steps:

- Reduce ink tack
- Change to an easier releasing blanket
- Lower press speed
- Decrease the pressure of the impression cylinder

Paper split in printed solid due to paper weakness or excessive ink tack.

Picking is more evident in solids, particularly in those near the back edges of the press sheet and at the tail edges of images. To distinguish between picking and other causes of spots in the printing, select a spot in the printing, then find the sheet where the spot first appears by thumbing down through the delivery pile. Examine the spot under magnification to see if there is a depression or disruption of the paper. If neither one is evident, picking is not the cause of the spot. If a craterlike spot is found, it may be the result of true picking or of the lifting out of foreign inclusions in the paper.

Sheetfed Letterpress

Paper-related causes of poor runnability for sheetfed letterpress include a lack of sheet flatness, curl, wrinkles, puckers, and tight or wavy edges. Additional causes are holes, scrap and turnovers in the load, and stuck sheets. Static electricity also can interfere with sheet feeding and delivery, causing ink setoff and damage of the printed sheet. The remedies for these static problems are the same as those mentioned previously in this chapter. Letterpress printing is more susceptible to serious static problems since it does not introduce moisture into the paper, as does offset lithography.

Screen Printing

Screen printing is by far the most flexible of all established printing processes. Its unique features include the need for little or no pressure and the ability to lay down ink films many times thicker than other printing processes, even to the point of producing embossed effects. The vast majority of screen printing is performed sheetfed. Screen printing can be done on many different substrates, paper being one of them. Papers used in screen printing can be rough or very smooth, because picking of the paper's surface is not a problem and smoothness is not a factor except where it relates to ink drying or smudging after printing. Screen printing can also be done on very porous or nonporous papers. Inks are formulated accordingly.

Paper used for screen printing must be flat, free from wavy or tight edges, and free of imperfections like wrinkles, buckles, cockles, and welts. These defects may prevent complete contact of paper and screen during ink transfer. The paper must also have sufficient dimensional stability to resist shrinkage and curling and to maintain register between the individual printing and drying processes of successive colors. Most paper-related problems in screen printing occur during drying because of the exceptionally thick ink films that are deposited on the paper, and to the complexity of the drying process. Screen printing paper therefore must have enough bulk and rigidity to resist the warping effect of the thick ink films during drying and to prevent the sheets from sagging when they are vertically supported. In addition, large sheets can present problems if the paper curls from the heat used for drying and causes printed areas to contact parts of the dryer before the ink has dried. Printers can remedy these problems by using papers with heavier basis weights (higher grammage) that have the required stiffness and bulk. Grain direction in sheets that are supported vertically during drying is important. For maximum stiffness, grain should be perpendicular to the horizontal support of the sheet.

3   Web Paper Runnability

Web Offset Lithography

Feeding

For web paper to produce a trouble-free run, it must be defect-free, contain mill splices that hold, and be uniformly wound in rolls. Web paper defects may be introduced during the papermaking process or during transit and storage. Manufacturing defects include holes, bursts, calender cuts, cracked and stuck edges, defective splicing, rope marks, corrugations, and variable winding tension. Defects created during transit and storage include gouges, crushed cores, dents, and water damage.

Manufacturing defects are usually found throughout the roll and are not detectable until the roll is being printed. Storage or handling damage, on the other hand, can be easily seen up front because the damage is on the outer surface of the roll. Such damage may be caused by the common practice of lining up several rolls of web paper at the infeed end of the press with the wrappers removed. When the wrapper is removed before the roll is in position for mounting on the reel stand, the outer layers may pick up dirt that can be carried into the press, become gouged when rolled across the floor to the reel stand, or absorb moisture that can cause blistering in the oven. Only the roll being mounted on the reel stand should have its wrapper removed.

Web paper must be flat enough to pass through the printing nip of the two blanket cylinders without wrinkling or becoming distorted. Rolls that unwind with even tension and flatness across the web and without localized distortion contribute to good register and reduce wrinkling and waste. Paper with loose edges or slack centers that cannot be pulled out under maximum press tension is referred to as being baggy. **Bagginess** at the center of a roll is referred to as a slack center; bagginess at the edge of a roll is called a slack edge. Slack edges can result from moisture being picked up by rolls that have been exposed to the atmosphere or by moisture streaks introduced at the mill.

Delivery and Folding

Moisture acts as a plasticizer for paper fibers, giving them the ability to bend without breaking. The more the moisture content of fibers is reduced, the more rigid the fibers become. A fiber with no moisture will break with the slightest bend. A problem that can occur with web folding, but that does not exist with sheetfed printing, is severe fracturing of the fibers due to dryness. Regardless of the paper's moisture going into a web dryer, the retained moisture after exiting is very low, making it difficult to fold the paper without breaking the fibers and cracking the coating. The result of severe fiber breaking is for the sheet to physically separate along the fold line, a condition known as **tear-at-the-fold** (TAF). While it is unusual for sheetfed printed papers to experience tear-at-the-fold, heatset web papers can be vulnerable to TAF if the papermaking furnish has not been properly formulated for heatset printing or the web oven temperature is so high that it removes all the moisture from the paper. Better designed folders, inks that dry at lower oven temperatures, and better fiber mix in the base paper have reduced the potential for TAF problems.

Another web folding problem, not to be confused with tear-at-the-fold, is **cracking-at-the-fold,** which is usually associated with coated papers and occurs when the coating is not flexible enough to stretch around the outside radius of a fold. Both printed web and sheetfed coated papers can crack along the fold line.

Remoisturizing the web and applying moisture at the fold line may reduce both cracking and TAF. Fewer folding problems are encountered when the stronger, wire side of the paper is kept to the outside of the fold. It may also be helpful to reduce roller pressure, use rubber-covered rollers during folding, avoid heavy ink coverage at the fold line, provide for the escape of entrapped air during intricate folding, and score at the fold line for heavier-weight papers.

Off-press folding. If paper loses excessive moisture during heatset web drying, it is difficult or impossible to correct the situation after the paper has been sheeted and sent to the bindery. Because high-speed bindery folding can subject paper to more severe conditions than on-press folding, the printer and the bindery should take special precautions to prevent moisture loss caused by heatset drying. Moisturizing devices and rubber rollers on the bindery folder can minimize cracking. Because web offset dryers are sometimes operated at too high a temperature, the temperature of the web exiting the dryer should be monitored and controlled to the lowest setting possible. The more moisture left in the sheet, the fewer static, cracking, and tearing-at-the-fold problems.

Thermalert MI, a miniature infrared temperature sensor. *Courtesy Raytek Corporation.*

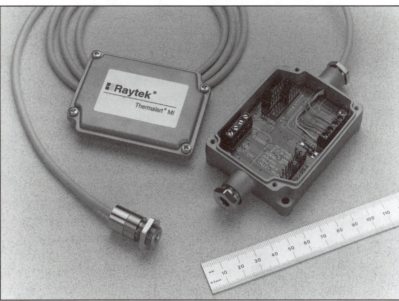

Other binding considerations. An unusual problem is encountered when signatures that have been printed by web offset are combined with covers printed by sheetfed offset. The web offset signatures are delivered and stacked with very low moisture content. The covers, having been printed by sheetfed, contain moisture in reasonable balance with the atmosphere. When the signatures and covers are bound, trimmed, and exposed to normal relative humidities, the signatures take on moisture and grow, while the covers, being in equilibrium with the atmosphere, remain the same size. This results in the signatures extending beyond the edges of the covers. Buckling at the edges of the book can also occur.

To keep moisture loss at a minimum, press dryer temperatures should be kept as low as possible. This step will also reduce problems due to static electricity, curl, and cracking during the feeding, gathering, and trimming of signatures. Partially restoring moisture and applying a silicone solution to the printed web via moisturizing equipment also can help to minimize these problems, as well as reduce ink smearing. To minimize dryer problems, use an optical pyrometer to measure the temperature of the web as it exits the dryer.

Absorbency of Paper

Ink absorbency is a critical factor in web printing. The absorbency of uncoated papers depends on such factors as refining and the fiber and filler composition of the paper, and it is determined primarily by the surface properties of the paper. As paper is made smoother and its surface compacted by calendering, its ink absorbency decreases. Surface sizing decreases ink absorbency and increases ink holdout by partially filming over the voids, pores, and capillaries at the surface, thereby reducing vehicle penetration. The degree of surface sizing can be varied, within limits to control ink absorbency. The absorbency of coated papers is controlled by the coating composition and calendering.

In heatset web printing, setoff due to lack of paper absorbency is not a problem, but too rapid absorption of the ink vehicle can reduce printed ink gloss. The same is true for gravure and flexographic printing, where inks also dry by evaporation, with the aid of heat.

Newspaper inks do not really dry, but absorption of the vehicle by the paper leaves the pigment trapped by the paper's surface. Newsprint is made to provide instant vehicle penetration for minimizing ink smudging during printing and folding on high-speed presses. The high opacity and color of newsprint help to counteract ink solvent strike-through and printed show-through.

Contamination Problems

The strength requirement for web offset paper is less than that for sheetfed offset because web paper is printed on both sides at the same time, producing less blanket wrap, and is always run grain-long, which is its strongest direction. In addition, the ink tacks in web printing are usually lower. This reduced strength requirement, along with lower-tack inks and the nature of web paper handling, allows web presses to print lower-basis-weight papers. At a basic size of 25×38 in. (635×965 mm), basis weights normally range from about 20 to 80 lb./ream (30–118 g/m^2). Heavier weights can be run, but they are usually delivered in sheets since they do not handle well in press folders. Heavier-weight sheets are also prone to delaminate because of the lower internal bond strength associated with these papers.

Coating pick. Coating pick usually occurs when the force required to split the ink film is greater than the surface strength of the coating. Coating pick is normally seen at the tail edge of a printed image. It is best observed by using a 10× magnifier and illuminating the area with a low-angle light.

Tail pick is best observed using a 10× magnifier and a low-angle light.

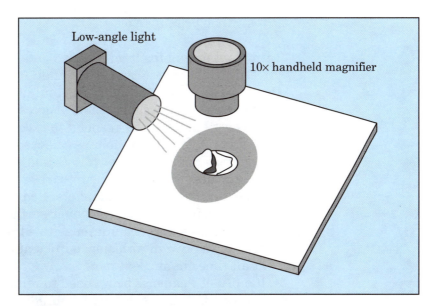

It is logical to conclude that if picking is seen in the black printed image, the picking occurred in the black unit. While this may be true, it is not uncommon for images that are printed by an earlier unit to pick on later units. Consider a four-color press with a color sequence of black, cyan, magenta, and yellow (KCMY). The first-down black ink is transferred to the paper without the occurrence of picking and immediately begins to build tack. The rate of tack buildup depends on solvent evaporation into the air and the absorbency of the paper. This first-down black ink coming in contact with succeeding blankets will pick on these later blankets if the ink tack builds to the point of exceeding the paper's surface strength. This type of picking can occur on one or all of the succeeding blankets, depending on the rate of tack buildup, and is known as **carryover piling.** The name comes from the fact that the ink is carried over from one unit to another and the picking occurs during this carryover phase.

To locate the source of carryover piling, printers must inspect not only the printed sheet and the suspected unit's blanket, but also all of the succeeding blankets. For example, inspecting the final print might show coating pick in the black printer. It would be logical to conclude that the picking occurred in the black printing unit. In this case, however, inspecting the black blanket would show no sign of picking if carryover piling was the problem. Inspecting succeeding blankets would show the black picking on one or more of the blankets. It is always important to check the blankets when investigating coating pick.

Lint. Lint originates from loosely bonded surface fibers; if it mixes with the ink, it can cause buildup in the printed image. Because fibers absorb water, this buildup produces slender white voids. Following are some sources of lint problems:

- Uncoated papers may respond to excessive web tension by "fluffing up." These problems can occur as the web, under high tension, passes over rollers and turning bars. Some of the surface bonds may be ruptured, causing loosened particles to transfer to the blankets. Reducing web tension and abrasive action on the paper surface as it passes through the press can minimize this type of lint and debris. To prevent abrasion, sufficient air must be present at all times in air float bars.
- If a brush cleaner is being used to remove slitter dust and loose surface fibers, it may be abrading the paper and loosening surface fibers that can be picked up by the blanket. To remedy this problem, set the brush cleaners to exert lighter pressure on the web.

Register

To maintain register in web printing, the paper must run through the press without weaving. Weaving can be caused by poorly wound rolls, malfunctioning guiding devices, and inadequate web tensions. Misregister can occur in the running direction or from side to side in the paper web. Misregister in the running direction can be caused by the piling of paper coating on the blanket, which changes the blanket's diameter and causes the web to stretch; by a roll wound with varying tension; or by an out-of-round or starred roll. Cutoff misregister may result from a roll being out of round or from excessive shrinkage in the dryer. Side-to-side misregister may be caused by:

- Uneven moisture content across the web
- Welts caused by leaving rolls unwrapped in a high-humidity area

- Distortions like corrugations and wrinkles
- Slack edges caused by moisture pickup at roll ends
- Tight edges with a baggy center caused by moisture loss at roll ends

Outer diameter distortions such as welts may require slabbing paper from the roll to remove the distortion. Misregister due to baggy or tight edges may be minimized by various web adjustments to flatten out the web. Following are some of those adjustments:
- Higher web tension
- A crowned or bowed roll to spread out the web
- Festooning of the web prior to printing
- Building up the ends of an infeed idler roller with tape or paper under slack web areas
- Adjusting the eccentric-mounted infeed roller to balance web tension

A condition known as "fanning out" of the web occurs when web tension is lower between the printing units than at the infeed. This situation causes web width to increase after the first color is printed, resulting in succeeding colors printing short. Bustle wheels are used in the center of the web ahead of later printing units to narrow the web and increase the printing width.

Bustle wheels.

Blistering and Delamination

Blistering. Heatset web blistering is caused by the pressure created when moisture in paper is vaporized, or turned to steam, in the web dryer. Unless the water vapor can escape quickly enough through the coating and ink film, the pressure will build to the point where an explosion occurs. Blisters never occur in uncoated paper because there is no coating to interfere with the escaping vaporized moisture.

Blistering.

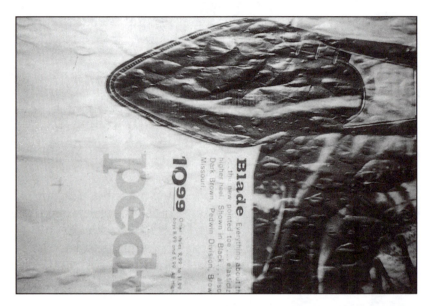

The blister resistance of coated papers depends on their moisture content, internal bond strength, and porosity. The moisture content of paper determines the amount of water available. The higher the moisture content, the more water that there is to vaporize. Internal bond is a measure of the strength of the bonds between the paper fibers. It determines the amount of pressure the paper can withstand before blistering occurs. Porosity is that property of paper that allows passage of water vapor from the inside the sheet to the outside. Porosity is the "valve" that controls the level of pressure buildup.

The blister resistance of a paper is determined by the relationship between moisture content, internal bond, and porosity. A paper with very high porosity can therefore have high moisture and weak bonds, but still not blister. In other words, the pressure cannot build to the point of blowing the sheet apart because a high-porosity paper does not restrict the flow of moisture vapor (steam). On the other hand, a paper with low porosity will not blister if the internal bonds are strong enough to resist the pressure or if the moisture content is low enough to keep the pressure below the level of blistering.

Blisters that occur during heatset drying are oval-shaped, sharply defined, bubblelike formations that are visible and usually appear on both sides of the web. Blistering usually occurs in heavily inked areas because the ink further reduces the coating's porosity. Since the greatest reduction in porosity occurs when solids back up solids, blisters are most likely to occur between these solid areas. One method for reducing blister potential is to print the solid as a 90% screen.

Blistering is a lesser problem for the common-impression-cylinder type of web offset press because the steam in the paper printed on this press has a better chance to escape through the unprinted side. Since sheet moisture has been significantly reduced during the printing of the first side, there is little available moisture to cause blistering during the printing of the second side.

Most papermakers build a sheet to possess as much blister resistance as possible while maintaining the required gloss and smoothness of the coated surface. It is possible to achieve more blister resistance by using larger, coarser fibers but only at the expense of gloss and smoothness. Printers ordering paper to be made should let the papermaker know in advance the type, design, and length of the dryer to be used and the expected temperature of the printed web as it leaves the dryer. A compromise between moisture content, gloss, and smoothness can then be made to provide for higher blister resistance.

Printers can also reduce the blistering potential of coated rolls by not unwrapping the rolls until they are needed at the infeed station. Exposing the outer paper layers to a humid atmosphere for any length of time can cause them to blister in the dryer due to moisture pickup. A roll of paper that blisters at the beginning may not blister after a few revolutions if the problem is caused by moisture pickup by the outer layers.

If paper tends to blister, try the following:

- Reduce the temperature of the dryer. (This change, however, may require a slower press speed.) A silicone applicator reduces and in many cases eliminates ink smudging when heat is reduced.
- If the dryer has two or more zones, reduce the heat in the first zone.

- Use a preheater, if available.
- Increase the press speed, if possible. This reduces both the rate of rise in temperature and the maximum temperature of the web.
- Use low-energy heatset printing inks that will dry at a lower temperature.
- If feasible, reduce chill-roll temperature so that dryer temperature can be correspondingly reduced.
- Use alcohol or wetting agent in the fountain solution to reduce the amount of water pickup.
- Use screen tints instead of solids or reduce color underlay.

Fiber puffing. Closely related to blistering is fiber puffing. Tiny bundles of fibers in coated groundwood-containing papers sometimes explode, much like popcorn, when going through the press dryer. The result is a rough, unattractive surface somewhat resembling sandpaper. The printer can minimize this problem by controlling the dryer's temperature. It has been well said that the dryer should be used to dry the ink, not cook the paper.

Blistering and fiber puffing are not the problems they were a few years ago. During the 1960s, blistering was very common. It has occurred far less frequently, however, since web printers began using lighter paper and longer web dryers with improved designs, and papermakers learned more about formulating coatings for web papers.

The tendency for paper to blister increases with an increase in the paper's basis weight. It is more difficult to develop internal bond strength in heavier weight papers, and the greater mass of these papers increases the total amount of available water. Higher-basis-weight papers are usually made with less moisture, on a percentage-by-weight basis, than lighter-weight papers to lessen this tendency to blister.

Delamination. Another potential problem in printing higher-basis-weight papers is the tendency for **delamination** during printing. Because the fiber bonds are somewhat weaker, the paper will fail as it is being pulled from the blanket. By definition, delamination occurs in the printing units of blanket-to-blanket perfecting presses and differs from the blistering that occurs in the web dryer. Visible as elongated blisters with indefinite edges that usually appear on only one side of the sheet, delamination occurs where solids or heavy halftones are backed up by similar printed areas. Delamination can

Delaminated web resulting from sharp flexing of web due to alternating web wrap.

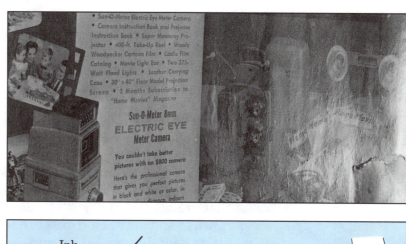

S-wrap.

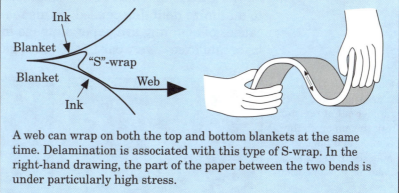

A web can wrap on both the top and bottom blankets at the same time. Delamination is associated with this type of S-wrap. In the right-hand drawing, the part of the paper between the two bends is under particularly high stress.

occur with smooth uncoated papers as well as with coated papers. If the web tends to wrap on both blankets, it may snap back and forth from one blanket to another. This motion causes sharp and rapid flexing and internal shear stresses that rupture the paper's internal structure, resulting in delamination. Following are some procedures that may stop delamination:

- Reduce ink tack on at least one side of the web to prevent the web from snapping back and forth on the two blankets.
- Reduce press speed, thereby decreasing the force required to overcome the pull of the inks.
- Use grater rolls to increase web wrap on the lower-unit blankets.
- Run the wire side for the heavier, more demanding form.
- Use additives in the fountain solution to improve blanket release.
- Preheat the web to improve blanket release.
- Change to easier-release blankets.

Doubling and Slur

Doubling occurs when some of the ink from dots printed by one unit is transferred from the paper to the blanket of the next printing unit, and then is transferred onto succeeding press sheets but not in register with the true, full-impression dots. Doubling of halftone dots can occur when the paper prematurely contacts or "prekisses" the blanket as it enters the printing nip, producing a weak transfer of ink from dots that are out of register with the true dots. Doubling increases the tone values of halftones, resulting in a distorted printed image. In sheetfed printing, premature contact of the paper and blanket can be caused by wavy- or tight-edged sheets with areas that are not flat and by static electricity. Sheet hold-down brushes and air or electrostatic hold-down devices help to minimize doubling caused in this manner. Other possible causes of doubling are paper slippage in the grippers, backlash, and excessive wear in the press gear train or bearings.

Doubling *(far right)* occurs when dots transfer out of register from the paper, to the blanket, and back to paper. Slurring is a smearing or elongation of dots.

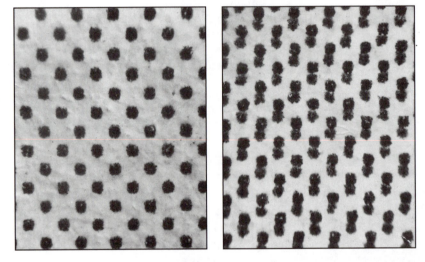

Doubling in web printing can vary from impression to impression, causing up-and-down variations in tone values and color. The opportunity for doubling occurs when slack or hard paper edges cause a web to weave. Other possible causes are insufficient web tension and excessive play in the bearings or gear train of the press.

Dot slurring refers to smearing or elongation at the trailing edges of halftone dots; it can also occur at the trailing edges of line and type composition. Dot slurring can be caused by excessive pressure in the impression nip between the plate and blanket or between the blanket and paper, which may produce a mechanical slippage. The causes of dot slurring include a loose or slipping blanket, an embossed blanket, too soft a blanket, too soft an ink, or too much ink. Dot slurring can also result from printing wavy-edged or tight-edged paper. On a single-color press, the defective paper will cause slurring, but on a multicolor press it will show up as doubling.

Tinting

Tinting appears during printing as a light scum on unprinted areas of the plate. Unlike ordinary plate scumming, it can be removed with a water sponge but it quickly returns when printing is resumed. Because it occurs only when printing on coated paper, tinting was believed to be caused by water-soluble material being extracted from the coating and attaching to the plate surface. It was thought that this deposit formed an ink-receptive film on the nonimage areas of the plate.

Tinting is no longer prevalent, however, and paper is rarely found to be the cause when it does occur. Tinting's more probable causes are related to the degree of plate desensitization, the types of inks or fountain solution, and press chemistry. To avoid tinting, printers should desensitize plates well and use inks that are sufficiently water-resistant and not subject to emulsification in the moisture of the dampening system.

Rotogravure

Practically all gravure printing in the United States and in many other countries is web gravure, also known as rotogravure. Gravure prints well on lower-quality, lightweight papers and is the major process for long-run, high-volume printing of Sunday newspaper supplements and magazine sections, preprinted newspaper inserts, coupons, catalogs, magazines, and a wide variety of packaging applications.

Gravure printing is a basically different process from either offset or letterpress printing and has its own paper-related problems. The most serious printability problem in gravure printing is a lack of contact between the individual cells of the gravure cylinder and the paper during printing impression. This lack of contact prevents ink from transferring from the cells to the paper and results in missing dots described as skips, snow, or speckle. Irregularities in paper surfaces such as holes, pits, or fiber bundles produce skips or missing dots, particularly in the highlight and midtone areas. Smoothness under printing impression is the most essential paper requirement for good gravure printability.

In addition to smoothness, absorbency and compressibility are also important paper properties. Compressibility can help the paper contact the cells of the gravure cylinder when under printing pressure, helping to minimize skips. In addition, skipping may be reduced by increasing the effective printing pressure, which is dependent on both the hardness and the pressure of the rubber impression roller. Electrostatic-assist technology can reduce the problem of skips by helping the ink transfer from the cells to the paper.

Electrostatic assist is a technology used by gravure printers to improve the transfer of ink from cylinder cells to paper.

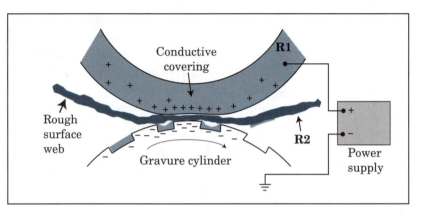

Shrinkage of wide webs between successive printing units can cause cross-deckle, or side-to-side, misregister. Shrinkage across the web can result from drying the ink after each color is printed or by the existence of high web tension that causes the web to narrow. Misregister can occur if the web lacks flatness or wrinkles during printing.

Picking of the paper's surface and accumulation of unwanted material on the printing surfaces generally do not occur in gravure printing as they do in offset lithography and letterpress printing. The highly fluid gravure ink allows the paper to separate from the gravure cylinder without the danger of picking or linting. Also, the gravure cylinder, as it rotates through the ink fountain and under a doctor blade, is self-cleaning. Debris that accumulates during printing can cause printing problems, however, by increasing the viscosity of the ink and scratching the printing cylinder.

For good runnability, rotogravure printing requires rolls that unwind with even tension and flatness across the web. Loosely wound paper at the roll core during roll winding at the mill can create runnability problems. Rolls should also be free from defects that cause web breaks. Gravure places great demands on roll quality because of wider webs, higher speeds, and the use of lightweight papers. Rolls that have slack edges, are baggy, and unwind with uneven tension can cause web breaks and wrinkling, particularly on wider gravure presses. Wrinkling can result in web breaks as the web is slit and folded. Rolls that cause the web to wander as it is cut into ribbons can be troublesome.

Increasing the web tension to smooth out the web increases the likelihood of a web break caused by a minor roll defect. The roll defects are holes, cracked edges, calender or hair cuts, and faulty splicing. Web papers should have adequate tensile strength and elongation properties to minimize their tendency to break under the higher tensions that may be required to level out the web and run the paper.

Flexography

Flexography is a process of rotary relief printing that has replaced letterpress as the major relief printing process. It is widely used for printing narrow-web, corrugated board, flexible packaging, milk cartons, and paperback books. The Cameron Book Production System, which produces books in-line from a paper roll, uses flexible relief plates. Flexography has also been adapted to print newspapers.

Flexography uses flexible rubber or photopolymer plates and rapidly drying, fluid inks. The inking system is much simpler than that of other printing processes. Flexographic inks do not set, but dry by evaporation or absorption with or without the aid of heated air. Advancements in flexographic platemaking, inks, electronic controls, and ink metering systems have led to a technology capable of high-quality process-color printing.

There are fewer paper problems in flexography than in other printing processes. Flexo is capable of printing on a wide variety of paper surfaces and other substrates. Compared to letterpress or offset lithography, it is more tolerant of surface strength and smoothness variations as well as surface debris. Picking is not a problem and dryer temperatures need not be as high as for web letterpress and offset printing. Nevertheless, smooth and level surfaces are essential for good halftone detail and to achieve lower printing impression with minimum "squeeze out" and dot distortion. As do other rollfed printing processes, flexography requires paper rolls that feed with even tension and are free from defects. Misregister and web breaks can occur in flexography for the same reasons they do in other printing processes described in this chapter.

Letterpress   A great variety of papers, both coated and uncoated, are used for commercial letterpress printing. Paper requirements vary with the end use of the printed product, the desires of the customer, and the desired printing quality. Papers used for printing periodicals by letterpress are, for the most part, lightweight coated papers printed with heatset inks. Dimensional stability is required for good register — a fact that is applicable to other printing methods also.

Paper-related problems in letterpress printing generally involve printability. Varying ink holdout and printed gloss can be caused by a nonuniformity of paper gloss and ink absorbency. Variation in pinpoint smoothness of the paper or an uneven surface created by a wild formation can cause halftones to lose detail and solid printed areas to take on a mottled, or "galvanized," appearance.

Pits, or low spots, in the paper are detrimental to letterpress printing. If the rigid letterpress plate cannot transfer ink to these low areas, white unprinted areas and missing halftone dots result. A paper that varies in caliper, is rough, or is insufficiently compressible can result in missing or broken halftone dots. Nonuniform packing, improper makeready, or plates that are not level also can cause this problem. When excessive squeeze is used to print a paper that is rough or that varies in caliper, an embossed print usually results. A firm, smooth paper having good formation and resilience is needed to ensure letterpress reproduction without excessive squeeze.

Since letterpress prints with a harder impression and with a greater ink film thickness than offset lithography, it tends to have a greater show-through. This problem is more serious with papers having a lower basis weight (lower grammage).

Linty paper, surface and coating debris, and pickouts and picking that accumulate on the printing plate and rollers create the same problems for letterpress printing as they do for offset lithography.

While blistering of coated paper can be a problem with heatset web letterpress printing, as it is for heatset web offset, it is not as common because both sides of a letterpress sheet are not printed and dried at the same time. Paper for heatset letterpress printing must have sufficient strength to be folded and bound after being subjected to heat and moisture loss in the dryer. Other paper-related causes of poor runnability for webfed letterpress are loosely wound rolls that unwind with uneven tension and the lack of flatness across the web.

Newspaper Printing

Newsprint, the lowest-priced paper used for printing, is basically a weak paper because of its fiber makeup; it gives poorer reproduction and has less endurance than other types of paper. The growth of multicolor web offset printing of newspapers has created a demand by newspaper publishers to upgrade newsprint printability to compete more effectively with other advertising media.

The most important requirements for letterpress newspaper printability are opacity, smoothness, and ink absorbency. Since little time can be given to makeready in the fast-deadline environment of letterpress newspaper printing, it is important that newsprint provide its own makeready via its printing cushion. In newsprint, ink vehicles are drawn into the pores and interfiber spaces of paper by capillary action. The number of pores and their size control ink absorption. Although a high rate of ink absorbency is needed, excessive ink penetration will contribute to show-through.

Variations in newsprint properties are better tolerated by web offset than printing by letterpress. Web offset has the advantage of printing finer screen halftones with greater detail in black-and-white and color reproduction. On the other hand, paper surface cleanliness is a greater concern for web offset than for letterpress. Twin-wire forming produces paper surfaces that exhibit less two-sidedness and have fewer linting problems.

The brightness of newsprint for print contrast is determined by mechanical pulps and the small percentage of chemical fibers that constitute their furnish. Little or no filler is used. In any printing process, the exceptionally high opacity of newsprint helps to minimize printed show-through. A reduction in basis weight (grammage), however, has tended to reduce opacity and increase show-through.

A major printing process for newspaper publishing is flexography. Flexography uses a resilient printing plate that, like web offset blankets, makes it more forgiving of variations in newsprint properties. Variations in surface smoothness and two-sidedness are important considerations in striving for improved color reproduction. Another advantage of flexography is its ability to print with water-based inks, which eliminate pollution problems and lessen dependency on petroleum solvents. Water-based inks greatly reduce ink ruboff as well as ink strike-through and show-through, which become greater problems as newsprint basis weight continues to be lowered. Problems associated with flexography are similar to those encountered with web offset printing.

Newsprint runnability problems involve tensile strength, roll quality, web imperfections, and moisture content. The greatest problem is web breaks, which are caused by calender cuts; hair cuts; cuts from fiber bundles, or shives; and slime holes. Other contributors to web breaks are wrinkles, poorly made splices, loose or uneven winding, damaged ends, water or glue having contacted roll ends, and roll turnovers. Careless handling and rough treatment during transit can also cause problems; the slightest nick on a roll end can produce a web break. Excessive clamp pressure or handling that produces an out-of-round roll can also cause poor runnability. Web breaks resulting from fiber cuts at the edge of the roll can be minimized by wetting the roll edges.

A Swedish study of more than a quarter of a million newsprint rolls showed the following causes of web breaks:

Web defects	9.1%
Roll defects	18.1
Transportation	4.6
Press or press operation	31.7
Unknown	36.5

The strength of newsprint is dependent upon its moisture content. Loss of moisture causes newsprint to become brittle and less capable of withstanding web stress and shock. Newsprint loses its built-in moisture very rapidly as it travels through a press and is exposed to low relative humidity. For best runnability, newsprint should contain 7–7.5% moisture. Statistical studies of web breaks clearly confirm that the frequency of breaks mounts steeply as the relative humidity in newsprint pressrooms decreases, and that humidity control reduces web breaks significantly. The National Newspaper Association has recommended that 45% relative humidity be maintained in the pressroom. Rolls should remain intact in their original wrapping until press time. Newsprint inventory should be rotated and used in the same sequence as it is received to prevent the accumulation of old and troublesome stock.

In trying to keep web breaks to a minimum, paper manufacturers and printers are also challenged by the practice of basis weight reduction. Since the 1970s, the basis weight of paper has been reduced from 32 lb./ream (52.1 g/m^2) for

The Cameron Book Production System. The web is conveyed through the first of two identical printing units. After printing on one side of the paper, the web is turned over for printing its second side. Flexible printing plates are mounted on the two continuous printing belts.

Printing belt

Dryer

Printing belt

Turning bar

Precision infeed

Dryer

Inking rollers

Mill rolls

Turning bar

Paper web

Inking rollers

Collator

Sheet conveyor

Cutoff

Book delivery

Three-knife trimmer

Formers

Transfer and divert

90° raceway

90° raceway

Stacker and counter

Cover breakers

Spine preparation

Combination end-sheet or paperback cover application

24×36-in. (610×914-mm) paper to 30 lb./ream (48.8 g/m^2), and lower.

Belt Press

Belt press printing, employed by the Cameron Book Production System, uses thin, flexible plates mounted on two endless plastic belts. For each revolution of the belt and corresponding length of paper, a complete book is printed from a roll and assembled ready for binding. Belt press printing uses letterpress inks and therefore requires a letterpress ink distribution system.

Rolls for belt press printing must have a minimal number of defects and unwind with even tension for trouble-free continuous in-line book production. Tolerances of caliper variation are narrower for belt presses than those required for other printing methods. A slight change in paper thickness from roll to roll or within a roll can cause problems in the form of an abrupt change in the bulk of the assembled books, with the consequence that covers made for designed bulk will be either too small or too large for the binding, or casing-in. Such variation in thickness among individual signatures is not a normal problem because thickness variations will tend to level out after the signatures are intermingled in the gathering operation.

4 Paper and Printability

Paper printability may be defined as the extent to which the properties of paper lend themselves to the true reproduction of images by a given printing process. In gravure printing (and sometimes letterpress), printability can be measured in terms of "missing dots" by using a test pattern and determining the number of missing dots. **Print quality** has been defined as the degree to which the appearance and other properties of a print approach the desired result. Print quality is determined by the successful integration of all the many variables involved in printing, including paper. The elements that produce quality image reproduction are print contrast, color saturation, ink gloss, and surface uniformity. Paper properties that help achieve these results are whiteness, brightness, gloss, smoothness, absorption, and surface uniformity.

The quality of an image depends on the whiteness and brightness of the outside light and the ability of the paper to reflect that light. The inks used to print process colors are transparent. These inks, when printed, allow outside light to pass through the ink film to the paper surface where the light is then reflected back through the ink film to an observer's eye. A paper that reflects equal amounts of red, green, and blue light at a high brightness level is called **white** paper. This paper has a spectral reflectance curve extending from the violet to the red regions of the visible spectrum and over a wavelength range from 400 to 700 nanometers.

Whiteness and Brightness

Paper brightness may be defined as the quantity, or amount, of diffused light reflected from the surface. Any color of paper can be bright — for example, bright red, bright green, or bright blue. To be white, paper must reflect *all* wavelengths of light in the visible spectrum at a high level. Papers that reflect the total visible spectrum are also known as "neutral" whites. Most printing papers, however, are anything but neutral. They come in many shades of "white." "Blue" or "cold" white describes papers that reflect a relatively higher percentage of light in the blue and violet region. "Warm" whites are papers that have higher light reflectance in the red or orange region of the spectrum. Gray papers, on the other hand, reflect all wavelengths more or less equally (depending on their shade) but at a low reflectance, or brightness, level.

Paper brightness is measured by comparing the amount of light reflected from the paper to the amount reflected from an ideal white standard. For measuring purposes, the paper industry defines brightness as the percent reflectance of blue light, as measured at a wavelength of 457 nm. Reflectance measurement at this wavelength is very sensitive to the detection of blue and yellow tints, as is the human eye. Most white papers are in the 60–90 brightness range, depending on type and grade.

How bright a paper should be depends on printing requirements, cost, and end use. The desire for a high printing contrast that commands the reader's attention may justify the added cost of high-brightness papers. Low-brightness papers are preferred for applications such as books that require minimum eye strain and ease in reading.

Print Contrast

Image quality also depends on the ability to see differences between density values within the image. The greater the density differences between midtones, highlight tones, and shadow tones, the easier it is to see detail. This difference in tone density is known as print contrast. Print contrast depends on the whiteness and brightness of the paper and the density of the ink. A lack of sufficient paper opacity and the resulting excessive show-through can reduce print contrast and detract from print quality. One measurement of print contrast is the density range between the paper and the solid ink film.

Maximum print contrast is best achieved by using a bright blue-white paper that has adequate opacity and is printed with the highest possible ink film density. White paper provides greater contrast than does colored paper to black and colored inks.

White Paper: A Source of Color

All the color a printer can print is contained in the paper being printed. White paper reflects the total color spectrum, and transparent inks essentially subtract selected colors from the paper. The inks that are used for process printing are transparent cyan, magenta, and yellow, plus black. The cyan ink film absorbs or subtracts from the paper the red wavelength of light, while allowing the blue and green light to pass through. The magenta ink film subtracts the green light, while passing on the red and blue light. Yellow subtracts the blue light from the white paper, while allowing the green and red to pass through. To summarize then, cyan absorbs or subtracts red, magenta absorbs or subtracts green, and yellow absorbs or subtracts blue.

The production of color in process printing can also be explained in the following way. White paper is white because it reflects equal amounts of red, green, and blue light. Printing process colors on white paper permits the reflected light to be modified or filtered in a way that produces colors, depending on the overprint of the cyan, magenta, or yellow ink films. For example, a cyan ink film filters out the red light, and yellow ink absorbs the blue reflected light, leaving only the green light from the paper to reach the observer's eye. Likewise, when a magenta ink film that absorbs green light is overprinted on yellow (which absorbs blue), the result is the red being reflected from the paper surface.

The quality of color depends on the ability of the paper to reflect red, green, and blue light at a high level of brightness. Of course, the source of the light that shines on the paper must also contain equal amounts of red, green, and blue light at a high level of brightness.

Smoothness

Smoothness is another paper property that affects ink gloss and color, as well as print contrast. Printed ink films that are glossy and have a high level of saturation must have a smooth and uniform surface. To achieve a level, or smooth, ink film, the thickness of the ink must be greater than the roughness of the paper. The average offset ink film thickness is 0.08 mils, which means that its optimum ink gloss is achieved on paper that has a smoothness of less than 0.08 mils. Paper roughness can cause microspots of reflected white light. The eye integrates this reflected white light with the ink color, resulting in a dilution of that color, which, in turn, results in a reduction of ink density and print contrast.

A smooth, uniform paper is especially important in high-quality image reproduction. Even though the ink film thickness is greater for letterpress and gravure, both methods still require a smooth surface for complete ink transfer.

Typical ink film thicknesses (wet, full-strength solid on smooth paper).

Type of Ink	μm	Mils (1 mil = 0.001 in.)
Offset lithography	2	0.08
Letterpress	3	0.12
Gravure	12	0.5
Screen	60	2.5

Some of the paper roughness in letterpress and gravure can be overcome in the printing nip to the degree that the paper is able to conform under pressure. Structural deficiencies such as a wild formation or insufficient compressibility can cause incomplete image transfer — for example, missing dots in gravure or broken prints in letterpress.

Mottle

A blotchy variation of ink density or gloss within a printed image is referred to as mottle. **Gloss mottle,** caused by paper, occurs when the paper surface contains dull and gloss spots. These spots, approximately ⅛–¼ in. (3–6 mm) in diameter, are usually caused by fiber clumps in the base sheet. During the calendering operation, more pressure is exerted on the coating that covers these clumps, causing this area to be glossier and more dense than surrounding areas. There is a direct relationship, particularly in sheetfed printing, between paper gloss and ink gloss. Any gloss mottle present in the paper will usually be seen in the printed ink film.

Another cause of gloss mottle is nonuniform ink setting. A paper surface that does not have uniform absorbency may cause differential drainage of the ink solvents and vehicles. Areas that drain less of the solvent and vehicle will produce higher ink density and higher gloss. Areas that are open and drain more of the solvent and vehicle will produce lower ink density and a reduction in gloss. This variation in ink density and gloss results in a blotchy or galvanized image.

Nonuniform ink absorption into a paper's surface can be caused by poor formation or by an insufficient coverage of fibers by the coating. As basis weight is increased and as greater percentages of long fibers are used to obtain strength, the likelihood of substantial differences in the uniformity of fiber distribution is increased. These greater differences in fiber distribution create mottle, which is more prevalent in heavier-basis-weight papers such as cover, tag, and paperboard.

A second type of mottle that occurs because of differential drainage of ink solvent is **back-trap mottle** (BTM). BTM occurs at the time of printing and is caused by paper differentially absorbing the ink solvent while traveling through the press. This nonuniform drainage creates an ink film that is composed of areas that are tackier and more viscous than surrounding areas.

Back-trap mottle occurs in both web and sheetfed offset printing. Consider a four-color press with a cyan, magenta, yellow, and black (CMYK) color sequence. Cyan, being the first-down color, contacts the following magenta, yellow, and black blankets. Some of the printed cyan transfers back from the paper to the magenta, yellow, and black blankets. The amount of transfer depends on the "wetness" of the cyan ink as it comes in contact with these blankets. If the cyan ink film is uniformly wet the transfer from the paper to the blanket will be uniform and the final print will be free of mottle. If, however, the paper has a high absorption rate and varies in its ability to absorb ink solvents, it will cause the cyan ink to drain in a nonuniform manner. This nonuniform drainage will create areas within the printed image with varying degrees of set. An ink film that has areas that vary in tack and viscosity will transfer back from the paper to succeeding blankets in a mottled pattern, hence the name back-trap mottle. Three conditions need to exist for back-trap mottle to occur: inks that set rapidly, papers having a high degree of absorptivity, and a multiunit printing press. Following are some steps that can be taken to overcome BTM:

- Change to a slower setting ink.
- Use a less-absorbent paper.
- Change the color sequence on the press. Since mottle nearly always occurs in the first-down ink, print this ink on a later unit, giving it less time to set.
- Print the job in two passes — for example, instead of six colors in one pass, print four in the first pass, two in the second pass.
- If back-trap mottle occurs on only one side of the paper, print on the other side of the paper if the job permits.

A third form of mottle is graininess, a finely patterned non-uniformity in a printed area. Graininess is usually caused by differences in ink acceptance and absorbency in a paper's surface. These differences may be caused by a lack of paper or printing smoothness; a wild, nonuniform paper formation; or, for coated papers, insufficient coating coverage. Graininess in halftone images refers to a nonuniformity of the print and a lack of an even tone value. The uneven tone value has a grainy or sandpaper-like appearance — sometimes described as "salt and pepper" — which is caused by irregularities and defects in the halftone dots. Microscopic examination of halftones is helpful in determining which of the many possible causes may be involved. Paper-related causes can be insufficient printing smoothness, a wild formation, a surface with a nonuniform ink receptivity and absorbency, blanket piling, uneven or insufficient coating, and doubling due to a lack of flatness in the paper's surface. Defects in the press, plates, dampening system, and inks can also cause graininess.

Ink Gloss

Sheetfed ink gloss. In sheetfed offset printing, ink gloss is a function of ink vehicle retention and paper gloss and smoothness. Most inks are made to lose solvents to facilitate setting and to retain the rest of the elements, such as resins, waxes, and drying oils, that gives finish to the ink film. A reduction in ink gloss will occur if the pore structure of the paper permits the resinous or vehicle portion of the ink to drain into the paper coating structure, along with the solvent. The extent to which solvent and vehicle are absorbed into the paper surface depends on the rate the ink crosslinks or polymerizes, as well as the paper's pore structure. An increase in paper gloss will increase the gloss of a printed ink film and enhance the brilliance and color intensity of the printed image.

The color density and gloss of printed images is strongly influenced by the ink holdout and gloss of a paper's surface. This can best be illustrated by using colored inks to print identical images on uncoated, matte-coated, dull-finish enamel, and glossy supercalendered coated papers. When printing with colored inks, differences in the surface and ink holdout of the paper will result in noticeable differences in intensity and gloss.

Web offset ink gloss. In web offset printing, the quick evaporation of ink solvent by heatset drying reduces the time ink has to drain into the paper, thereby providing good ink holdout and high ink gloss. Ink gloss is further enhanced if the paper also has high gloss, smoothness, and good ink holdout properties. Coated papers have more of these characteristics than uncoated papers. Failure to obtain the desired gloss in web offset printing can be caused by a number of factors:

- There may be too much penetration of the ink into the paper before it reaches the dryers. Ink may therefore have to be formulated with a less-penetrating vehicle. If a suitable ink cannot be formulated, a less-absorbent paper with better ink holdout should be used. (Note: less-absorbent papers may have higher blister potential.)
- A coated paper with higher gloss may be required, since a higher paper gloss contributes to a higher printed gloss.
- The paper, if preheated on the infeed, may be hot enough to lower the viscosity of the inks and increase penetration into the paper. Reducing or omitting preheating may help.
- Ink gloss may be reduced by too high a temperature in the dryer, which can cause excessive penetration of the ink's resinous binder. Sometimes called "fried ink," this problem can be remedied by reducing the dryer temperature or increasing the press speed. Reformulating the ink may enable the dryer to operate at a reduced temperature.
- The press may be running with too much fountain solution, preventing the smooth ink lay necessary for high gloss.
- There may be excessive ink penetration, or "dryback," in the dryer. Possible remedies include reducing web temperatures by cutting down heat in the dryer or increasing press speed, using inks that have a better high-temperature holdout, and reducing web tension in the dryer to prevent overstretching of the web and roughening of the paper's surface.
- The chill roll is not cold enough.

Viewing Paper and Printed Images

Evaluating and judging paper and the quality of printed colors requires standard viewing conditions. Since natural daylight varies and is not always available, printers must use standardized artificial illumination. TAPPI T 515 describes the spectral, photometric, and geometric characteristics of a standard artificial light source. Also described are illuminating and viewing conditions and the procedures for visually evaluating color differences in paper and printed images.

Color-matching booth (Spectralight II®) provides four common light-sky conditions (horizon, daylight, incandescent, and cool white) and ultraviolet. *Courtesy GretagMacbeth.*

Color-matching booths are designed to illuminate paper samples by simulated daylight and with a neutral gray background. To ensure more accurate visual comparisons in the booth, individual paper samples should be the same size, placed in close proximity, and viewed at a 45° angle. Since differences in the texture and finish of paper can distract from a visual comparison of color, samples should have the same grain direction and their same side (felt or wire) should face the observer. The viewing positions of the samples should be interchanged to avoid a possible bias caused by viewing them in a one-relationship dimension. Color matching or assessment is complex because it is both psychological and physical. Although the human eye is incredibly sensitive to color, it cannot make quantitative measurements or establish a color memory. Color measurement is used widely to ensure that white or colored papers conform to established tolerances as they are being made and to provide a mathematical record for maintaining permanent and reproducible color standards.

Opacity

When light strikes an ordinary paper surface, one fraction will be reflected, a second fraction will be absorbed, and the remaining fraction will be transmitted through the paper. Paper can transmit light in two ways: as parallel rays that do not scatter, and as scattered, or diffused, rays. The total light transmittance, parallel plus diffuse, determines the degree of opacity.

Opacity results from light being absorbed and diffused as it passes from air to fiber and back to air. Pure cellulose fibers are transparent. Printing papers are generally somewhat translucent. Groundwood and unbleached fibers create opacity because of their greater light absorption. Filled papers have a high opacity, resulting from the high number of light-scattering fiber-to-air, air-to-filler, and fiber-to-filler interfaces. Fillers vary in their ability to scatter light and to raise opacity. Dark-colored pigments and dyes increase opacity by their light absorption. Titanium dioxide is unexcelled in its opacifying efficiency and is very effective in increasing brightness. Because titanium dioxide is also a more costly pigment, its required use accounts for the higher cost of many opaque papers.

Show-through of images from the back side of the sheet will reduce print contrast and interfere with the visual appearance of the image. The amount of show-through is determined by the paper's opacity, or ability to absorb and scatter light. The degree of opacity depends on several factors, including paper coating and filler composition, dyes, basis weight, and contrast between the printed image and paper. Sufficient opacity and absence of objectionable show-through often may be difficult and costly to attain with white papers that are high in brightness.

Because tinting dyes for blue-white papers are more efficient in light-scattering than those for yellow or neutral white papers, blue-white papers have a higher opacity than their yellow-tinted counterparts. For the same reason, yellow papers will have less opacity than their white counterparts. Colors like blue, green, and gray have a higher opacity than white because of their high light absorption.

Another factor influencing opacity is the contrast between image and paper. An image printed with yellow ink will have less show-through than one printed with black ink. The degree of opacity is also determined by the paper's finish, bulk level, degree of refining, and calendering.

This opacimeter (Model BLN-3) measures and gives a digital readout of contrast opacity in accordance with TAPPI T 425.
Courtesy Technidyne Corporation.

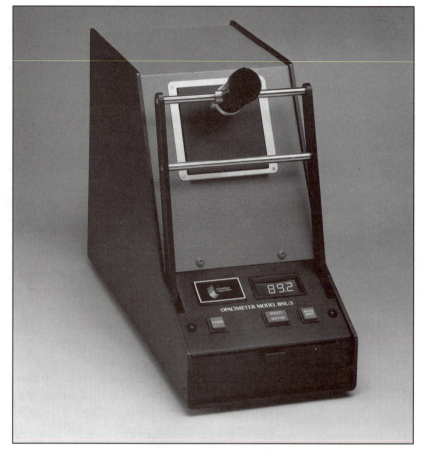

The opacity of papers ranges from a few percent for transparent papers to 100% for opaque papers. Opacity is measured by the TAPPI, or **contrast ratio,** method. This is the ratio of the diffuse reflectance of a single sheet of paper when backed by a black, light-absorbing surface to its reflectance when backed by a white, highly reflective surface. Light transmitted through the paper is absorbed when the paper is backed with the black surface, whereas light is reflected back and transmitted through the paper a second time when the paper is backed with the white reflecting surface. The total reflectance from the measured side of the paper will therefore be greater with a white backing because the added light portion is being transmitted back through it and reflected from this side. (For greater details, see TAPPI T 425.) Normally, it is required that papers have the maximum percent opacity consistent with cost and various paper properties.

The **diffuse opacity** (previously known as **printing opacity**) method differs from the contrast ratio opacity method of measuring in that it replaces the white reflecting surface with a thick stack of the paper being tested. (This method is described in TAPPI T 519.) From a printing standpoint, the opacity of paper is its ability to hide the printing on its reverse side. Show-through of a printed image from the back side of a sheet of paper is caused by the differences in total paper reflectance on the side facing the observer, resulting from nonprinted and printed areas on its opposite side. Although the printing opacity method more accurately measures the differences in reflectance observed as show-through, the contrast ratio method is generally used because of its speed and convenience.

Show-through may result from lack of opacity or from strike-through. **Strike-through** is caused by excessive penetration of the ink into, and sometimes through, the paper. Strike-through, which may not be fully apparent until some time after printing, tends to make the paper more transparent, thereby increasing the visibility of the printed image when observed on the reverse side of the paper.

Show-through is influenced by printing composition. The overhanging from side to side of printed boundaries, solids, and heavy ink coverage contributes to show-through. To avoid show-through, heavy coverage should be backed up by heavy coverage in register, wherever possible. Type and line composition has less show-through when it is printed in back-to-back register.

5 End-Use Requirements

The myriad of printed products using paper and paperboard fall into such broad categories as advertising, communications, dissemination of information, business transactions, recordkeeping, packaging, and household use. Determining the paper requirements for these diverse categories can be a complex process.

Advertising

Advertisers use papers of all types and in a broad range of basis weights (grammages). Paper used for printed advertising must first of all be suited to the printing process; offset lithography and rotogravure are the major processes. The paper should also provide the color, texture, and aesthetic background desired by the art director and the quality of printed reproduction expected by the customer. Practical requirements are also important. For example, advertising that contains return mail cards for customer response requires that paper meet the minimum thickness specified by the postal department.

Annual Reports

The paper for annual reports should be able to provide a clean, crisp reproduction of financial text and provide high-quality printed reproduction of pictorial subjects. If a suitable paper that serves both purposes cannot be found, different types of papers may be used within one report — one type for the financial information, another type for the pictorial sections. The preferred papers for printing annual reports are dull-finish enamels and matte-coated papers. High-gloss coated papers generally are not used because of their glare. The printing process used to print annual reports is offset lithography.

Books

In book manufacturing, paper must meet both bookmaking requirements and the requirements of the printing process. Bookmakers focus primarily on the aesthetic qualities of paper, choosing a shade and surface texture compatible with the subject of the book to establish a mood-setting background for the reader. A cream-white shade and antique finish would be appropriate for books on historical subjects, whereas a blue-white, high-finish paper would be appropriate for contemporary books with multicolor illustrations. High brightness may be desirable for some books, whereas a softer shade is preferred for others.

In papers for book manufacturing, consistency of shade is critically important. Opacity also is an important property because it minimizes show-through of type composition in places where solids may be backed up only by line composition or by no printing at all. A primary requirement for books is that they be manufactured to a consistent bulk and within prescribed limits so that the assembled book will fit its predesigned cases or binding, as well as its shipping container. High-bulk papers are required for many books, such as fiction and children's books. Low-bulk papers are needed for reference books like bibles and encyclopedias. Papers for many textbooks must comply with National Association of State Textbook Administrators (NASTA) specifications.

In the bindery, paper must be strong enough to resist being cut by binding threads (for sewn binding) and strong enough to resist tearing at stapled areas for saddle-stitching. In adhesive binding, paper must form a strong bond between the body and cover of the book to ensure the integrity of the book. In addition, the book's edges must withstand trimming without tearing or shattering.

The printing processes used for book printing are letterpress, sheetfed and web offset lithography, flexography, and, to a limited extent, gravure.

Papers used in manufacturing books with the belt press of the Cameron Book Production System must be made to narrower tolerances for thickness variation than those used for other printing processes. A slight change in paper thickness within a roll, or from roll to roll, can cause an abrupt change in the bulk of finished books. The averaging out of bulk variations among various signatures, as accomplished by other printing processes during gathering and binding, is not possible in belt press printing.

The type of paper used in manufacturing a book depends on the type of book and its end use. Groundwood content papers are used for books having a temporary or one-time use. For longer-life books, papers from bleached, all-chemical wood pulps are required. For maximum longevity and archival use, alkaline-sized papers are required. Coated or uncoated papers are both used in bookmaking, depending on the printing composition of the book and the quality of reproduction desired. Basis weights for book papers, at a basic size of 25×38 in. (635×965 mm), range from approximately 20 to over 100 lb./ream (44 to over 148 g/m^2).

Endleaf paper, which secures the body of the book to its hard cover, must have high tear and folding strength and must accept moisture from the glue that attaches it to the cover, without welting or waving. Papers used for book jackets or covers must withstand repeated handling and provide the proper surface for cover printing. Printed book jackets are usually made of coated-one-side (C1S) label paper. The decorative covers of paperbacks are generally made of coated-one-side cover or bristol.

Business Forms

The paper most often used for business forms is "business forms" bond, or register bond. It is manufactured to meet the particular requirements involved in the printing, conversion, and use of business forms. The basis weight of register bond, in the basic size of 17×22 in. (432×559 mm), generally ranges from 12 to 24 lb./ream (45–90 g/m^2), although lower basis weights are sometimes used. White and colors are generally used for multiple-ply forms. Register bond is designed to provide rapid ink absorption that avoids ink tracking on forms presses, along with sufficient tear and tensile strength for printing and perforating performance on high-speed line printers and for the deleaving of carbon paper from snapout forms. Register bond must take line-hole punching without having "hanging punches," fuzz, or lint. Dimensional stability is also a critical requirement of register bond, as its name implies. This stability allows the sprocket holes of continuous forms to register with the sprocket-driven mechanism of the collator during assembly of the various paper plies making up the form set and during subsequent use on line printers. Register bond must be able to receive sharp, clean carbon images from interleaved carbon paper, a necessity for legible copies, and be capable of being refolded and stacked following computer printing. Caliper must be controlled closely for consistent performance and packaging requirements. For production of continuous forms, roll quality and the absence of defects in the web are also prime requirements.

For business forms used as optical character recognition (OCR) documents and for computer input information, register bond must meet specific requirements. These include minimum permissible levels for brightness and opacity, maximum permissible levels of optical brighteners, and maximum permissible limits for dirt count and size of dirt specks. Porosity, thickness, and basis weight (grammage) limits may also apply, depending on the specific OCR equipment used.

Other papers used for business forms are ledger, bristol, adhesive-coated, safety, and duplicating papers. A lightweight, one-time carbon is produced especially for multiple-ply forms. Carbonless papers are used increasingly for business forms.

Papers used for personalized, computer-generated letters must meet the specialized needs of forms printing and computer printout, while providing the quality of printing sought for personalized letters and advertising. Personalized, computer-generated letters are preprinted in one or more colors as a continuous line-hole punch form on specially designed web offset presses that may have heatset dryers for handling coated paper. Individualized information, including addresses, is inserted by a computer line printer or by ink jet printing.

In general, the printing processes used for business forms bond are web offset, letterpress, flexography, and offset letterpress.

Business, Professional, and Personal Stationery

Bond papers are commonly used for business and professional stationery. Envelopes may be made from a matching paper or from a standard envelope paper. Grades of bond include watermarked and unwatermarked bonds made from chemical (wood) pulp and watermarked, cotton-content bonds. The characteristics of good bond paper include erasability and a good service for typing.

Personal stationery is often printed on white or pastel papeterie, a heavily filled uncoated paper with a smooth, vellum, or embossed finish, often used also for greeting cards. For wedding and other announcements, a special type of paper suggesting elegance is used.

Papers used for business, professional, and personal stationery must be suitable for letterpress, offset lithography, thermography, and steel-die engraving. Aesthetic requirements include a uniform surface texture, cleanliness, good formation, stiffness, and crackle.

Catalogs

Coated and uncoated papers in a broad range of basis weights and grade levels are used for printed catalogs. Mail-order catalogs are generally printed on lightweight paper to reduce mailing costs. Lightweight coated paper or a roto-type news is used for the long-run mail-order catalogs and is usually printed by rotogravure. Web offset is used extensively for both shorter and longer printing runs.

Checks

Paper for check printing must have a uniformly smooth surface for writing, printing, and the imprinting of magnetic ink character recognition (MICR) material. Essential requirements include strength, stiffness, and the stamina to undergo physical handling and pass through a check-sorting process before finally being returned to the writer. Letterpress and offset lithography are predominantly used for check printing.

Envelopes

Paper selection for envelopes depends both on aesthetic considerations and on functional requirements of the envelope. In addition to a standard envelope paper, coated and uncoated book papers are used to achieve desired levels of print quality. Register bond is used to print envelopes produced with their inserts and as a finished self-mailing piece from an in-line operation on web business forms presses. Some envelopes are printed in various colors to get attention or garner a response to direct mail advertising. Flexography, letterpress, and offset lithography are the major printing processes for envelopes. Thermography and steel-die engraving are also used to produce envelopes, but to a lesser extent.

Financial and Legal Applications

Lightweight, opaque printing papers are normally used for the printing and mailing of prospectuses, stockholder reports, and proxies. Permanent and durable papers like high-grade bonds and ledgers are needed for printed legal documents such as contracts, leases, wills, and mortgages. Letterpress and offset lithography are the two major processes used to produce these papers.

Flexible Packaging and Labels

Printing for flexible packaging such as gift wraps, box wraps, food wraps, book jackets, and labels has special requirements. Gift-wrapping paper must have adequate strength and a surface with adequate ink holdout and smoothness for printing. Box wraps require paper that can properly combine and laminate to paperboard. Food-wrapping paper must comply with applicable governmental regulations and with the requirements of packaging operations, which include print quality and sanitation. Label papers must be suitable for printing, varnishing, lacquering, bronzing, embossing, and diecutting. Other prime label paper requirements include freedom from curl caused by printing operations, the ability to perform well during automatic labeling, and the ability to adhere firmly to the labeled surface. Flexography and rotogravure are the primary printing methods for flexible packaging. Labels are printed by gravure, letterpress, sheetfed offset, and flexography, with screen printing used to a minor extent.

Folding and Rigid Cartons and Containers

Printed paperboard is used to make folding cartons for products like food and cigarettes, as well as printed rigid containers for products like cereal, milk, cosmetics, and drugs. The types of printed paperboard include lined corrugated board, combination furnish paperboard, and bleached-white solid paperboard, which may be coated or uncoated. In addition to printing and aesthetic requirements, paperboard must meet the fabrication needs of the specific form and type of packaging and its contents. Paperboard must have the strength and rigidity to be diecut, folded, scored, and formed or fabricated into a package on high-speed converting and packaging machinery. Paperboard must also be able to withstand gluing, lamination to other materials, and overcoating; be resistant to fading, abrasion, and moisture; comply with hygienic and sanitary specifications and the governmental regulations applicable to the packaged product; and be free of toxic substances. The processes used to print paperboard are flexography, gravure, letterpress, and sheetfed offset lithography.

Greeting Cards

The papeterie type of paper made specifically for greeting card manufacturing has a uniformly textured surface, which can be smooth, vellum, or embossed. Other papers, used for aesthetic effects, include genuine and imitation vegetable parchment and cast-coated, dull, matte, suede, flock-treated, and metallic-coated papers. Greeting card paper should have a bright surface without glare. In addition to its aesthetic and printing qualities, it must score and fold smoothly with no cracking and be suitable for such operations as bronzing, embossing, flocking, diecutting, and thermography. Adequate stiffness and rigidity are required for large-size, single-fold cards. Paper for greeting cards is printed predominantly by sheetfed offset. Letterpress is used for imprinting. Screen printing is used to a limited extent.

Magazines and Periodicals

To reduce mailing costs, large-circulation magazines are generally made from lightweight, groundwood-coated publication papers ranging in weight, at a basic size of 25×38 in. (635×965 mm), from 30 to 34 lb./ream (44–50 g/m^2). Magazine covers and advertising inserts are generally printed on heavier-weight, higher-quality coated paper. Uncoated papers are used for inserts and reply/return cards. Magazines having a high circulation, like general and special-interest consumer magazines, are printed in long runs by gravure. Web offset is used extensively for long-, medium-, and short-run magazine printing.

Maps

The paper for map printing must have good dimensional stability and be flat enough for hairline register requirements. Adequate opacity is essential for producing maps that have no distracting show-through. Cotton content papers may be required for long-life maps. Wet-strength paper is sometimes needed for maps that are used outdoors and subject to wetness. Map paper must have exceptional tear, tensile, and folding strength to withstand unfolding, handling, and refolding without falling apart. Maps are printed almost exclusively by offset lithography.

Menus

Paper for menus should meet certain aesthetic standards, some of which may require special finishes, surface treatments, or unique coloring. Menu paper should also have adequate thickness and rigidity and be able to withstand printing, embossing, and repeated handling and refolding. Letterpress and offset lithography are the processes used to print menus.

Music

Music printing requires paper that has good opacity and is free from dirt specks. It must give sharp, dense reproduction of music notation and have a soft fold, so that sheets or pages remain flat and do not spring back when turned by the musician. Offset lithography is the major process for printing music.

Newspapers

Newsprint — whose fibrous composition is largely groundwood, thermomechanical, or another type of mechanical pulp with the minimum percentage of chemical wood fiber added for strength — is manufactured specifically for newspaper printing. It is not surface-sized and must be highly absorbent to allow for the rapid penetration of news ink without the aid of heatset drying. The trend in newsprint is toward a smoother, stronger, less two-sided, and more lint-free surface for the improved quality of multicolor printed newspapers. Twin-wire forming produces a more lint-free and less two-sided newsprint than single-wire forming.

Since newsprint is an inherently weak paper, roll and web defects can easily precipitate web breaks on high-speed presses. In addition, moisture content must be maintained at a high level — close to 8% — to prevent brittleness and minimize web breaks.

Rotogravure supplements are printed on a "roto news" paper, which is of higher quality than newsprint. Roto news is made with more finely screened pulp, may be made on slower machines, contains more filler than regular news, and is calendered to the higher finish needed for rotogravure printing. Essential requirements for roto news paper include proper receptivity and holdout for gravure inks, softness and compressibility, freedom from abrasiveness, and freedom from defects in rolls.

Supercalendered uncoated rotogravure papers containing mechanical pulp and fillers are used as a premium roto paper for the Sunday supplements and magazine sections of newspapers. Newspaper inserts may be printed on newsprint or roto news. To produce more effective printed advertising and capture reader response, newspaper inserts can be printed on higher-quality coated and uncoated papers printed on multicolor heatset presses.

Most newspapers once printed solely by letterpress are now printed by web offset. Flexography is currently used for some newspaper printing, but may be used to a greater extent in the future.

Postcards

Heavyweight paper, or bristol, is used for postcard printing to provide adequate stiffness for mailing. Glossy-coated bristol, including cast-coated, is used for the pictorial side, while a lower gloss coating suitable for writing purposes is used for the reverse, or message, side. Government postcards are printed on an uncoated bristol. Adequate stiffness and thickness and a printing surface suited to the printing process are primary requirements. Offset lithography is the major process used for printing pictorial postcards.

Tags, Tickets, and Tabulating Cards

Printing for tags, tickets, and tabulating cards requires specialized equipment and specific types of paper. Tag papers are made for maximum strength and durability. Coated tag paper may be used for improved print quality. Wet-strength tag is needed for laundry and outdoor use. Ticket stock must have good strength, must tear properly at perforations, and may be required to have a built-in protection against counterfeiting. Tabulating cards are printed on a tag-type paper made for the demanding requirements of keypunching and computer information input. Tags, tickets, and tab cards are printed by letterpress, offset lithography, and, to a limited extent, flexography.

Telephone Directories

Very lightweight uncoated papers whose basic ream weight, at a basic size of 24×36 in. (610×914 mm), is 22.5 lb. (36.6 g/m^2) or less are made for the specific requirements of telephone directories. A substantial percentage of mechanical fibers are used for economy and to obtain the high opacity demanded for directory printing. Low- and consistent-caliper surfaces that are lint-free and provide clear, legible printing of fine type are essential. Paper shade consistency is necessary to avoid visible shade variation of directory edges. Directory paper for yellow pages must provide clear reproduction of their advertising content. Strong tag is used for directory covers. White coated tag or cover is used increasingly to achieve attractive color printing. Web offset is the major process for printing directories, while sheetfed offset is used for printing directory covers.

6   Paper Grades and Specifications

Selecting and Ordering the Right Paper

Paper choices should be made at the beginning of the production cycle, based on a complete knowledge of end-use requirements and customer expectations. It is not unusual for paper to be specified by someone who may not know its end-use requirements or the capabilities of the particular printing process. This lack of understanding may lead to increased waste, higher cost, failure to meet customer needs, and missed deadlines.

Paper selection is usually based on aesthetic considerations and technical requirements. A property of paper that influences aesthetic judgments is its whiteness. There are multiple shades of white paper available, enough to cause miscommunication between art director, publisher, customer, and printer. Is it warm white, cream white, cool white, or bright white? One mill's cream white is not the same shade as another mill's cream white. To help bridge this communication gap, a sample of the selected paper should accompany the job folder throughout the printing process. Colored paper also varies from mill to mill and a conscious effort should be made to clearly identify the chosen color. Again, a paper sample attached to the job ticket is a good way to protect against frustration and disappointment after the job is printed.

Other properties that influence the aesthetic selection of paper are the finish and surface texture. These properties vary — as do color, shade, and brightness — from mill to mill, underscoring the need for a paper sample to accompany the job throughout the printing process. Another important reason for exercising this precaution is the practice of selecting a paper from one mill's swatch book and instructing the printer to use that paper, or its equivalent.

Beyond aesthetic considerations, paper must meet the numerous technical requirements of the printing process and allow the printer to reproduce the printed subject in a manner that meets customer expectations. Paper must have sufficient opacity to avoid objectionable show-through, and it must meet the physical and environmental demands of folding, binding, and converting operations. The following case history illustrates how costly it can be to select the wrong paper for end-use requirements. A designer selected a paper for cookie bags on the basis of its excellent printability. The paper had good ink holdout and was a smooth, dull, bright white sheet. The paper was designed for high-quality color reproduction, not for flexible package printing. When cookie bags made with this paper arrived at supermarkets, the bags looked as if they had been through a war. The job was rerun on paper designed for packaging and having acceptable color reproduction that easily met customer requirements. Choosing the wrong paper for the job ended up costing everybody a great deal of money, time, and sleep. Aesthetic and technical requirements mandate that knowledgeable people such as papermakers, designers, and printers assist each other in selecting the right paper for the end-use requirements.

Overall value analysis should be used in paper selection. The cheapest paper may prove to be the most costly if it fails to perform as expected or causes production costs to exceed estimates. Paper availability also may be a consideration if the chosen paper is a making order with a minimum quantity run and is not carried in stock. If not enough paper is ordered or excessive waste in production causes a shortage, it may be impossible to reorder a small quantity.

A knowledge of the kinds of paper available and the proper procedures for specifying and ordering paper is necessary in selecting the right paper for a printed product. For example, paper merchants carry equivalent papers from various mills, and it is not uncommon for them to suggest that one mill's paper be substituted for another's. The person placing the order should not only be aware that paper characteristics may vary from mill to mill, but should also be prepared to make choices based on a knowledge of these differences. Otherwise the "equivalent" paper may not meet end-use requirements or customer expectations. This chapter describes numerous kinds of paper and paperboard used for printing, along with grade variations within a given type of paper and typical printing applications. Since the performance of a paper can be determined only after printing, converting, and using it, it may be helpful to acquire printed samples of jobs similar to the job being planned, dummies made from the selected paper, or proofs with the actual or similar printing composition.

In inquiring about and ordering papers, it is important to provide complete and accurate information about the end-use requirements and aesthetic consideration of the job. In addition, there should be no discrepancies between the verbal entry of the order and its written confirmation.

The systematic use of a prepared checklist containing all possible information needed will avoid errors and oversights and give the merchant and paper manufacturer the information required to deliver the proper paper to the printer at the right time and destination. Following is some standard information that should appear on checklists for sheets and rolls.

Basis Weights and Grammage

Although many types of paper are manufactured in almost identical weights when expressed as a common denominator, this fact is not readily apparent when their basis weights are related to their different basic sizes and ream areas.

Internationally, the weight of all paper and paperboard is expressed as grammage, which is the weight in grams of one single sheet of paper whose area is one square meter (39.37×39.37 in.). When the basic weights of papers, as used in the United States, are converted to grammage, their common denominator or weight relationship becomes readily apparent. For example, a 20-lb. bond and a 50-lb. book paper have respective grammages of 75 and 74 g/m² or nearly, but not exactly, the same weight. (See Table 11, *U.S. Basis Weights Expressed as a Common Denominator in Grams per Square Meter*, in the Appendix.)

Basic size of paper in the United States.

Basic Size (inches)	Single-sheet area (sq. in.)	500-sheet ream area (sq. ft.)	Papers
17×22	374	1299	Wedding, bond
23×35	805	2795	
24×36	864	3000	Tag
25×38	950	3300	Printing, label
20×26	520	1806	Cover
22½×28½	641	2227	Bristol
25½×30½	778	2700	Index bristol

Ordering Paper in Sheets

Specify the number of sheets, followed by their total weight. Example: 100,000 sheets of 50-lb. stock, with a sheet size 25×38 in., is written as 25×38 − 50 (100M) = 10,000 lb. If the number of cartons or skids is specified, it should be verified that this number will provide the total quantity of sheets desired. The total quantity of sheets may have to be adjusted upward or downward to avoid having the mill or merchant break cartons or send a partial skid load. Specify the grade by its brand, proprietary, or agreed-upon name.

When the paper is not a stocked item and the purchaser has a set of specific requirements, a making order is required. Making orders are subject to a permissible plus-or-minus percentage variation in the delivered quantity, whose magnitude depends on the quantity. When a making order states "not more than" or "not less than" the ordered quantity, the permissible one-way variation in delivered quantity is double that which applies to a plus-or-minus variation. For example, if the permissible variation is ±5% on a making order, the one-way variation becomes 10% if the order reads "not more than" or "not less than" the ordered quantity. Paper users should thoroughly understand this aspect of making orders and ask the paper supplier to provide the percent variation applicable to specific orders.

Size and ream weight. Specify the dimensions and weight per 1,000 sheets, followed by the corresponding basic size and basis weight, as a double-check for correctness. Example: If a printing paper whose basic size is 25×38 in. (635×965 mm) is ordered in a 35×45-in. (889×1143-mm) sheet size, the order should show the weight per 1000 sheets of the ordered size. In this case, it would be 35×45 − 266M. This specification should then be followed by the basic size and weight for that grade category which, for printing grades, is 25×38 − 80. When calculating costs, always be sure that applicable upcharges for lightweight papers are not overlooked.

Caliper and bulk. If there is a thickness specification for the paper in addition to basis weight and finish, it should be stated as an average, minimum, or maximum caliper in thousandths of an inch, or points caliper (micrometers for metric units), depending upon what thickness is actually wanted. Thickness is subject to manufacturing tolerances, as is basis weight.

Finish. Identify finish by names like antique, wove, vellum, or laid. If the paper is embossed, identify it by its pattern, number, or name. If there is any doubt, submit a paper sample in the desired finish along with the order. For deckle-edge or laid-finish papers, indicate their grain and the direction of the deckled edge or laid lines.

Color/shade. If the grade is made in more than one shade of white or a color, specify the desired shade. To avoid a misunderstanding, submit a sample of the shade or color desired.

Grain direction. State whether the grain is to be long or short, or indicate the dimension for grain direction. Example: If the grain is to run the long dimension of the sheet, it should be written either "25×38 grain-long" or "grain in the 38-in. direction." If grain direction can be either long or short, specify "grain optional." Although the direction of the grain may also be underscored, as in 25×<u>38</u>, it is best not to rely on this method to indicate grain direction.

Trimming. Most sheetfed paper for offset printing must be cut to exact size, and all corners must be square. This is particularly necessary for sheetfed perfecting presses and jobs that are printed "work and tumble" or "work and flop." Orders for paper printed in this manner should state this requirement.

There is a trend toward the precision sheeting of offset printing papers, without the need for guillotine trimming. Precision sheeting produces sheets whose edges are cleanly cut and without dust and "welding"; it is a good system for maintaining sheet squareness and dimensional accuracy.

Pressroom conditions. Specify whether the pressroom is conditioned or unconditioned. If it is conditioned to a constant relative humidity and temperature, state the readings on the order.

Special requirements. If the paper must meet specific requirements such as special inks (like high-gloss, high-tack, or metallic inks), unusual folding or binding applications, varnishing, lacquering, bronzing, or an out-of-the ordinary use, the paper supplier should be alerted. If the selected paper is not going to meet these requirements, it is better to know at the outset.

Packaging. Always indicate the method of packaging and its pertinent specifications. These specifications include junior or full-size cartons, either unsealed and marked in reams or some fraction thereof, or sealed as a designated number of sheets and skids. Cartons may be palletized for unitized handling and better protection. For proper use by the printer's handling equipment, skid specifications should include weight and height limitations; the number of sheets per skid; the height, direction, and distance between runners; and leg construction, location, and spacing. For uncoated papers, the order should state if there is a preference for packing the paper wire-side or felt-side up.

Delivery and shipping instructions. The order should state the delivery date required and the days and hours when the paper can be received at its destination. Other required information required may include the name of the railroad for a rail siding, platform and unloading restrictions, and whether the destination is a warehouse or the printing plant. Sidewalk or platform delivery should also be noted.

Ordering Paper in Rolls

Because ordering paper in rolls differs considerably from ordering paper in sheets, the person placing roll paper orders should use a checklist to ensure satisfactory performance on web printing equipment. A quantity of paper ordered in sheets represents a known usable area. Roll paper, on the other hand, is ordered and invoiced on the basis of its gross roll weight, which includes the weight of the wrapping and the weight of a nonreturnable core. Rolls having returnable, metal cores are normally invoiced for the net weight of the paper, with a separate charge and accounting for the core and a refund of its charge when it is returned to the paper manufacturer.

The total area for a roll of given dimensions and weight depends upon the type of paper and its thickness. A thinner paper, wound to a 40-in. (1016-mm) diameter, will have more surface area than a thicker paper wound to that same diameter. A paper with the same thickness but higher basis weight will weigh more for the same diameter roll. Roll paper is best ordered by length or footage. If using this method is not possible, the paper orderer can estimate amount of paper from formulas (given in the appendix). Some manufacturers indicate the total footage or length of paper on each roll.

Orders for rolls of paper must make allowance for waste, which includes the prepress waste of wrapping and roll stripping, core and core waste (which can amount to 3% or more), and on-press and binding waste. Making orders of rolls (like making orders of sheet paper) are subject to a permissible plus-or-minus variation in delivered quantity.

Roll dimensions. Roll width and diameter should be individually stated. Since paper manufacturers have a plus-or-minus width tolerance, printing requirements that rolls not exceed or be less than a specified width should be clearly indicated so that the manufacturer's tolerances can be properly fitted to the specific requirement.

Maximum diameter is usually desirable for minimizing the number of roll changes. Manufacturing tolerances for diameter are normally ±1 in. (±25.4 mm) from the ordered diameter. Caution should be taken when ordering maximum diameter, to ensure that this maximum diameter plus the manufacturer's tolerance does not exceed the capacity of the printing equipment, requiring that rolls be trimmed to a usable diameter. Mills may have additional charges for narrow-width rolls and rolls of small diameter.

Basis weight and thickness. A manufacturing basis weight tolerance generally applies to rolls, as it does to sheets. When ordering basis weights higher than normal for web printing, precautions should be taken so that the paper's thickness does not create problems with on-press folding and handling or cause coated paper to blister.

Side out. If the printer prefers that either the wire or felt side of the paper be wound on the outside of the roll, it should be indicated on the order. A stronger fold generally results when the wire side is at the outside of a fold.

Splicing. Heatset printing generally requires the use of heat-resistant splicing tape. Since a supplier not used to supplying paper for heatset printing may overlook this need, heat-resistant splicing tape should be specified on the order. Splices may be made straight across or diagonally across the web. Diagonal splices have less tendency to catch on parts of the press and distribute their thickness over a greater area in a folded signature. Splice locations can be indicated by flagging or by marking on each end of a roll.

Core specifications. Always specify core type — returnable or nonreturnable — and core dimensions. Include such details as inside diameter, ends with or without slots, and dimensions of the slotted ends for the printer's keyways.

Printing requirements. The process by which the paper will be printed is vital information. Printers should indicate whether the paper will be printed on heatset or nonheatset web presses. For coated paper, heatset requirements should be clearly specified and should include the manufacturer, model name, and length of the heatset drying equipment. If heatset drying equipment is to be used (like flame-impingement dryers that place extra demands on paper for blister resistance), this fact should be known to the paper supplier, along with the amount of ink coverage and the paper's exit temperature from the heatset dryer.

Since the types of paper and specifications required for web offset and sheetfed offset printing are generally different, printers should distinguish between rolls for web printing and rolls for in-plant or in-line press sheeting.

Roll packaging. All pertinent information for roll identity and use should appear on the packaging. This information should include grade name, order numbers, roll dimensions, weight, mill roll number, number of splices, and direction of unwind. For easy identification in warehouse storage, these specifications may appear in two different locations on the roll wrapping. It may also help to indicate certain identifying information on the end of an unwrapped roll near its core.

Delivery and shipping instructions. If rolls should be shipped on their ends or sides for a specific reason, this should be stated on the order. Any special instruction or restrictions that apply to receiving, unloading, roll handling, and equipment capacity also should be noted, along with the delivery date required and the days and hours when paper can be received. For rail shipment, the name of the railroad servicing the printer's rail siding should be indicated.

Paper Sampling Programs

Sampling the many types and grades of paper used for printing is no easy task and cannot be left to chance. It requires that printers constantly review and update the various sample books and files to make certain that they represent the quality, shade, and color for each grade and indicate the items still being manufactured. Samples of current quality are particularly relevant for jobs that must meet critical paper specifications. Rather than attempting to sample too many different types of papers and keep them updated, experienced buyers may elect to sample only those papers used most frequently and to request samples of paper used less frequently on an as-needed basis.

A properly maintained, reliable, and readily accessible sampling of papers can be a useful and essential tool for printers. A new sampling program should begin with current quality samples identified by their date of receipt. File samples should be systematically kept current according to a schedule arranged with paper suppliers. Suppliers should agree to automatically update the samples when a change occurs in color, shade, or quality or when items of a sampled grade are added or deleted.

To be practical and useful, sample filing systems should protect samples from dust, dirt, and exposure to the atmosphere and provide fast and convenient sample replacement retrieval. Sample swatch books, loose-leaf binders, and filing cabinets or drawers are commonly provided by paper merchants and suppliers. The usefulness of a sampling program may justify appointing someone to keep it updated.

Proper procedures for visual comparison. When two or more paper samples are compared for shade, color, or brightness, each sample should be backed up by several other samples of itself. This procedure eliminates possible errors in visual judgment resulting from the influence of show-through caused by insufficient opacity of a single-sheet thickness of a sample. During a visual comparison for shade, brightness, or color, the position of samples should be interchanged to avoid a possible bias caused by having viewed them in one relationship only.

In visual paper comparisons, finish patterns such as laid finish and the influence of grain direction upon surface finish, gloss, and brightness should not be overlooked. For uncoated papers, differences between the wire and felt sides can influence the way in which they are visually assessed. Consequently, samples of different papers should be compared when their grain is running in the same direction and, with uncoated papers, when their same side — felt or wire — faces the observer.

Illumination has a pronounced influence upon the visual comparison of white and colored papers. Printers should use northern daylight or artificially simulated daylight provided by color-matching booths. The 6500 K intensity of illumination, described in TAPPI Official Test Method T 515, is the preferred level for visual comparison of white and colored papers. White papers containing optical or fluorescent brighteners will appear to have different brightness levels, depending upon daylight, indoor incandescent, or indoor fluorescent illumination. For this reason, it may be advisable to examine these papers under the different available lighting conditions, including fluorescent lamp light.

Paper Types

Adhesive-Coated Paper

Used primarily for printed labels, adhesive-coated papers have an adhesive that is either activated by water or heat or is permanently tacky. Gummed papers, with water-activated adhesives, have either a conventional or dry type of applied gumming. The dry type of gummed paper is preferred by printers because of its ability to remain flat and its lower tendency to curl over a broader range of relative humidities.

When selecting a gummed paper for printed labels, printers should specify the surface to which the labels will be adhered. Gummed papers are made with different adhesive formulations geared to the specific requirements of the target surface. Gummed papers are fabricated with a variety of surfaces and from different types of paper, including uncoated white and colored paper; glassine, glossy-coated, cast-coated, and low-gloss-coated white and colored papers; papers with a metallic surface (such as gold or silver); and foil-mounted paper.

Two essential considerations in selecting a gummed paper are the type of surface desired for printing and the type of gumming that will adhere to the target surface. Since gummed papers are more prone to curl than other papers, extra precaution should be taken to keep them wrapped when not being processed.

Heat-seal papers are coated with an adhesive that becomes tacky when heated. These papers are used for instant and permanent adhesion to surfaces like plastics, glass, and vinyl (for example, for phonograph records). Heat-seal papers, because of their high instant tack, are well suited for high-speed packaging. Selection of the proper heat-seal paper involves evaluating the surface to be labeled, the method and machinery to be used, and the dwell time for heat activation.

Intense heat, such as that used for ink drying, must be avoided when printing heat-seal papers.

Pressure-sensitive adhesive-coated papers have an adhesive that is permanently tacky at normal temperature and adheres to a surface by contact and applied pressure. Because of their unique properties, adhesive-coated papers require special printing and handling care. Helpful suggestions are available from suppliers of these papers.

Bible Paper

Bible paper, once printed only by letterpress, is the forerunner of lightweight printing papers. Bible papers have exceptionally high opacity for their basis weight, which extends from 17 to 40 lb./ream (25–59 g/m^2) based on a 25×38-in. (635×965-mm) sheet size. In addition to bibles, lightweight papers are also used for handbooks, manuals, dictionaries, financial and legal printing, and professional reference books because they reduce bulk and mailing costs. The subsequent savings in postage and distribution realized with lightweight papers can often far outweigh their high initial costs.

Special adjustments and techniques are usually required for the efficient handling of lightweight papers during printing. Such information is available from the manufacturer. Web offset, however, has made it easier to print lightweight papers, and a value analysis may reveal substantial savings.

Blanks

Blanks are thick types of paperboard produced on a cylinder machine with surfaces designed for printing. The thickness of blanks ranges from 15 to 48 pt. (0.38 to 1.22 mm), thickness being determined by the number of plies laid down by the paper machine. Uncoated blanks may be white-lined on one or both sides for printing, while coated blanks are coated on one or both sides. Grain direction is an important consideration relative to the blank's conformance to the curvature of the press cylinder and to the blank's end use. Heavier blanks are best handled on presses having large cylinder diameters, which reduces excessive bending. Excessive bending and ink tack must be avoided to prevent separation of the plies. Blanks are used for printed signs, point-of-purchase and window display signage, streetcar and bus cards, posters, and calendar backs.

Bond Papers

The basic size for bond papers is 17×22 in. (432×559 mm) with standard basis weights of 13, 16, 20, and 24 lb./ream (49, 60, 75, and 90 g/m^2). Bond papers are classified as writing paper and differ from book or printing papers in several important ways. Bond papers must have permanence; durability for handling, folding, and loose-leaf binding; and adequate internal and surface hardness for pen-and-ink writing, erasure, and typing. Stiffness and rattle are required for letterheads and documents. Some compromises in printing properties, such as reduced opacity and dimensional stability, are made to meet these other end-use requirements.

Bond papers are made in various grades. **Utility bond** has no watermark and is made from chemical wood pulp. It is used for printed products like letterheads, invoices, statements, forms, price lists, short-term policies, and direct-mail advertising enclosures. **Watermarked bond,** also an all-chemical wood pulp sheet, is a stronger, brighter, better-quality bond than unwatermarked bond.

The best bond is a premium-quality, air-dried, cockle-finish, all-chemical wood bond made by some manufacturers. Next in order of quality and cost are the cotton-content bond papers, formerly designated as "rag content." Quality levels are watermarked as either 25, 50, 75, or 100% cotton-fiber bond paper, with the watermarked 100% cotton fiber bond being a premium sheet. These grades of bond are exceptionally well-formed on slow-running paper machines and are air-dried for added strength and to produce a cockle finish. Cotton-containing bond papers add class and a distinctive character to printed letterheads and documents, and they can be matched with envelopes of equal quality. An erasable type of bond paper allows corrections to be made. Because bond papers have a hard surface, inks must be carefully chosen and special care must be exercised during printing.

In addition to business, professional, and personal stationery, high-quality bond papers are used for insurance policies, certificates, statements, deeds, and long-life documents. Some bond paper grades are available in colors and in finishes such as laid and linen. Register bond or business forms bond is a special type of bond made for the specific requirements of manufacturing continuous printed forms. Some bond papers are designed for uses other than printing.

Bristol Paper

The basic size for bristol paper is 22½×28½ in. (572×724 mm), with basis weights of 67, 80, 100, 120, 140, and 160 lb./ream (147, 176, 219, 263, 307, and 351 g/m^2). Uncoated printing bristols are made from chemical wood pulp (free of groundwood), in white and colors. Finishes are "smooth" and "vellum."

A vellum-finish bristol is widely used for offset lithography because of its higher bulk, pleasing surface, and ability to set inks quickly with minimum setoff. Because of their excellent strength and bulk, printing bristols are used for cover applications.

Index bristols have a basic size of 25½×30½ in. (648×775 mm), with basis weights of 90, 110, 140, and 170 lb./ream (163, 199, 253, and 308 g/m^2). They are are made with a smooth finish in white and colors, and they are available in different grades, including those made from all-chemical wood pulp and 25, 50, or 100% cotton fiber. Because of their toughness, stiffness, good writing and erasing surface, and resistance to repeated handling, index bristols are used for file cards and records, index systems, ruled forms, mailing cards, diecut novelties, and covers. A typical application for cotton-content index bristols is the filing cards used in libraries, institutions, and government agencies.

Postal bristol is made specifically for postcard use, in either white or light cream color. It has a smooth, uniform finish designed for pen-and-ink writing and a caliper suitable for mail-processing equipment.

Coated bristols — used for heavyweight cover applications and for pictorial postcards — are available with coating on one or both sides and in white and colors. Standard thicknesses are 8, 10, 11, and 12 points (0.20, 0.25, 0.28, and 0.30 mm).

Business Forms Bond (Register Bond)

Business forms bond is a type of bond paper manufactured for the specific requirements of nonheatset web printing and continuous business forms. The basic size for business forms bond is 17×22 in. (432×559 mm), with the most common basis weights being 12, 15, 18, and 20 lb./ream (45, 56, 68, and 75 g/m^2). In forms printing, both colored and white register bonds are used to differentiate the sheets (plies) in a set of forms. Specific paper requirements for forms printing include rapid ink absorption, adequate strength and stiffness for printing, dimensional stability for registration of collated forms, and a surface capable of accepting clean, sharp carbon impressions. Other requirements include close control of caliper, exceptionally good roll quality, and the ability to be refolded and stacked at high speed for computer printouts.

Carbonless Papers

Carbonless papers are replacing many carbon interleaved forms because they simplify paper work, produce smudge-free copies, and eliminate the messiness associated with the use and disposal of carbon paper. Carbonless papers are technically different from regular papers. They incorporate a chemical transfer system and use a reaction between two different chemical coatings to transfer images. The back side of the top sheet in the carbonless set is coated with encapsulated chemicals. The intermediate sheets have a receptor coating on the front side and an encapsulated coating on the back side, with the last sheet of the set having a receptor coating only. When pressure is applied to the top sheet of the set by typing, writing, or "crash printing," an image is formed by the reaction between the chemicals liberated from the collapsed capsules and the contacting receptor coating. Special precaution must be taken not to damage the encapsulated chemicals by excessive pressure and friction during handling, printing, cutting, and trimming. The proper side of each paper used in the set must be printed so that the sheets are collated in their required sequence. Manufacturers of carbonless papers provide specific instructions for the printing and processing of these papers.

Coated Printing Paper

The basic size for coated printing paper is 25×38 in. (635×965 mm), with basis weights of 60, 70, 80, and 100 lb./ream (89, 104, 118, and 148 g/m^2). Coated papers, also known as **enamels,** are manufactured for sheetfed offset in various grade levels and designated as 1, 2, 3, or 4, or premium. Grade levels are determined primarily by brightness, with premiums being brighter than the others.

The finishes of coated papers range from the superhigh gloss of cast-coated enamels to the "glossless" look of matte-coated papers. **Cast-coated paper,** whose surface is produced by a casting process is a special and separate type of paper. This paper has an exceptionally smooth, level surface and a mirrorlike gloss. Cast-coated paper bulks higher because it is not supercalendered.

The gloss range of dull-finish enamels is normally 25–35. Dull enamels, like high-gloss enamels, are supercalendered but use different coating formulations to produce a dull surface. Dull coated enamels are used where good ink holdout and a lay of ink approaching that of glossy enamels is wanted, but without a glossy paper background. Dull enamels are used for annual reports, catalogs, product brochures, and books and for printing jobs requiring high-quality multicolor reproduction with minimal paper gloss.

Below dull coated enamels are the coated matte grades. The basic size of coated matte papers is 25×38 in. (635×965 mm), with standard basis weights of 50, 60, 70, 80, and 100 lb./ream (74, 89, 104, 118, and 148 g/m^2). These papers combine some of the advantages of both uncoated and coated dull papers. While they do not have the high degree of ink holdout that fully coated paper has, their lithographic reproduction is far superior to that of uncoated papers. With a glare-free background and a maximum gloss of 0–20, matte-coated papers handle like uncoated paper on press. They generally have a higher bulk and opacity than enamel papers of the same weight because they are not supercalendered and have less coating and therefore more fibers.

Embossed enamel and matte-coated papers are available in various embossed patterns. They offer the high reproduction fidelity of a coated paper along with a textured background.

Coated papers for web offset — made for the specific requirements of heatset drying and for running on a web press — are available in high-gloss enamel, dull-finish enamel, and in a matte surface similar to that used for sheetfed offset. The upper limit of their basis weight, at a basic size of 25×38 in. (635×965 mm), generally does not exceed 100 lb./ream (148 g/m^2) because of blistering and folding considerations.

Cover Paper

The basic size of cover paper is 20×26 in. (508×660 mm), with basis weights ranging from 50 lb./ream (135 g/m^2) to as high as 19 pt. in thickness (0.48 mm). Cover paper's primary functions are physical and aesthetic. A cover paper must have sufficient strength and durability to protect its contents adequately under normal use. It may be required to match the color and surface texture of the inside paper or to be distinctly different in appearance. Additional requirements may involve diecutting, embossing, varnishing, lacquering, the printing of metallic inks, scoring, stapling, and drilling.

Coated cover papers are used because of their enhanced print quality and ink holdout. Surfaces may have a glossy or dull finish. Most coated covers match the whiteness or color and the finish of a companion coated paper. Coated covers are available in white and numerous colors and in different finishes, grades, and basis weights. Colors may be brilliant, bright, pastel, or subdued, depending on the needs of the designer. Finishes include plate, smooth, wove, vellum, laid, and felt, as well as embossed finishes having various patterns.

Deckle-edge cover papers are sometimes used. Duplex covers are made by laminating two cover papers having a different color or finish. Coated bristol papers and tag papers often fulfill the strength requirement for a thick, stiff coated cover.

Specialty cover papers include plastic-laminated and pyroxylin-coated covers, which are water-, soil-, and grease-resistant and require special inks for their printing. Other specialty covers are coated with mica, gold, or silver. Their surfaces may be embossed, flocked, or velour-textured. The embossed patterns can resemble the texture of leather or cloth. In creating attractive, functional covers for booklets, annual reports, catalogs, and advertising, graphic designers can choose from a wide variety of attractive and functional cover stocks.

Label Paper

The basic size for label paper is 25×38 in. (635×965 mm), with basis weights of 60 and 70 lb./ream (89 and 104 g/m^2). Label papers coated on one side (C1S) are designed for the diverse requirements of printed label manufacture, application, and end use. Beyond the printing process, these requirements may include varnishing, lacquering, bronzing, and embossing. Other considerations are the labeling application, laminating, compatibility with adhesives, and the lamination of or combination with other materials. The coated side of labels may be white or colored and may be supercalendered, cast-coated, or matte-finished.

Labels are used for such applications as box wraps, cigarette packaging, metal can and bottle labels, posters, book jackets, food wraps, pressure-sensitive labels, and lamination to paperboard. When selecting a label paper, printers should give the paper supplier all requirements pertaining to the paper's printing and finishing operations, method of application, and end use.

Latex-Treated Papers

Latex-treated papers have fibers that are impregnated with latex to ensure durability, high-edge tear resistance, wet strength, flexibility, and leatherlike properties. They may be stretched, stamped, punched, and embossed in the same manner as leather. Embossed patterns with leather and fabric designs may be applied. Latex-treated papers may be coated for improved printability and resistance to oil, grease, and water. They are used for rugged printed covers, charts, maps, labels, banners, tags, book covers, and children's books.

Ledger Papers

Ledger papers are made in heavier basis weights than bond papers. They are available in basis weights of 24, 28, 32, and 36 lb./ream (90, 105, 120, and 135 g/m^2), and their basic size is 17×22 in. (432×559 mm).

Ledger papers must have good strength, good stiffness, and a hard surface suitable for pen-and-ink writing, erasing, ruling, and data entry. These papers are used for the machine posting of data, which requires a smooth to slightly rough or "postal" finish. Ledger papers are made from all-chemical wood pulp, from a combination of wood and cotton fibers, or from 100% cotton fiber. Typical uses include loose-leaf and bound ledger books, inventory and accounting record systems, wills, deeds, and other long-lasting documents.

Lightweight Coated Printing Papers

Lightweight coated printing paper grades are usually made from groundwood fibers and have the lowest brightness of the printing grade family. Lightweight coated groundwood papers are used extensively for high-volume web offset or rotogravure printing of magazines, catalogs, and preprinted newspaper inserts and coupons. Their basic size is 25×38 in. (635×965 mm), and their basic weight ranges from 30 lb. to 40 lb./ream (44 to 59 g/m^2).

Manifold and Onionskin

Manifold and onionskin papers are essentially lightweight bond papers. Manifold papers are available in either machine or unglazed finish, and in a finish machine-glazed on one side for producing distinct carbon copies. Onionskin papers are air-dried and have a cockle, smooth, or calendered finish. Their fiber content may be all-chemical wood, or 25% or 100% cotton fiber. Both types of papers are often ordered grain-short for maximum rigidity in the press-running direction and for better blanket release. Regular basis weights, at a basic size of 17×22 in. (432×559 mm), are 8 or 9 lb./ream (30 or 34 g/m^2). Representative uses of manifold and onionskin papers are airmail stationery, lightweight reports, catalogs, manuals, envelope enclosures, advertisements, and carbon copies of correspondence and legal documents.

Newsprint

Newsprint is manufactured largely from groundwood pulps and is used primarily for the printing of newspapers. Newsprint traditionally has not been surface-sized because it needs to be highly absorbent to allow for the rapid penetration of news ink without the aid of heatset drying. Newsprint used for quality multicolor newspapers is usually sized, however, to give it a stronger and more lint-free surface. The quality of newsprint has also been improved by twin-wire paper machines that produce a sheet with less two-sidedness.

Most newspapers once printed solely by letterpress are now printed by web offset and flexography. Since newsprint is an inherently weak paper, roll defects can easily precipitate web breaks on high-speed presses. Moisture content must be maintained at a high level, close to 8%, to prevent brittleness and web breaks.

Rotogravure supplements are printed on a "roto news" paper. **Roto news** is made with more finely screened pulp, contains more filler than regular news, and is calendered to the higher finish needed for rotogravure printing. Proper receptivity and holdout for gravure inks, softness and compressibility, freedom from abrasiveness, and rolls free from defects are other essential requirements of roto news paper. Supercalendered uncoated rotogravure papers containing mechanical pulp and fillers are used as a premium roto paper for the Sunday supplements and magazine sections of newspapers.

Newspaper inserts may be printed on newsprint or roto news. However, for more effective printed advertising and reader response, higher quality uncoated and coated papers printed multicolor on heatset presses can be used for newspaper inserts.

Paperboard

The term "paperboard" refers to paper products that have a higher basis weight (grammage), greater thickness, and more rigidity than paper. Paperboard normally has a thickness of at least 12 pt. (0.012 in. or 0.30 mm). Some exceptions to this rule are liner board and corrugating medium (whose thickness may be less than 12 pt.) and drawing paper (which may exceed 12 pt. in thickness).

Solid unbleached sulfate (SUS) paperboard grades are used as a facing material for corrugated containers, as a corrugating medium for the fluting material in corrugated containers, and in the fabrication of cartons and beverage carriers. Solid white bleached paperboard, called **solid bleached sulfate** or **SBS,** is widely used for the packaging of food and nonedible products such as plates, dishes, and blister packaging. Recycled paperboard is converted into containers, folding and set-up boxes, cores, and corrugating medium and is used in the manufacture of chipboard.

The function of paperboard cartons, boxes, and containers is not only to protect the product, but also to advertise and sell it at the point of purchase and to provide instructions for its proper use. Paperboard cartons are used for milk and other beverages. White-lined or coated gray boxboard made from recycled fibers is printed for cereal, soap, and cracker boxes. Strong white-lined unbleached board is printed for applications such as beverage carriers. Solid white (bleached) paperboard of various thicknesses, either coated or uncoated, is printed for folding cartons used to package products like food, cosmetics, candy, and cigarettes.

Parchment

Artificial parchment, with its mottled appearance, is produced by a special procedure during papermaking. It is available in white and pastel colors and in various weights. Artificial parchment is used for printed products like wine lists, certificates, testimonials, diplomas, announcements, guarantees, and coupons, and where a dignified background for printing is desired.

Vegetable parchment is a unique paper made by passing paper through a sulfuric acid bath that fuses its fibers into a homogenous mass. It has a high wet strength and is greaseproof. Because of its unique appearance and durable hard surface, vegetable parchment is used for etching and drawing applications; wills, deeds, diplomas, and stock certificates; reproductions of historical and religious documents; and other permanent records. Because of its greaseproof surface, vegetable parchment is ideal for certain package enclosures. Special inks are required for printing parchment paper because of its greaseproof surface.

Safety Papers

Safety papers must be able to expose forgery or document alterations made by either mechanical erasure or chemicals. They also must meet the rigid durability specifications needed in the handling and treatment of bank checks. Safety papers are available with a protective background in various designs and colors. The standard basis weight, at the basic size of 17×22 in. (432×559 mm), is 24 lb./ream (90 g/m^2).

Check paper must have a smooth surface for imprinting sharply defined, unbroken MICR characters and for printing pictorial backgrounds. Other critical requirements include adequate bursting and tear strength and the ability to maintain rigidity to withstand repeated handling and many passes through high-speed check-sorting equipment. While the largest use for safety papers is printed checks, they are also used for many other negotiable documents that need protection against forgery, such as bonds, deposit slips, coupons, tickets, merchandise certificates, certificates of title, warranties, and legal forms.

Tag Papers

The basic size of tag papers is 24×36 in. (610×914 mm), with basis weights of 100, 125, 150, 175, 200, and 250 lb./ream (163, 203, 244, 285, 325, and 408 g/m²). Tag papers are made from long-fiber sulfate pulps that have exceptional strength. These papers are calendered to a smooth, hard finish and are available in white, manila, and various other colors. Coated tag papers are used where better printability is required. Typical applications are tags, file folders, job tickets, jackets, heavy-duty envelopes, and covers.

Text Papers

Text papers are made in many different finishes and textured surfaces, in bright and natural white shades, and in many different colors. Some are watermarked and have deckled edges that lend a degree of elegance and beauty to the paper. Text papers are made in wove, antique, vellum, and felt finishes, which may have light, medium, or heavy pattern-depth embossing. They come in a gamut of colors, including strong bright colors, subdued colors, and pastels. Many grades are available in matching envelopes and cover weights. Text papers offer varied and visually appealing backgrounds for graphic design and are especially suited for programs, announcements, menus, annual reports, and corporate advertising brochures.

Uncoated Groundwood Printing Paper

The basic size of uncoated groundwood printing paper is 25×38 in. (635×965 mm), with basis weights ranging from 20 to 45 lb./ream (30 to 67 g/m²). Uncoated, machine-finish groundwood printing papers are similar to newsprint but have a smoother surface and higher brightness. They are manufactured with various percentages of fillers to enhance their brightness and printability. Printing applications include catalogs, directories, periodicals, bus transfers, way bills, ballots, and paperbacks.

Supercalendered uncoated groundwood papers are increasingly used for rotogravure printing. These supercalendered papers have a higher percentage of clay filler and more highly refined mechanical pulps than machine-finished groundwood printing papers, providing a superior finish for gravure printing. The print quality of supercalendered uncoated ground-wood approaches that of lightweight coated groundwood paper. Printing applications include magazines, catalogs, and the supplement and magazine sections of Sunday newspapers.

Uncoated Free Offset (No Groundwood)

Uncoated free offset papers have a basic size of 25×38 in. (635×965 mm) and basis weights ranging from 45 to 120 lb./ream. (67 to 178 g/m^2). These papers are available in both sheetfed and web offset varieties and in many grades, finishes, and colors. Finishes include various smooth, wove, vellum, antique, and embossed patterns. White offset papers range in brightness from approximately 75 to 90, or above. Opaque offset grades offer more opacity and brightness than standard grades. Colored offset lines come in six or more colors. Their uses run the gamut from commercial printing to such applications as personalized computer-generated letters and "business forms" promotional mailings. For book manufacturing, uncoated free sheets can be made to a specified bulk and shade, as well as for specific printing processes and binding requirements.

Wedding Papers

The basic size for wedding papers is 17×22 in. (432×559 mm), with basis weights of 28, 32, 36, and 40 lb./ream (105, 120, 135, and 150 g/m^2). These papers are made with a very uniform fiber distribution and a nonglare refined surface. Wedding papers are made from chemical wood, cotton fibers, or a combination of cotton fibers and wood fibers. Whether finished as vellum, plate, or linen, wedding papers must have an appearance of quality and the ability to produce sharply engraved characters. In addition to wedding stationery, wedding papers are used as stationery for executive, professional, and personal use, and for commercial announcements and invitations. Bristol weights are used for business cards, acknowledgments, and announcements.

7　Handling Paper Complaints

Printers are responsible for getting the job out on time, meeting customer needs, and recovering any losses associated with problems caused by paper or other input materials. Paper merchants and papermakers are responsible for meeting the needs of printers and their customers and, if necessary, replacing any defective material and providing compensation for losses that are directly related to paper.

Although the printer's and papermaker's responsibilities are very similar, the emergence of a complaint can initially put more pressure on the printer. Most paper manufacturers will replace a particular paper or compensate for lost time and wasted material if they have evidence showing that the paper is defective or the most probable cause of a problem at the printing plant. Evidence of paper problems comes primarily from paper mill records and the pressroom. Mill records will usually show that the paper met specified standards when it was shipped because the manufacturer's policy is to recycle or send paper to the seconds market if it doesn't meet set standards. The evidence that a paper is defective is usually found in the pressroom, so it therefore becomes the responsibility of the printer to provide the necessary proof that paper was the cause of a particular problem.

Some printers handle paper problems by either switching manufacturers or by mentioning the problem to the suppliers and absorbing the loss. Other printers will report a problem, with no supporting evidence, and expect the supplier to automatically pay for all losses, becoming frustrated and angry when this does not happen. While the above approaches to paper problems offer some degree of satisfaction, they do not provide insight into solving present and future paper problems, nor do they support fair and equitable settlements.

For this reason, the printer should have a solid complaint handling system in place to manage paper problems. As part of this system, the problem should be immediately reported to the paper merchant or mill, and supporting evidence and data should be gathered, recorded, and submitted. The printer is essentially the only one in a position to collect the real time data and samples necessary to support a paper problem. The pressroom is, in a sense, the "scene of the crime," where clues and evidence exist for supporting a claim. The pressroom is also the source for evidence that determines whether or not a paper is responsible for a given problem.

Reporting and Verifying Paper Problems

Reporting of a Problem

The first action a printer should take when a paper problem arises is to notify the merchant or mill representative. This early warning of a potential problem gives the paper supplier an opportunity to provide input before waste and lost press time is incurred. If a decision must be made to continue the job with the paper that is causing a problem, it should be made in cooperation with the paper supplier. Continuing to use problem paper without informing the paper supplier or allowing for input may lead to disagreements that frustrate later attempts at a financial settlement.

Identifying the Paper

To be able to recommend other paper as a possible cure for a paper problem, paper manufacturers need information that will pinpoint specifically when the paper was made, the paper machine on which it was made, and its exact location across the paper machine reel. Knowing this, papermakers can advise the printer to try paper from another part of the order or even from an entirely different order. It is not unusual for a change in paper to solve the problem. Acquiring information about paper that runs trouble-free can be as important to the paper manufacturer as getting information about problem paper.

Gathering Supporting Evidence

Complaint handling process. It is in the printer's best interest to have a complaint handling process that makes it easy to collect the appropriate samples, data, and information needed to support a claim. Following is a brief outline of a complaint handling system, including some general procedures that should be followed in collecting evidence at the time of printing.

- Establish a process to report complaints, collect samples, and assemble evidence of paper problems.

Having a good com-
plaint handling
system in place
improves the chances
for a fair settlement.

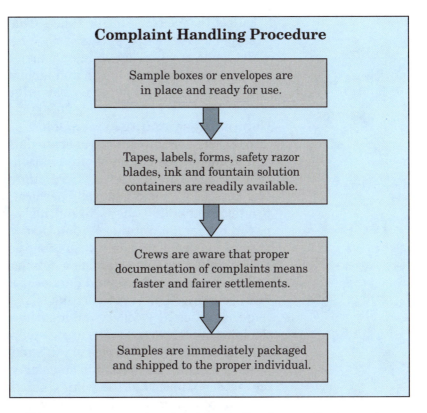

Complaint Handling Procedure

Sample boxes or envelopes are
in place and ready for use.

Tapes, labels, forms, safety razor
blades, ink and fountain solution
containers are readily available.

Crews are aware that proper
documentation of complaints means
faster and fairer settlements.

Samples are immediately packaged
and shipped to the proper individual.

- Educate everyone involved in production on the importance
  of collecting vital information and train them to use the
  proper collecting procedures.
- For a problem involving press sheets, collect and staple
  together twelve consecutive sheets from the *feeder;* for roll
  problems, strip three to four wraps from the roll when the
  problem occurred. *Immediately label the samples.*
- Collect twelve consecutive sheets or signatures (showing
  the problem) from the *delivery* and immediately staple and
  label these samples.
- Collect ink and fountain solution samples from the trays
  and immediately label the containers. Use plastic bottles
  with watertight lids for the fountain solution and plastic
  or metal cans with lids for the ink. *Don't use paper cups for
  samples!* Paper cup containers will absorb water and solvents and may tear and leak.
- If the problem stems from blanket contamination, pull
  samples of the debris from the blanket using tape. Don't
  fold the tape back onto itself or attach it to paper. Instead,
  attach the tape to a piece of clear plastic. Because the
  debris may be carried in with the paper, it is important to

collect twelve consecutive sheets from the feeder. Again, staple and label the sheets.
- Set aside any unused problem paper, cover the paper with a moisture-barrier material, and label it as complaint paper, with job name and paper mill identification numbers.

Complaint sampling system. Most paper mills have extensive testing capabilities to generate data for solving paper- and print-related problems. In addition to paper technology they have the ability to test inks, fountain solution, and blankets. Since mills generally perform tests in response to a printer's complaint, they will routinely ask for samples of the paper, ink, and fountain solution that was on the press at the time of the problem, along with other pertinent information.

The printer should establish a detailed process for collecting and saving the evidence and data accrued while the problem was occurring. The way to do this is to set up a sampling system that efficiently collects all identifying information from the labels, tickets, and cards associated with each carton, skid, and roll, along with samples of ink and fountain solution. The basis of a sampling system is an easily accessible depository for material, placed at the point where information and samples are collected. This depository may take the form of large individual envelopes or boxes with distinct markings that identify the containers as complaint material. These boxes or envelopes should contain small metal or plastic containers, with lids, for collecting ink and fountain solution. Markers for labeling, tape for collecting debris from blankets, and razor blades for cutting paper and scraping blankets should also be included in the complaint boxes or envelopes.

All paper, ink, and fountain solution samples, along with written remarks and records associated with the job, should be placed in these containers and kept until the complaint is settled. Since it is in the merchant's interest to identify paper problems, most papermakers are glad to provide help in setting up a complaint system, and they may even supply the material needed to collect and save the samples.

Sampling. To be helpful to the papermaker, samples of paper problems must be obtained in the proper amounts and must be properly arranged and labeled. Following is the proper sampling procedure for a picking problem that occurs due to differences in sheeted roll paper.

Multiple webs of paper, usually from three to five rolls, are cut together for filling skid and carton orders. It is possible that each roll within this set has different properties such as smoothness, gloss, strength, or absorption. This variation in rolls used to generate sheeted paper will be reflected in the skids or cartons. Since the picking problem may be caused by paper from only one of the rolls, it is important to sample at least twelve consecutive sheets to be sure the offending sheet is included at least twice in the sample. Twelve sheets that include the offending sheet at least twice from both the feeder and delivery will show a pattern that points to paper as the probable cause of the picking.

Collecting and keeping sheets in consecutive order is important for complaint analysis.

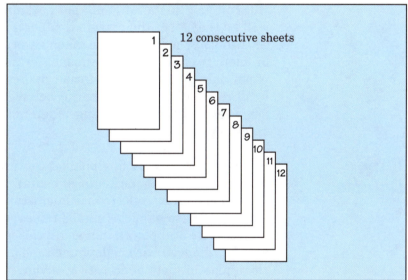

In assembling samples, it is essential to keep the sheets in consecutive order. This is best accomplished by stapling the sheets together when they are collected. The sheets should also be labeled according to position: the top sheet should be labeled top #1, through to the bottom sheet, which would be labeled bottom #12. Samples should include 12 consecutive sheets from the feeder and 12 consecutive sheets from the delivery, taken at the time the problem is occurring. The samples should show the problem, whether it is a printing problem, a curl problem, or a contamination problem.

Immediately after the initial paper samples have been collected, labeled, and placed in the complaint box, paper from another order, or a competitive grade, should be run with the paper that is experiencing the problem. Again, samples should be saved, labeled, and placed in the complaint box, to be retained until the complaint has been resolved.

Inks samples from both the fountain and ink can should be placed in appropriate sample containers (small metal cans, not paper cups), and fountain solution from the fountain trays should be collected in watertight plastic containers. These samples should be labeled and added to the complaint box. The accurate and immediate labeling of samples is extremely important. Waiting too long to label the samples greatly increases the chances of mixing up the samples and is a major reason for confusing information.

Another risky practice is pulling the defective job, then putting it back on press to show the problem. Often the job will run just fine after being put back on the press. It may well be that all of the marginal paper was used in "fighting" the problem, or it may have taken several impressions for the problem to show. It is not unusual for interactions between paper, ink, and fountain solution that cause printing problems at one time to disappear or behave differently when the job is rerun, because of changes in temperature, ink, or length of run.

Paper Defects

Debris. Particles causing blanket contamination such as surface debris, picking, pickouts, or contamination from other sources should be collected for microscopic and chemical analysis. These particles can be removed from the blanket with a knife and placed in a small closed container or they may be removed with cellophane tape and mounted on a clean plastic sheet of acetate or mylar. Never adhere the tape to itself or to paper. As particles are collected, identify and label the sample by the printing unit or units from which particles were taken. If possible, try to match one or more of these particles with the defect it created in the printed sheets by sorting through the printed pile to locate the original defect. Circle the defect, being sure to include the six sheets immediately preceding and the six sheets immediately following this sheet and marking their printing sequence. Staple one of their corners to keep them in proper sequence.

Collect twelve consecutive sheets of the unprinted paper. With a single pass, wipe across the edges of a lift of the unprinted paper with a black cloth. If there is a significant accumulation of white particles, enclose the cloth in an envelope as part of the evidence.

Blanket piling. To report on blanket piling, state whether the piling is occurring in the image or nonimage areas, on which printing units it is occurring, and the color involved in the piling. If at all possible, remove the blanket showing the piling condition and retain it so that the paper supplier may examine it. Otherwise, collect some of the piled material by scraping it from the blanket and placing it in a small container, or remove the material with cellophane tape and mount it on a plastic sheet. If piling is occurring on more than one press unit, collect samples from each unit and immediately label the samples. A photograph of blanket piling after a stated number of impressions is helpful. Collect several press sheets and mark the areas where print quality has deteriorated due to piling. Indicate the number of impressions these sheets represent from the previous washup. A sample of fountain solution and ink from the fountains should be submitted as part of the supporting evidence.

Blistering. Evidence and information needed to support a blistering claim should include twelve consecutive printed sheets or signatures that illustrate blistering, the roll number, approximately 10 ft. (3 m) of the full roll width of the unprinted paper, the temperature of the web as it leaves the dryer, and the press speed. Be sure to *immediately label the samples* as they are being collected.

Curl. It is sometimes difficult to collect samples of curled paper and have them show the same condition of curl after they have been shipped to the paper supplier. Photographs of the paper before and after printing may best illustrate how a curl problem looked at the time of printing. These photographs can include the paper's labeling or identifying information. When samples of paper are shipped for evidence of curl, they must be shipped flat and be well protected from bending. A newly opened carton or skid should be photographed immediately, as should paper that has been opened for a period of time. Information that needs to be reported about a curl problem includes the relative humidity and temperature of the pressroom at the time the curl occurred, the direction of the curl, whether the curl is to the felt or wire side, and whether it is across or with the grain direction. It is also important to know when the curl became evident — that is, before printing, after printing, when the first side was printed, or when the second side was printed.

Damaged blankets. The folded or defective sheet or the material or object that caused blanket damage should be recovered and saved, along with the six printed sheets immediately preceding and the six printed sheets immediately following the printing impression at which damage occurred. The unwashed damaged blanket or blankets should be kept as part of the evidence, and the printing unit or units on which damage occurred should be noted.

Misregister and wrinkles. For misregister and wrinkling problems related to paper, collect twelve consecutive press sheets and mark the areas containing the problem. If unprinted sheet paper has wavy or tight edges or some other visible distortion, take photographs illustrating its condition and collect twelve sheets of the unprinted paper. As soon as a new carton or skid of the same lot is opened, take photographs and collect twelve sheets to illustrate its condition.

For misregister and press wrinkling problems related to roll condition, take photographs of a laid-out, unwound strip from the roll or the web as it feeds into the press. This procedure will show uneven tension, bagginess, or other visible distortion. Collect twelve press sheets or signatures and mark the area that illustrates the problem. Take 6–8 ft. (2–3 m) of unprinted paper (full width) from the trouble-causing roll and mark the boundaries of areas that are baggy, slack, distorted, or otherwise believed to be causing the problem. Identify them by their roll number. Do not fold samples; ship them in a large-diameter mailing tube.

Low printed gloss and mottle. Mark areas of the press sheet or signature to illustrate the problem. Collect the six sheets or signatures immediately preceding the sheet illustrating the problem and the six immediately following this marked sheet. Keep the sheets in sequence and number them "prior to the problem" and "after the problem." If the paper has not been backed up, back up 50–75 sheets and collect twelve consecutive sheets. This procedure will show whether only one side of the sheet has a mottle problem or whether mottle is common to both sides.

Identify the first sheets or, for a roll, 6–8 ft. (2–3 m) of the full roll width. In addition, for each printing unit, completely fill a small ink can with an ink sample, seal the can, and identify the ink by brand name and number.

Web Breaks

Web breaks are a serious problem for all forms of web printing and can occur anywhere on the press, from infeed to cutoff. Breaks result in costly downtime, paper waste, and, frequently, damage to printing plates and blankets. Excessive web tension contributes to web breaks by stretching the paper and reducing its resiliency. On the other hand, most papers have tensile strengths well in excess of the normal infeed tension used for web printing. It usually takes a local weakness or defect in the web, or excessive tension on its edge, to initiate a web break. Following are known causes of web breaks and suggested preventive measures and remedies.

- Excessive tension on one or both edges of the web due to moisture loss and shrinking is making the web tight-edged and baggy. This condition can start tears at one or both edges and cause web breaks. Keeping rolls wrapped, making certain their wrappings are undamaged, and humidifying their storage area during winter are preventive steps.
- There is excessive tension on one edge of the web due to a tapered roll — that is, one having a nonuniform diameter. Sometimes turning the roll end-for-end will help this situation. Tapered rolls should be reported to the mill.
- A roll has a stuck or cracked edge or a dent, nick, or cut on its end. Any edge defect is a weak spot where a tear can start and produce a web break.
- There are wrinkles; slime spots; foam spots; calender, blister, fiber, or hair cuts; or bursts, all potential causes of web breaks. While these defects cannot be entirely avoided in paper manufacturing, their occurrence should be minimal.
- Bad mill splices can cause web breaks.
- An out-of-round, or wobbling, roll gives a jerky web infeed and subjects the web to sudden high tension.
- Faulty press alignment can cause web breaks.

A sample of each web break, including both ends of the break, should be collected and identified by its roll number and its position in the roll — that is, near the core, middle, or outer diameter part of the roll. Also record the location on press where the break occurred. Evidence of the manner in which breaks occur is helpful in determining and eliminating their causes.

Paper Defects That Cause Web Breaks

Blade scratches. A blade scratch is a fine, hairlike indentation in the coating surface that runs in the grain direction. It is caused by a particle becoming lodged behind the paper machine coating blade during the coating operation. If the scratch becomes deep enough to sever the web, it is called a blade cut. If a larger particle becomes lodged behind the blade and produces a wider path, it is termed a **blade streak.**

Blister or calender cuts. A blister or calender cut is a cut in the web that is usually diagonal to the machine direction. It normally results from excess paper that accumulates as a blister at the entrance of a calendering nip and cuts the paper as it passes through the nip. The area adjacent to the cut often appears translucent due to the excessive calendering pressure applied because of the extra paper thickness.

Calender cut.
Courtesy Kimberly-Clark Corp.

Bursts. Bursts are irregular separations, or ruptures, of the web; bursts have several causes and are referred to by different names. An **air shear burst** is produced when air becomes trapped in the roll during winding. A **caliper shear burst** is caused by nonuniform nip velocities due to variations in the paper caliper of the roll during winding. This results in a machine-direction shearing force that exceeds the web strength. A **cross-machine tension burst** appears across the grain and is caused by an abrupt change in cross-machine sheet caliper, or by winding the roll too tightly. A **full machine-direction burst** refers to a complete separation, or rupture, of the web that parallels the machine direction. It is caused by winding the roll so tightly that its wound-in tension exceeds the ultimate tensile strength of the paper. The only recourse in running rolls with bursts is to remove the ruptured outer laps. The roll should be rejected if the bursts extend too deeply into it.

Burst.
*Courtesy Kimberly-
Clark Corp.*

Cracked edges or edge tears. A cracked edge, or edge tear, is a broken edge of the web that usually extends only a short distance inward from the edge. These cracked edges usually result from paper that has been manufactured with too little moisture. Cracked edges or edge tears are likely to create web breaks.

Dished or telescoped rolls. Dished or telescoped rolls have the appearance of roll edge misalignment, which may be convex or concave. Dishing occurs during roll winding; telescoping occurs when some inner part of the roll slips in the direction of its axis after winding. Telescoping can take place during shipping or handling, or as the roll is unwound. Causes of telescoping are too "soft" a winding, nonuniform cross-machine caliper, and excessive web tension while unwinding.

A telescoped roll.
*Courtesy Consolidated
Paper, Inc.*

End damage and stuck edges. End damage and stuck edges can be serious and costly. Examples of end damage are edge nicks or tears, gouges, and bruises caused by rolls being struck with sharp objects or handling equipment or being tipped on their ends. A stuck web occurs when one or more web layers are stuck to each other because water or glue gets on the end of the roll. All of these defects can initiate web breaks.

Roll with damaged edge.
Courtesy Kimberly-Clark Corp.

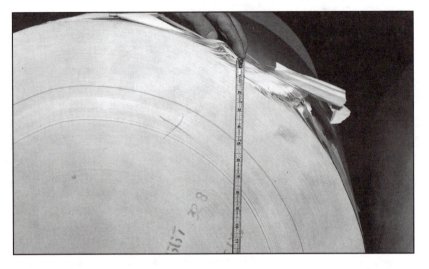

Fiber cuts. A fiber cut in a web is normally short, straight, fairly smooth, and randomly located. Frequently the fiber, or shive, that produced the cut as the paper passed through calendering is visible adjacent to the cut. A **hair cut** is a smooth, curved cut. As the paper containing the hair passes through calendering, the hair cuts the web. Fiber and hair cuts can start web breaks, especially when they are located at the edge of the web and oriented in the cross-web direction.

Fiber cut.
Courtesy Kimberly-Clark Corp.

Hair cut.

Holes. Holes can result from slime or agglomerates of fines and fibers that lift from the web. A hole in the paper machine wire or a small plugged area in the wire can also produce holes. Holes are an obvious cause of web breaks.

Slime hole.
Courtesy Kimberly-Clark Corp.

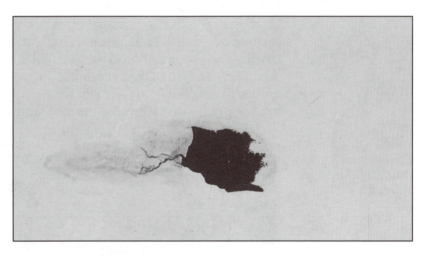

Moisture welts. Moisture welts, or wrinkles, are bands of raised welts or soft wrinkles that appear near the outer roll diameter and run in the machine direction. They result from moisture absorption and an expansion of the paper in its cross-grain direction. These welts or wrinkles form when rolls are exposed to high humidity, or when cold rolls are exposed to warm air for any length of time. Moisture welts rarely extend far into the roll. They can be removed by slabbing off the outer wraps. If not removed, moisture welts can cause weaving of the web and misregister.

Out-of-round rolls and crushed cores. Out-of-roundness and crushed cores can result from storing a roll on its side, excessive clamp pressure with roll-handling equipment, or dropping or bumping the roll. An out-of-round roll will "hump" as it unwinds, producing a jerky web travel with varying web tension and causing misregister. To avoid out-of-roundness, rolls should be stored and shipped on their ends, the clamping pressure of roll lift trucks should be controlled to the minimum necessary for safe transportation, and rolls should never be dropped or subjected to severe impacts.

Ridges or hard spots. A ridge, or hard spot, is a defect that appears as a ring extending around the roll circumference. It is caused by a nonuniform cross-grain caliper. Higher caliper areas build up into ridges, causing the paper within the ridge to stretch. This stretching can also cause press wrinkles and misregister in that area.

Rope marks and corrugations. Rope marks, chain marks, and corrugations are bands of relatively uniform width that extend around the roll, possibly all the way through the roll, parallel to the machine direction. Within these bands are diagonal markings that resemble a rope or have a tire-like pattern. The latter are softer areas caused by lower caliper and a greater stretching of the web under high tension during winding and calendering.

Corrugated roll.
Courtesy Consolidated Paper, Inc.

Splices. A poorly made splice will cause a web break. To prevent this kind of break, the spliced ends should be parallel and in exact alignment and the draw across the splice should be even. In addition, careful attention should be paid to keeping the splicing adhesive away from other wraps of the roll to keep them from sticking together. If printers are having problems with mill splices, the matter should be discussed with the mill to determine the best splices for that particular operation.

Starred rolls. A starred roll has an end with a "star" pattern caused by tightly wound paper surrounding loosely wound paper so that the higher tension of the outer layers squeezes the inner layers. Dropping, bumping, or clamping a roll or subjecting it to impact will cause its inner layers to buckle or shift and will transform the circular winding pattern to a starred one. A starred roll is no longer round. It has flat sections across its face that cause it to hump and unwind with jerky draws. If starring is not severe, however, a roll may run without trouble.

Static and curl. Static and curl problems normally appear in web printing only if the paper is delivered as sheets rather than as signatures. Static that builds up as the paper passes through the press can prevent it from delivering and jogging properly at the sheeter. Loss of moisture in the paper can contribute to static problems. Remoisturizing the web is an effective way to combat static, but the web must be cool in order to retain any applied moisture. Reducing the temperature of the chill rolls sometimes helps, but if problems persist, the printer should consider installing a special remoisturizer.

Web wrinkles and creases. Web wrinkles and creases can develop and run lengthwise as the web passes through the press. Causes are moisture welts and a web having slack edges due to moisture picked up while in the roll. A slack-edged web will be forced to contract sideways as it passes through the printing nip. This will produce wrinkling, which, in turn, can cause a web break and misregister. Following are steps for minimizing wrinkling:
- Increase web tension. Stretching the web tends to tighten slack edges.
- Keep rolls wrapped until they are printed to prevent moisture loss or gain at their ends.
- Build up the ends of the infeed idler roller with tape or paper just under the web's slack edges.
- Add as many infeed rollers as can be mounted into the infeed system. The greater the amount of web festooning, the greater will be the tendency for the web to flatten out.
- Use a curved spreader roll at the infeed to flatten the web.

8   Technology and Measurement

Paper Composition

The raw materials generally used to make paper are cellulosic fibers; pigments such as clay, calcium carbonate, titanium dioxide and plastic; dyes for shade and solid colors; adhesives (also known as binders), such as starch and latex; and an assortment of additives. The fibers give bulk, strength and foldability to paper, while the pigments contribute to printability by increasing surface smoothness. The binders, or adhesives, bond pigments to each other and to the fibers. Additives are used for such purposes as improving the flow properties of coatings, reducing coating foam, and controlling the migration of water from coatings. Dyes are used for creating the desired shades in printing papers as well as the strong, solid colors of specialty papers.

The selection and proportions of these materials is based on the printing process, the converting operation, functional and end-use requirements, and cost considerations. For example, coatings, which consist of pigments, binders, and additives, must be formulated for the needs of the printing method and product end use. Offset coated papers contain more binder than letterpress, flexo, or gravure papers because of the higher force required to split an offset ink film. Binders for offset printing must also resist water in order not to weaken during the printing operation. The type of binder used, such as acetates, styrene butadienes, acrylics, or starches, depends on the degree of water resistance, the level of pick resistance, ink setting time requirements, web drying ovens, and desired paper gloss.

A typical coating pigment contains 80–90% clay. Titanium dioxide, calcium carbonate, and plastic pigments make up the other 10–15%. Titanium dioxide and calcium carbonate, being bright white pigments, are used to increase the whiteness and brightness of paper. Because titanium dioxide is eight to ten times more costly than clay or carbonate, it is used only when the required brightness and opacity cannot be achieved by other pigments. Calcium carbonate is a brighter pigment than clay and is used to increase a paper's brightness, but its opacity is not as great as titanium's. Plastic pigments, because of their thermoplasticity, soften under the calendering temperature and pressure making it easier to obtain higher levels of paper gloss. It is not unusual for high-quality printing papers to contain all four pigments.

Fiber

Trees are the primary source of paper fiber, because of their availability and lower cost. Cotton and linen fibers are used for specialty papers such as bonds and writing papers. Fibers processed from trees or other sources are referred to as pulp, which is processed in pulp mills. There are two primary processes for making pulp. The mechanical process uses the whole tree—excluding bark, roots, and leaves—and grinds it into pulp using giant grindstones. This type of pulp, known as groundwood, has a low brightness and fibers that are weaker than fibers produced by the chemical processes. The major use of groundwood pulp is in lightweight newsprint. It is not uncommon, however, for printing papers to contain 25–30% groundwood fibers.

The other processes for producing pulp use chemicals to extract the fibers. Fibers from this process are brighter and stronger than groundwood fibers and are more costly to produce because only about 50% of the tree is converted into fibers and because chemicals are used. The most common species of trees used in making pulp are hardwoods such as maple and oak, and softwoods such as pine and spruce. Softwood fibers are longer and stronger than hardwood fibers and are used where paper strength is important—for example, bags and boxes. The hardwoods, with their shorter and thinner fibers, are best suited for smooth printing surfaces. Most papers, however, including printing papers, contain long fibers for strength. It is possible to analyze paper for the type of fiber it contains; this process is described in TAPPI T 401.

Fiber Length, Printing, and Strength Properties

As the ratio of the long-fiber content to the short-fiber content of a paper is increased, its strength properties increase. Long fibers produce a wilder, less uniform formation and a reduction in surface levelness and smoothness. The demands for strength generally conflict with those for printability.

Effect of fiber on paper properties.

Property	If fiber length is increased	If fiber length is decreased
Bursting strength	Increases	Decreases
Folding endurance	Increases	Decreases
Formation	Becomes wilder	Becomes less wild
Print quality	Becomes poorer	Becomes better
Surface levelness	Decreases	Increases
Surface smoothness	Decreases	Increases
Tearing resistance	Increases	Decreases
Tensile strength	Increases	Decreases

Mechanical Refining Fibers

Refining is a process that mechanically alters fibers in a way that increases their ability to bind to each other, enhancing other desirable properties. Initial refining slightly increases tearing resistance because fiber bonds are developed that resist fibers' capacity to pull away from each other when paper is torn. With further refining, tearing resistance continues to decline because of the reduction in fiber length and fiber cutting. Maximum tear can, therefore, be achieved only with minimal refining.

Bursting strength, folding endurance, and tensile strength increase with increased refining because of the greater degree of fiber bonding that occurs during papermaking. If refining

Effect of refining on paper properties.

Property	If refining is increased	If refining is decreased
Apparent density	Increases	Decreases
Caliper	Decreases	Increases
Compressibility	Decreases	Increases
Dimensional stability	Decreases	Increases
Formation	Becomes more uniform, less wild	Becomes less uniform, wilder
Hardness and softness	Harder	Softer
Ink holdout of uncoated paper	Becomes greater	Becomes less
Internal bond strength	Increases	Decreases
Porosity	Decreases	Increases
Smoothness	Tends to increase	Tends to decrease

is continued far enough, these strength properties will independently reach their peak value and then decline because of the extreme fiber cutting and shortening that results from prolonged refining. For example, onionskin paper, which is highly refined, has a high tensile strength but low tearing resistance. The caliper for any given basis weight will decrease gradually with continued refining because, as fiber bonding becomes progressively greater, a denser fibrous network results. As the paper becomes denser with continued refining, it also becomes harder and less compressible.

Added refining also produces paper that is less porous and therefore less absorbent of printing inks. By increasing the cutting and reduction of fiber length, papermakers can achieve a better formation, as well as a smoother, more level surface

Effect of refining on paper properties.

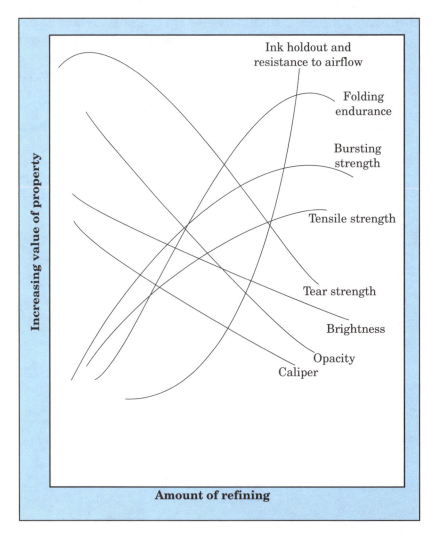

Ink holdout and resistance to airflow

Folding endurance

Bursting strength

Tensile strength

Tear strength

Brightness

Opacity

Caliper

Increasing value of property

Amount of refining

for printing. In addition, internal bond strength is raised with increased fiber bonding.

Increased refining is detrimental to dimensional stability because refining increases the bond between fibers which, in turn, reduces the space between the fibers. This reduction in fiber space reduces the amount a fiber can change before affecting other fibers. Fibers that swell or shrink because of moisture loss or gain transfer this change to the paper when they are tightly bonded together, producing dimensional changes in the paper.

Refining also adversely affects optical properties. Refining decreases opacity because closer fiber bonding and a reduction in interfiber air spaces results in less light scattering and a more transparent paper. Brightness is also decreased because a greater portion of incident light will penetrate deeper into and be absorbed by the denser structure of a more refined paper, allowing less light to be reflected by the paper.

For a hypothetical paper, the manner in which each of these properties changes independently of the others with continued refining can be visualized by a graphic representation of their values versus refining. (See illustration on facing page.) The extent of refining for any given paper depends on a careful balance of the various optical, structural, surface, and mechanical properties required for its end use.

Fillers

Fillers of various types and amounts are added to the paper-making furnish to increase opacity, brightness, and smoothness; reduce ink strike-through; and decrease roughness due to fiber size. As the percentage of filler in paper is increased, the paper's voids and capillaries are reduced in size, increasing the ability of the paper to absorb fluids. An increase in filler content usually increases the absorbency of paper.

Dimensional stability is improved with increasing filler content because filler is inert to moisture, which reduces the paper's reaction to moisture changes. From a printing standpoint, a filler content of 15–25% is generally desirable for uncoated papers. Other use requirements and paper characteristics, however, may dictate that a lesser percentage be used. The amount of filler in a paper is expressed as its **ash content.** The percentage of ash in a paper is determined by placing a weighed sample in a crucible and subjecting it to a high temperature until all carbon residue is completely burned. The residue of ash remaining after combustion consists of inorganic materials such as fillers and coating pigments. The procedure for determining the ash content of paper is described in TAPPI T 413. Qualitative analysis of the ash content of paper to identify its mineral constituents requires elaborate analytical procedures, as described in TAPPI T 421. Sophisticated equipment is used to identify the many chemical components of paper and to shorten the time required for chemical analysis.

Filler's Influence on Paper Properties

Fillers are used primarily because they improve optical properties and printability, increase opacity and brightness, and improve the print quality of uncoated papers. Since fillers are relatively inert to moisture, as compared to fibers, they tend to make paper less sensitive to changes in relative humidity and to improve its dimensional stability. Fillers reduce stiffness and bulk and make paper softer, which may or may not be advantageous. Fillers reduce the physical strength properties of burst, fold, tear, and tensile strength. Internal bond strength is also reduced as the percentage of filler is increased.

The opposing effects of fillers on paper properties show why compromise must often be made in determining the extent to which fillers will be used in paper to meet the demands of a printing process or end-use requirements.

Effect of fillers on paper properties.

Property	If filler content is increased	If filler content is decreased
Brightness	Increases	Decreases
Bursting strength	Decreases	Increases
Caliper	Decreases	Increases
Dimensional stability	Increases	Decreases
Folding endurance	Decreases	Increases
Ink absorbency for uncoated paper	Becomes more uniform	Becomes less uniform
Internal bond strength	Decreases	Increases
Opacity	Increases	Decreases
Picking resistance	Decreases	Increases
Rattle	Decreases	Increases
Smoothness	Tends to increase	Tends to decrease
Stiffness	Decreases	Increases
Tearing resistance	Decreases	Increases
Tensile strength	Decreases	Increases

Printability

The printability of a paper's surface can be defined as the degree to which its surface properties enhance the production of high-quality prints by a particular printing process. The printability of a paper surface is influenced by surface and other paper properties. Surface properties that influence printability are smoothness, levelness, the degree to which and the uniformity with which the surface accepts ink transfer from the printing plate, and the paper's absorption of the ink. The levelness of paper refers to the evenness of its surface contour and to surface irregularities that are large and farther apart than the fine, pinpointed ones that determine its smoothness. The surface irregularities and point-to-point variations in actual thickness that describe the degree of levelness are 0.1 in. (2.54 mm) or greater in size and occur at about the same distance apart. Levelness is influenced by formation; a wild formation reduces levelness.

Printability is often difficult, if not impossible, to assess and predict from measurements of various paper properties. Consequently, printing tests are used to give a direct indication of printability. Methods used to measure, control, and predict printability include procedures that have been found, through experience, to best correlate with the printability observed during field performance. Proof presses and laboratory instruments like the Prüfbau and IGT printability testers and the Huck gravure printability tester are used. It is not uncommon to use actual printing presses to evaluate printability. Many efforts have been made to replace subjective evaluation with a single number. To date, no generally accepted method has been devised to quantify printability because it is really a composite of properties such as printed ink gloss, print density, paper smoothness, and paper gloss. Expressing these specific properties as a single number for printability is impractical because the relative importance of these properties is different for different printing jobs. Recognizing and working with these specific properties, however, is a positive step toward better scientific control of printability.

For the visual assessment of print quality, the following general aspects can be considered:
- *The completeness of the printed image areas and the sharpness of their edges.* Ideally, no breaks should occur in the solid areas. There should be no missing or broken halftone dots, sometimes described as "breaks" or, when applied to gravure printing, as "skips" or "snow." Completeness of image transfer is greatly influenced by the **printing**

smoothness of the paper. Printing smoothness refers to the completeness of contact between the paper's surface and the ink film on the printing plate or blanket under printing pressure. The extent to which a paper surface contour will change under printing pressure to contact ink on the printing plate or blanket more completely is known as its **conformability.** Structural deficiencies like a wild formation and insufficient compressibility can cause incompleteness of image transfer.

• *The uniformity of ink absorbency and gloss of a paper's surface as evaluated in solid printed areas and halftones.* Nonuniformity of a paper surface's ink absorbency and gloss produces a gloss mottle, with a density mottle in solid prints and a mottle and graininess in uniform halftone areas. A **mottled,** or **galvanized,** appearance in solid prints is defined as a visible, gross nonuniformity in ink density, color, or gloss, or any combination thereof. **Graininess** refers to the nonuniformity of a printed area, but with a finer and more patterned nonuniformity of ink lay than mottle. Differences in ink acceptance and absorbency from point to point in a paper's surface can be caused by a deficiency in printing smoothness; a wild, nonuniform formation; or an insufficient coverage of the fibers by coating for coated papers. A wild formation with nonuniform fiber distribution can produce a rough surface, different degrees of densification, and ink absorbency of a paper's surface during calendering. Uneven ink penetration from point to point in the surface produces a mottled gloss appearance in heavily inked areas.

• *The color density and gloss in printed areas, which are strongly influenced by the ink holdout and gloss of the paper's surface.* Paper gloss predominantly influences printed-ink gloss. The combined effect of a paper's gloss and ink holdout also influences the color density of the print. Variations in these properties can produce differences in the color and gloss intensities of printed ink films and the contrast and impact of the print. High printed-ink gloss may or may not be desirable depending on the end use of the printed product.

Surface Sizing and Paper Properties

Surface sizing increases the surface strength of uncoated papers and is required to obtain the level of strength needed for offset printing. Because it fills many of the voids and spaces among the fibers, surface sizing improves ink holdout;

Effect of surface sizing on paper properties.

Property	If surface sizing is increased	If surface sizing is decreased
Brightness	Decreases	Increases
Bursting strength	Increases	Decreases
Tendency to crack with sharp fold	Increases	Decreases
Ink holdout	Increases	Decreases
Opacity	Decreases	Increases
Porosity	Decreases	Increases
Stiffness	Increases	Decreases
Surface strength	Increases	Decreases
Tensile strength	Increases	Decreases

increases bursting strength, tensile strength, and stiffness; and reduces opacity, brightness, and porosity. A high level of surface sizing is detrimental to folding since it binds the outer fiber layers together and interferes with their movement when the paper is folded sharply.

Coating Weight and Paper Properties

Coatings are designed to completely cover the paper's fiber structure, while fillers are designed to fill in and around the fibers. Coatings are applied over a fiber mat, or base sheet, that has been filled and smoothed prior to coating. This filling and smoothing operation is usually done in line with the coating operation. The amount of coating applied depends on the roughness of the base sheet and the smoothness and paper gloss required for a particular grade. As coating weight is increased for a given basis weight or grammage, the base stock weight must be correspondingly reduced. Reducing the base stock weight lowers caliper, opacity, stiffness, and strength. These opposing effects limit the maximum coating weight. Increasing coating weight reduces porosity and increases the blister potential of heatset web papers.

Blister Resistance

Papers for heatset web printing have the potential to blister in ink-drying ovens if the moisture content, porosity, internal bond, and dryer temperature are not within acceptable ranges. Coatings, fillers, and surface sizing all increase the potential for blistering by reducing sheet porosity. While the best test for blister resistance is the press dryer itself, there are other methods that can indicate blister-prone paper. One method

uses a hot oil bath, the temperature of which can be adjusted
to chosen values. A paper's blister resistance is measured by
first preconditioning it to a constant relative humidity and
moisture content and then plunging it into a hot oil bath. By
varying the temperature of the oil bath, the tester can determine the temperature at which the paper will blister. This
method, as well as others, does a good job of comparing one
sheet of paper to another; it may be risky, however, to use the
test results to predict whether a paper will or will not blister
on a given press, with a specific dryer, for a particular job.
The accuracy of such a prediction may be somewhat improved
if the test results have been correlated with the performance
history of a given coated paper on heatset web presses.

Another method, described in TAPPI T 526, simulates the
sealing of both sides of a coated web, as would be the case
with back-to-back heavy ink coverage. First, the paper sample is conditioned to a constant relative humidity. Next, clear
lacquer is applied to both of its sides in a prescribed manner.
The oven of the blistering apparatus is adjusted to a selected
temperature. The lacquered test sample is placed in a trans-
porter, which passes it through the oven at a precisely controlled dwell time. The exposed sample is then examined for
blistering. The dwell time and oven temperature can each
be independently varied until blistering occurs. While this
method does not take into account the penetration of solvents
or oils into the paper, it does measure the ability of the paper's
internal bonds to resist the expansion of paper moisture.

Compressibility

Compressibility is the ability of paper to change its surface
contour and make contact with a printing plate or blanket
within a printing nip. **Resiliency** is the ability of paper to recover its original thickness and surface contour after release
of the compressive forces of the printing nip. The compressibility of paper is related to its hardness and density, and
depends on the degree of refining, the interfiber air volume,
and the extent to which the fibers were compacted during
manufacture.

Hardness, and its opposite property **softness,** indicates
the degree to which paper will resist indentation by some
other material such as a stylus, pen, pencil, type, or printing
plate. The softness, or compressibility, of paper is sometimes
measured as the time required for a given volume of air to
leak, or as the rate of air leakage between the paper's surface
and metal surfaces that are applied under pressure. How

deeply the metal surfaces impinge on the paper depends on the paper's softness and compressibility. The rate of air leakage measures relative softness. The slower the leakage, the softer the paper.

The combined interrelationship of compressibility, softness (or "printing cushion"), and resiliency influences the printability of a paper, particularly for letterpress and gravure printing. Compressibility and resiliency help to compensate for point-to-point variation in a paper's thickness by bringing small areas of the paper and printing plate into contact for satisfactory ink transfer during letterpress and gravure printing. Newsprint must be very compressible and resilient for letterpress printing since minimum makeready must be used to overcome surface roughness. Compressibility and resiliency are not as essential for offset and flexographic printing since the rubber blanket in one case, and the plate in the other, provide some resiliency.

While a soft, easily compressible paper is generally preferred to a hard, relatively incompressible paper for printing, some end-use requirements may dictate the reduction of compressibility, resiliency, and softness. Calendering, to obtain the required smoothness and finish, compacts the paper and reduces its compressibility. Papers have to be sufficiently hard for handling and folding and must have adequate strength, durability, erasability, and pick resistance. Offset printing papers are generally harder than those made specifically for letterpress or gravure printing in order to withstand the splitting forces of ink applied by a rubber blanket.

Dimensional Stability

Dimensional stability refers to the ability of a sheet or web paper to maintain constant dimensions in its grain and cross-grain directions under the environmental conditions and stresses applied during printing and converting. No paper is completely dimensionally stable. All papers will expand or shrink with changes in moisture content. If the fibers in a sheet of paper were free to expand or shrink individually without any restraining influence on each other, paper would undergo little dimensional change. Since fibers are bonded to each other at their numerous crossover points, individual fiber dimensions affect the total fiber structure, causing changes in paper dimensions.

The less that paper is refined and the higher its porosity, the less that it will expand or shrink for a given change in moisture content. Too little refining, however, will produce a

Multisection paper expansimeter (Neenah) that measures dimensional stability as a function of relative humidity in accordance with TAPPI UM 549. *Courtesy Technidyne Corporation.*

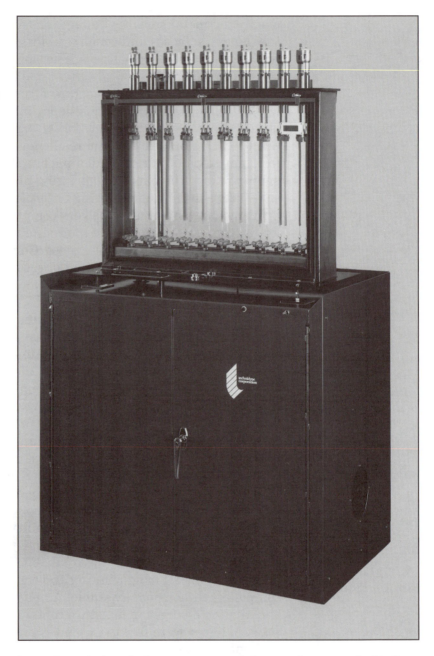

linty, loosely bonded structure with low pick strength. Refining is necessary for developing adequate strength to reduce the potential for picking, blistering, splitting, or delaminating. Printing papers are generally made to have the maximum dimensional stability consistent with other properties required for the printing method. Papers for continuous business forms require a high degree of dimensional stability so that they can be printed, assembled, and collated into multiple sets on pin-fed registration equipment while maintaining their matching "lengths." Papers other than those made specifically for printing purposes may be less dimensionally stable due to characteristics and properties needed for their intended use. It has been found that paper has its best dimensional stability in an environment of 35–50% humidity.

Formation

Formation indicates the structure of paper and the uniformity with which its fibers are interwoven and distributed. An ideal formation, if it existed, would resemble what one would see if looking through a ground glass or translucent plastic film.

Formation is significant because of its influence on other paper properties. The levelness and smoothness of a paper, for example, are greatly dependent on the uniformity of its formation. When compared to a paper having a closed, uniform formation, a paper with a wild formation will not have a level surface, but one with "hills" and "valleys." Calendering the wildly formed paper to level out and eliminate its "hills" will produce a surface of nonuniform density and ink absorbency, since the "hills" will be more compacted than the "valleys." Such a paper will tend to print with a mottled or galvanized appearance, particularly in solids. A wild formation will tend to cause greater variation in opacity and printing show-through, especially in light-basis-weight papers.

Formation is usually judged by viewing paper by transmitted light. The transmitted light will show dark and light spots, depending on the wildness of the formation. The degree of uniformity can be determined by comparing the paper in question with a set of standard paper that has been assigned formation numbers. Since formation is difficult to judge subjectively, instrumentation is used to analyze and rank it. TAPPI UM 432 describes a way to compare the formation of samples with an instrument.

Letterpress and gravure printing papers require good formation to help them attain the necessary degree of surface levelness. Offset printing is more tolerant of the effects of variation in paper formation, since it prints from a resilient rubber blanket. The degree of formation uniformity often must be balanced with other paper properties like strength and economic considerations. Increased fiber length and the high percentage of long fibers needed for strength contribute to a wilder formation. Additional refining, which tends to improve formation, may not be possible because of considerations such as dimensional stability and paper machine operation. Slow-running paper machines, with their "wire shake," produce excellent formation, but their use is impractical for many papers that must be produced at high speed for economic reasons.

Internal Bond Strength

The strength of paper and paperboard is usually expressed in two directions: the grain and cross-grain directions, or the X and Y directions, respectively. Paper strength is also figured in a direction perpendicular to the plane of the sheet, or in its Z-direction. Strength in the Z-direction is termed the **internal bond strength** of the paper, and the ply bond strength is defined as the transverse force required to delaminate a unit area of paper.

One method of measuring internal bond strength is the Z-directional tensile test, described in TAPPI T 541. A paper or paperboard sample is sandwiched between two flat blocks that have a 1×1-in. (25×25-mm) area and is adhered to each block with double-sided pressure-sensitive tape under a designated pressure. This sandwich assembly is placed in a

Z-direction tensile strength measurement.

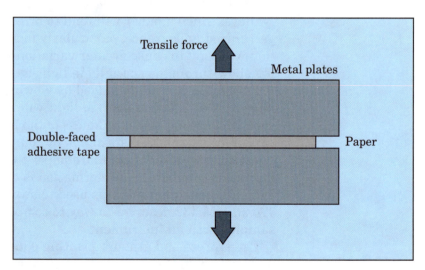

tensile tester, and an increasing tensile load is applied perpendicularly to the plane of the test sample. The tensile force, in pounds per square inch or kilopascals, required to delaminate the sample is a measurement of its internal bond strength.

Internal bond strength is also measured by the amount of work required to delaminate a unit area of paper. The test assembly consists of a paper sample sandwiched between, and adhered to, a metal base and a right-angle metal anvil. A pendulum, released from its high point, swings downward to strike the anvil that is adhered to the upper side of the test sample. The impact of the pendulum, applied at a right angle to the paper's surface, causes the paper to delaminate. The maximum point to which the pendulum swings after its impact is a measurement of the paper's internal bond strength.

Specimen assembly used in an internal bond impact tester (Scott Model B). Measurement is made of how far a pendulum hammer swings after striking the protruding angle and delaminating the paper sample.

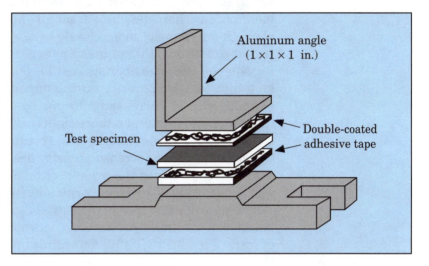

Internal paper bonds must be strong enough to withstand the delamination and rupturing that occurs when printing is done with tacky inks and has heavy solids, the repeated Z-directional stresses applied to both sides of a paper simultaneously on blanket-to-blanket web presses, and the internal forces that build up due to moisture being vaporized in web dryers.

Porosity

Compared to materials like plastics or metal, paper is highly porous. Fibers, sizing, fillers, and coatings account for only a part of the total volume of paper, while the remaining portion is air. The air volume of paper ranges from 60 to 70% for bulky papers and from 15 to 35% for dense papers such as glassine and bonds. The ratio of the volume of the physical components to that of the air space among the fibers for any given paper greatly affects such properties as hardness, compressibility, resiliency, and the ability to absorb fluids, inks, oils, and water. The porous structure of paper consists of (1) voids, or air spaces, which extend down from the paper's surface into its interior; (2) interfiber air spaces; and (3) pores, or channels, which extend completely through the paper's thickness.

Most uncoated printing and writing papers would be considered moderately porous when compared to saturating and filter paper, which is highly porous, or greaseproof paper, which is dense and nonporous. Coated printing papers are relatively nonporous in comparison to uncoated printing papers.

The porosity level of a paper results from the manner in which it is made. A paper made from all long fibers will be more porous than one made from all short fibers because short fibers compact more closely under the same manufacturing conditions. Fillers make paper less porous by occupying some of the interfiber spaces. The single most important step that controls porosity during papermaking is the degree of fiber refining. Increased refining, by producing greater interfiber bonding and a more tightly intermeshed fibrous structure, decreases porosity and results in a denser paper. Other factors that decrease porosity are surface sizing, coatings, wet pressing at the press section of the paper machine, and compaction of surface by calendering.

The porosity of paper is measured by its resistance to the passage of air under prescribed conditions. One method, as described in TAPPI T 460, determines porosity by measuring the time in seconds that it takes for 100 cm^3 of air under constant pressure to pass through a circular 1 in.^{2} of paper. Air under light pressure is provided by the constant weight of an inner cylinder that descends by gravity in a surrounding fixed cylinder partly filled with oil for an air seal. Air is permitted to escape through a fixed area of the paper held between clamping plates.

A timing device clocks the number of seconds required for the cylinder to descend and force 100 cm^3 of air through the paper. The Gurley densometer is commonly used for measuring porosity in this way.

A second method for measuring porosity, which uses the Sheffield porosimeter, is described in TAPPI UM 524. Measurement is based on the rate of airflow through a specified paper area. Filtered air, under a fixed low pressure, flows upward into a tapered glass column and then to the orifice plate of the gauging head, where it flows through the paper.

The rate at which air flows through the paper, which depends on its porosity, is indicated by the height of the air-suspended metering float in the glass column. Its position indicates the velocity of the airflow through the sample. A wide range of papers can be measured instantly and accurately by this method by simply changing the diameter of the orifice plate of the paper test area. The orifice diameter should be stated when reporting or specifying porosity measured in this way.

The above two methods of determining porosity—the time required for passage of a given volume of air through the paper and the rate of air passage through the paper—have an inverse relationship to each other. For example, as paper becomes less porous, the porosity readings increase when measured by the passage of a given volume of air and decrease when measured by the rate of air passage. As papers become less porous and more dense, they are more susceptible to curl and to greater dimensional changes caused by variations in their moisture content.

The porosity of the paper directly impacts the setting of "quickset" inks. Inkmakers produce these inks by adding gel varnish to the ink and reducing the viscosity (body) of the gel varnish with a low-viscosity ink oil. As the paper absorbs the ink oil, the viscosity of the printed ink film rises rapidly; that is, the ink "sets." Quickset inks will not set at all on nonporous surfaces such as foil.

Porosity is sometimes a consideration for runnability and end use. High porosity, sometimes referred to as an open sheet, may interfere with the vacuum pickup and transportation of sheet paper used on printing presses and on bindery, envelope, and other converting machinery. Porosity affects adhesive and coating penetration. If porosity is too high, the adhesives and coatings may strike through the paper, or their solids may penetrate excessively, leaving a starved adhesive bond or an inadequate ink film thickness at the paper surface.

Porosity can greatly affect dimensional change in paper. Papers like register bond for making continuous forms are made highly porous to minimize their dimensional change during printing, collating, and end use. Saturating, filter, and other absorbent papers also must be highly porous. Papers for the application of carbonizing inks and special coatings must have a very low porosity. Dense papers—those having low porosity—are more susceptible to curl and dimensional change during printing and converting.

Smoothness   From a printability standpoint, smoothness refers to surface contour and the degree to which the surface levelness approaches an optical plane such as smooth glass. Short fibers produce a more level paper than do long fibers. The manner in which fibers are dispersed as paper is formed on the paper machine wire has a great influence on formation surface levelness. A nonuniform fiber distribution ("wild formation") reduces levelness. Levelness normally decreases as basis weight increases.

Other papermaking factors that control smoothness are the extent of wet pressing, the use of smoothing presses, the paper machine felts, the amount of filler in the paper, and the degree of calendering. The application of coatings and supercalendering significantly increases smoothness. Blade coating and cast coating produce a more level surface than do other methods.

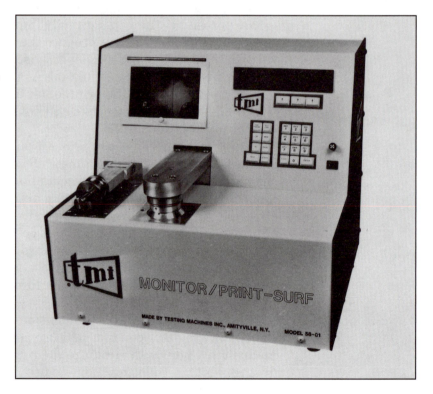

TMI Monitor/Print Surf™. The device is designed to measure surface roughness of paper and board under conditions similar to those experienced during printing. *Courtesy Testing Machines Inc.*

Smoothness is commonly measured by an air-leak tester. One way to apply the air-leak principle is to measure smoothness as the time it takes, in seconds, for a given volume of air to leak between a smooth glass test plate and the paper surface under a specified air pressure.

The method for measuring smoothness by this principle, described in TAPPI T 479, is used for the Bekk and the Gurley smoothness testers. Since no constant relationship exists

TMI Monitor/Smoothness™ is a "Sheffield-
type" tester for
smoothness and porosity that meets TAPPI
T 538.
*Courtesy Testing
Machines Inc.*

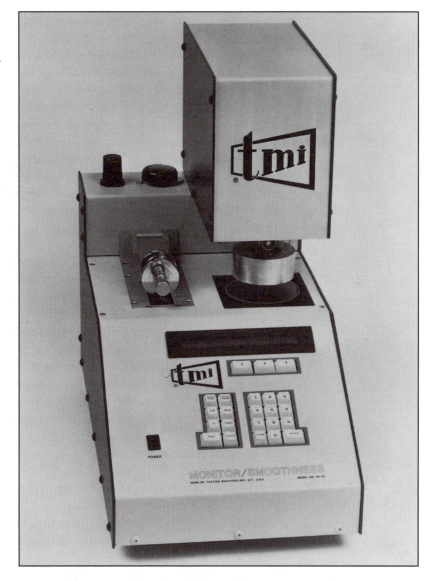

between test values obtained by these two instruments, the
name of the instrument should be designated in reporting
test values or specifying smoothness measured.

An instantaneous and accurate method of measuring
smoothness is to use the Sheffield paper smoothness gauge,
as described in TAPPI T 538. Smoothness is measured as the
rate of airflow between the annular groove in the upper gauge
head and the paper's surface.

Filtered air, under a fixed low pressure, flows upward into
a tapered glass column and then to the gauging head, where
it leaks across the paper's surface. The rate at which air leaks

across the paper, which depends on the paper's smoothness, is indicated by the height of an air-suspended metering float in the tapered glass column. Smoothness is measured instantly for all ranges of paper smoothness by this method.

The Bendtsen smoothness tester, described in TAPPI UM 535, also rapidly indicates smoothness as the rate of air leakage over the paper's surface. The values provided by measuring smoothness using these two basic manners have an inverse relationship. As the smoothness of paper increases, readings on the Bekk and Gurley instruments increase, whereas they decrease for the Sheffield and Bendtsen instruments. To avoid any misunderstanding, the instrument should be designated in reporting or specifying smoothness values.

Surface Strength Surface strength, or pick resistance, is the property of paper that enables its surface to withstand the force required to split an ink film as the paper is being pulled from an inked plate or blanket during printing. **Picking** designates any disturbance of the paper surface that occurs when the force to split an ink film is greater than the surface strength of the paper. Picking can occur as a partial lifting or complete removal of coating fragments from the surface, as a partial delamination of the paper substrate below the printed surface, or as a rupture consisting of a continuous removal of the paper surface. **Dry picking** occurs in the absence of water; **wet picking** occurs in the presence of water used during printing. Wet picking occurs when the water, used in the dampening system of an offset press, weakens the coating binders. A paper's surface strength increases with the use of long fibers, an increase of internal binder, a decrease in filler content, refining, and surface size.

Because of its speed and convenience, the Dennison wax test, described in TAPPI T 459, has long been used to measure surface strength. The wax test is useful for uncoated papers but is of no value for coated papers containing thermoplastic binders, such as latex or plastic pigments. Wax sticks calibrated to increasing adhesive power are melted on the paper surface. After cooling, the wax sticks are pulled away from the paper with a quick jerk perpendicular to its surface. The wax strength number is the wax with the highest number that does not disturb the paper surface. Both sides of the paper should be tested, since the felt side normally has a lower pick strength than the wire side. This test is used in paper mills to detect differences in surface strength that may occur during manufacture of the paper, but is of little use in predicting the performance of paper on a printing press. It does not consider pick strength in relation to grain direction. Due to limitations of the wax test in predicting pick resistance under actual printing conditions, laboratory pick testers have been developed to more closely simulate printing action.

The IGT printability tester is used to measure surface strength in accordance with TAPPI UM 591. It measures the pick resistance of coated and uncoated papers in a manner closely simulating the printing process, by the use of tack-graded inks, control of printing pressure, and a mechanical action similar to that of a printing press.

Surface strength measurement with IGT printability tester. The greater the distance from the start of motion to the start of pick or split, the higher the surface strength.

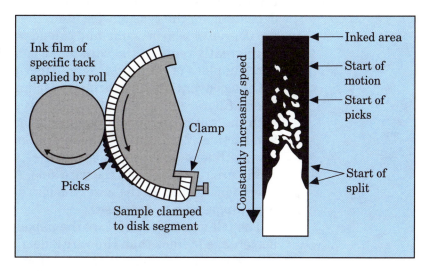

This instrument simulates printing speeds by beginning at zero and accelerating to a maximum rate. As printing speed increases, the force exerted on the paper by the ink film split increases until picking occurs. The length of the printed strip before picking starts indicates the printing speed required to pick the paper. The product of this printing speed and the viscosity of the ink used is an index of surface strength. This method can measure picking resistance in both the grain and cross-grain directions. One of its disadvantages is that it tests only a small area and that the results may not represent the order of the paper in question. Another instrument that is used to measure surface strength is the Prüfbau printability tester.

Other methods of measuring surface strength involve the use of a series of inks having progressively higher tack levels on proof presses. The tack of the ink, which causes picking, indicates surface strength. The best test for surface strength is the printing press, provided that variables such as inks, blankets, rollers, plates, and operating conditions are continuously controlled within prescribed limits.

Paper Sides

Paper made on a single-wire conventional fourdrinier machine produces paper with sides that are different. One side is referred to as the **wire side,** the other side as the **felt side.** Paper made on a twin-wire paper machine has two wire sides and will be less two-sided.

The wire side (or both sides for twin-wire formers) has the impression of the wire mesh left in its surface. This impression is called a **wire mark.** The diamond-shaped pattern of the wire may or may not be pronounced and easily seen, depending on the type of wire used, the type of paper, and the degree of wet-pressing and calendering. Papermakers have greatly reduced the wire-mark pattern by using plastic wires in place of bronze wires on paper machines.

On a conventional fourdrinier machine, the slurry of fibers, fillers, sizing, and other additives flow onto the wire, with the water component being drained away by gravity and suction. With the downward drainage through the wire, smaller fibers (or fines), filler particles, pigments, dyes, and sizing are removed from the wire side. As successive layers of fibers form a mat on the wire, the loss of fines through the wire progressively decreases.

The felt side, or top side, of the paper will have a higher percentage of fines than the wire side. On the other hand, the wire side will have a greater percentage of fibers aligned in the machine direction because they are fixed in this position during the initial drainage. Fibers in the upper layers that form the felt side will have a greater chance to align themselves in different directions since they remain in a water suspension longer. The wire side has a more pronounced grain, less fines and fillers, and more open structure. If there is a choice, the felt side of an uncoated paper is generally preferred for printing because it tends to be smoother.

The wire and felt sides of paper, as produced on a single-wire fourdrinier machine, can often be identified by one of several tests:

- Fold an uncoated sheet on itself so that both sides can be viewed at the same time. Let light strike the surface at an angle. Slowly turn the folded sheet and observe the rectangular or diamond-shaped impression that identifies the wire side.

• Use the procedure above, after first dipping the paper in water and allowing it to stand for a few minutes. Moistening will often restore the original texture and wire mark that was there prior to calendering.

A procedure that may be used for coated or uncoated paper is described in TAPPI T 455. Place a sheet of paper on a table so that its grain direction parallels the line of vision. While holding the sheet in position with one hand, pull upward with the other to start a line of tear parallel to the grain direction. As the tear progresses, gradually guide it so that it moves in the cross-grain direction and toward the outer edge of the sheet, producing a tear line following a curved path. Turn the sheet over with its opposite side facing upward and make a similar tear. The tear with the more feathered edge, especially in the curved portion of the tear, is the one produced when the wire side faces upward. The successful use of this method requires some experience, which may be gained by

Tearing determination of wire and felt sides of paper. The tear is made first in the direction of the grain and then is curved gradually to the right. The wire side produces a wider, feathered edge, according to TAPPI T 455. Use only for paper produced on a single-wire fourdrinier machine.

applying it to papers whose wire or felt side is known. Differences between the wire and felt sides of a paper made on a conventional, single-wire fourdrinier machine also may relate to runnability and end-use performance.

Since the wire side of paper has less fillers and fines than the felt side, it will withstand greater tensile stress and stretching at the outside of a fold. Thus paper has less tendency to crack when its wire side is on the outside of the fold. The wire side generally has greater pick resistance and, if there is a choice, it is the preferred side for printing forms having heavy ink coverage. For blanket-to-blanket sheetfed perfecting presses, there may be a preferred side up in order to achieve better blanket release and sharpness of printed images.

The felt side is preferred for pen-and-ink application, since it normally has less tendency to feather. It is also the side that is preferred for the printing of letterheads. Watermarked paper generally reads properly when its felt side faces the reader. Paper is usually laminated with its felt side outward. Envelopes are folded with the felt side out. The curl characteristics related to the wire and felt sides as paper gains or loses moisture are important considerations in deciding which side should be printed first to minimize curl.

Calendering

The main purpose for calendering is to impart a desired finish to paper. Calendering affects paper properties in different ways. As the degree of calendering is increased, smoothness increases and a higher gloss develops. Thickness, stiffness, and opacity, on the other hand, are reduced. Calendering decreases brightness somewhat by compacting the fibers and reducing the light-scattering ability of the paper. Using too much calendering pressure to obtain higher gloss or finish may result in crushing, weakening, and blackening of the paper. Calendering decreases porosity and ink absorption. The supercalendering of coated papers reduces porosity, thereby increasing the paper's tendency to blister.

Ink Absorbency

Although to date, there are no standard tests for surface ink absorbency that are applicable to the vast number of different printing situations, certain tests have been found useful. In the Vanceometer test, described in TAPPI UM 519, a metal roller is used to spread a film of oil of constant viscosity over the paper's surface. Immediately after application of the oil film, the paper's surface will have a high-gloss reflectance. As the oil is absorbed, gloss decreases to a final value of the paper itself. The instrument's glossmeter measures the rate of gloss decrease and thus the paper's absorbency. The Vanceometer is useful for measuring the ink absorbency of low-gloss paper but is not too satisfactory for high-gloss papers.

A practical test for measuring ink absorbency and ink hold-out is to pull solid impressions with a black ink using a proof press. A measured volume of ink is applied to a solid form of known area so that a constant amount of ink will be applied to the paper each time. A stopwatch is started at the instant of impression and the gloss of the print is observed. The disappearance of gloss in the ink film is the end point of the test. The total time for gloss disappearance is a measurement of ink absorbency. Although there is, unfortunately, no standard ink for this test, it does provide a means of comparing different papers. Ink absorbency can also be measured by using printability test instruments like the IGT and Prüfbau.

The K and N ink absorbency test uses a nondrying ink vehicle that contains an oil-soluble dye. The best use of this test is to compare individual papers to one another. The papers that are to be tested are arranged so that they overlap, with each paper having about two inches of the overlap showing.

Arrangement of paper samples for the K and N ink absorbency test.

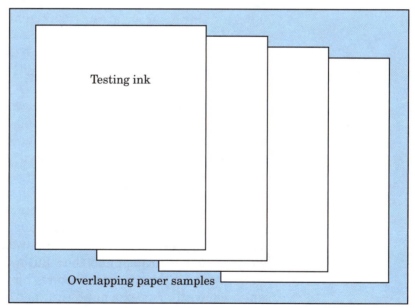

A thick layer of the ink is applied to the overlapped sheets and allowed to remain for two minutes, after which it is wiped off with a clean, soft cloth or paper tissue. Each of the tested papers will retain a colored stain, with the degree of color depending on the absorbency of the paper. The K and N test works best on smooth coated papers but is of little value on rough-finished papers. The density of the absorbed color can be measured with a reflection densitometer.

The K and N test will also indicate the comparative uniformity of absorbency of coated papers. Mottled color or visible variation in the density of the ink stain indicates nonuniform absorbency, which may or may not be an indication that the paper will mottle when printed.

Paper pH

Paper has a pH that depends on the papermaking process. An acid system will produce papers in the 4–6 pH range, while an alkaline system creates papers with a pH of 7 or more.

The term **pH** is a chemical abbreviation or symbol for the **potential of the hydrogen ion** (H^+). A positively charged hydrogen ion (H^+) produces acidity, whereas a negatively charged hydroxyl ion (OH^-) produces alkalinity. Pure water consists of a hydrogen ion (H^+) and a hydroxyl ion (OH^-). Its chemical formula is H_2O, which also may be written as HOH. An infinitesimally small percentage of these HOH molecules in pure water disassociate or break apart to form electrically charged ions:

$$HOH \longrightarrow H^+ + OH^-$$

The ionization of pure water produces neither acidity nor alkalinity, since there is an equal number of hydrogen (1) and hydroxyl (1) ions present. In other words, pure water, because it has an equal number of hydrogen and hydroxyl ions, is neutral. When acid-producing substances such as hydrochloric acid (HCl) are dissolved in water, an excess of hydrogen ions is formed and the solution becomes acid. Likewise, when alkaline or hydroxyl-producing substances like caustic soda (NaOH) are dissolved in water, an excess of hydroxyl ions is formed and the solution becomes alkaline.

Numbers for the pH scale extend from 0 to 14. They represent a logarithm, or exponent, that mathematically expresses the concentration of the hydrogen ions. When the pH number of a substance and its solution is exactly 7, it will have an equal concentration of hydrogen and hydroxyl ions. The substance is neither acidic nor alkaline; rather, it is chemically neutral. When its pH number is less than 7, it will have a greater concentration of hydrogen ions than hydroxyl ions and will be acidic. Likewise, when its pH number is more than 7, it will have a greater concentration of hydroxyl ions (OH^-) and will be alkaline.

The pH scale. As pH increases above 7, the concentration of OH⁻ ions exceeds that of H⁺ ions; alkalinity increases exponentially. As pH decreases below 7, the concentration of H⁺ ions exceeds that of OH⁻ ions; acidity increases exponentially.

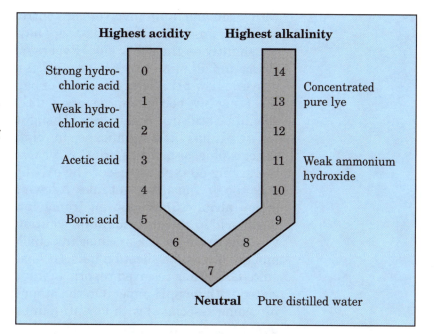

Changes in pH numbers represent exponential changes in the ion concentrations. A solution whose pH is 5 has ten times the effective acidity of one whose pH is 6, but a solution whose pH is 2, such as a mild acid, has 10,000 times the effective acidity of one whose pH is 6. The term pH indicates the intensity, not the quantity, of an acid or alkali, analogous to a temperature scale that denotes the intensity of coldness or hotness.

The pH value of paper may be determined by use of the glass-electrode pH meter. A pure water extraction of a given weight of the paper is made according to a prescribed procedure. The pH of the water extract is then determined with a pH meter. The pH of a coating, which may differ from its body stock, can be determined by carefully removing the coating with a razor blade, without disturbing or removing the fiber, then measuring the pH of a water extraction of the removed coating. TAPPI T 435 describes the procedures for cold-water extraction. A surface measurement method and pH meter are used, as described in TAPPI T 529, to perform a nondestructive determination of pH for paper used for books, documents, and archives.

There are many applications of pH during manufacture and use of paper. Control of pH within a narrow range is required during the multistage bleaching of pulp and in the preparation of the papermaking furnish. The internal sizing of paper with rosin and alum involves the control and measurement of pH. Rosin-sized, uncoated papers have a pH under 7 and are slightly on the acidic side. Papers made with synthetic sizing and alkaline fillers have a pH of nearly 7 or slightly above 7. Low pH affects the aging of paper and reduces its life. Long-life, permanent papers and those for archival use should be acid-free and have a pH slightly above 7.

The pH has little significance in relation to letterpress, flexographic, or gravure printing, or when inks other than the drying-oil type are used. The pH of paper does not influence the drying of heatset inks. A low-pH environment (below about 4.5), originating from a low-pH paper or too much acid in the press fountain solution, can retard or prevent the drying of ink or cause ink chalking for the drying-oil and quickset-type sheetfed inks. (It has been several years since GATF has received reports of ink-drying problems associated with low-pH paper. On the other hand, ink-drying problems associated with low-pH fountain solutions are frequently encountered. Fortunately for the printer, the pH of the fountain solution can be easily controlled.) A pH above 7, extending into the alkaline range, has been found to promote the drying of inks that contain drying oils.

Alkaline systems have replaced acid systems in many European mills and are being used increasingly by North American paper manufacturers.

Dirt

Although printers often use the word "dirt" to refer to all sorts of debris, **dirt** has a special meaning to the papermaker. It consists of any embedded foreign matter or specks that can be seen on the paper. Dirt is an aesthetic consideration and is undesirable. It may or may not interfere with print quality, depending on whether or not it can be lifted from the paper and transferred to a printing plate or rubber blanket.

The amount of dirt in paper can be numerically estimated. In accordance with TAPPI T 437, this involves a visual examination and counting of all dirt spots having an equivalent black area of 0.04 mm^2 or greater. The equivalent black area of each dirt spot is determined by matching its area with the area of one found on a photographic print having a series of round black spots, along with the areas of rectangles of graduated areas, on a white background. The test calculates the total area in square millimeters per square meter of paper examined. This yields a mathematical dirt count as parts per million. Freedom from dirt is especially important in papers that are used in optical character recognition (OCR) applications, where a speck of dirt can cause a false reading.

Water, Moisture, and Paper

Moisture

The moisture content of paper refers to the amount of moisture it contains. Relative humidity is the ratio of the amount of vapor actually present in the atmosphere to the greatest amount that it can contain, at a given temperature. For printing papers, the moisture content range is usually from 2% to 6%. The point at which the moisture content of a given paper is in balance with a specified relative humidity can differ, depending on the paper and its fiber and mineral composition. Relative humidity is a significant factor in determining the equilibrium balance of paper with a specified atmosphere.

The test to determine whether paper is in balance with the atmosphere is made by measuring the relative humidity and temperature immediately surrounding the sheets of paper. For skids or stacks of paper, a probe or sword-shaped blade is inserted between sheets so that its humidity and temperature-sensing elements are isolated from the external atmosphere. To measure the relative humidity and temperature of roll paper, four or five layers of paper are cut through with a sharp blade extending 7–10 in. (178–254 mm) inward from one roll edge. The probe is laid flat against the exposed paper and quickly covered by taping the outer layers back into place. TAPPI T 502 gives detailed steps for measuring the relative humidity and temperature for both sheet and roll paper.

Being hygroscopic, paper fibers have a strong attraction for water molecules. Fibers increase in size when they absorb water and decrease in size when they lose water. The diame-

Expansion of paper with and across the grain as moisture content increases.

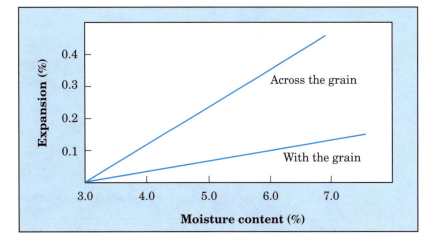

ter of the fiber changes more than its length when losing or gaining moisture. Because of fiber orientation and stresses built in during the papermaking process, this greater change in fiber diameter causes the cross-grain direction of the paper to change more than the machine direction.

These dimensional changes in paper, caused by changing moisture content, are a major cause of register problems, curl, and paper distortion. The degree of dimensional change for any given change in moisture content depends on the type of paper, its composition, and the extent of refining. Printing papers are manufactured to have the lowest dimensional

Change in values of selected paper properties with changes in relative humidity.

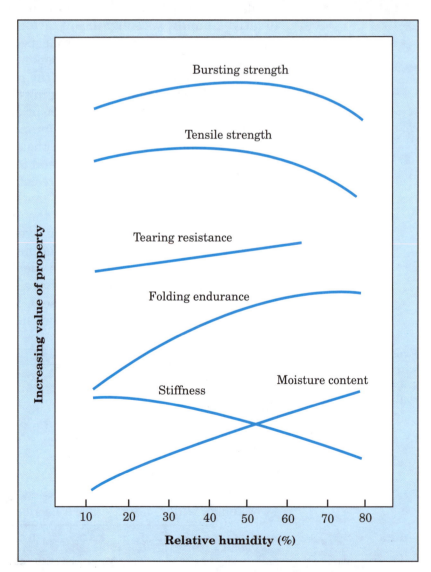

change consistent with their other required properties. Many papers not specifically designed for printing are less dimensionally stable because they have to meet other requirements.

Changes in the moisture content of paper can cause various types of distortion. For example, a moisture gain from the atmosphere produces wavy edges for sheet paper, and soft end rolls that unwind with baggy edges. Moisture loss can produce cockles or a puckered condition in a paper's surface or can result in curl by unbalancing the stresses existing between the paper's wire and felt sides. With moisture gain, paper tends to curl toward the felt side. The severity of the curl is reduced with a reduction in the two-sidedness of the sheet. Papers made on twin-wire machines are more uniform from side to side and less likely to curl due to a change in moisture. These distortions can be avoided or reduced by keeping the paper wrapped until it is used.

Sheetfed offset printing ideally requires that the moisture content of the paper be in equilibrium with the relative humidity of the pressroom. For multicolor printing and with multiple passes through sheetfed presses, it has been found that changes in sheet dimensions between successive printings is minimized when the moisture content is slightly higher than its equilibrium value for the relative humidity of a conditioned pressroom. Too low a moisture content results in a hard, brittle paper with reduced resiliency, printing cushion, and smoothness under printing impression. Brittleness also contributes to web breaks, cracking, and tear-at-the-fold problems. Paper prints better with a higher moisture content because of its increased resiliency and its ability to flatten out and conform to the printing surface under impression. Steel and copper plate engravings require a paper with high moisture content so that the paper will be sufficiently pliable to draw out and conform to the contour of the engraving dies, thereby producing sharply outlined images.

Too high a moisture content can cause coated web papers to blister in heatset dryers. Coated papers for heatset drying are therefore generally manufactured with a lower moisture content than their sheetfed counterparts. Adhesives are selected so as to maximize coating porosity. As the basis weight of coated paper is increased, its internal bonds are weakened, which may require a decrease in moisture content in order to avoid blistering during heatset drying. A high moisture content combined with a low paper surface pH may interfere with the drying rate of sheetfed oil-based inks.

The **equilibrium moisture content** of a paper depends on its fibrous and nonfibrous composition, the relative humidity of the environment to which it has been exposed, and its environmental history. Fillers and coatings decrease moisture content since they have little or no attraction for water. Since fillers are relatively insensitive to water, they increase the dimensional stability of paper in proportion to the amount in which they are present. Groundwood-content papers such as newsprint have a higher equilibrium moisture content than groundwood-free papers because they are mostly composed of water-loving materials such as fibers, lignin starch, and sugars.

The moisture content of paper is expressed as a percentage of its original weight. For example, a paper with a moisture content of 5% would lose 5% of its weight when dried in an oven. In determining percent moisture by the oven drying method (TAPPI T 412), a weighed sample is placed in a drying oven at 221°F (105°C) for about 1 hr. It is then withdrawn in a closed, airtight container and weighed again. Percent moisture is calculated by dividing the sample's dried weight by its original weight, then multiplying by 100. For rapid moisture determinations during paper manufacturing, moisture is measured by instruments based upon a relationship of moisture to electrical resistance or capacitance. These instruments are frequently calibrated by the TAPPI T 412 oven-dry method. Rapid on-line measurement of the moisture of a moving paper web is made with sensors using infrared or microwave rays.

The TMI series 400 moisture meter. This type of moisture meter, with a clamp-type electrode for measuring moisture in sheets of paper, is a precision measuring system with digital readout. *Courtesy Testing Machines Inc.*

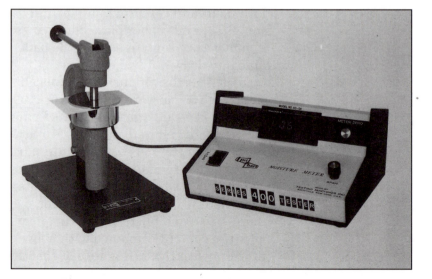

Web printers use moisture content numbers to determine blister resistance and foldability, whereas sheetfed printing and some converting applications use **equilibrium relative humidity** at a specified temperature to determine paper stability. Equilibrium relative humidity is that atmospheric humidity at which exposure of the paper will result in neither gain nor loss in moisture. The moisture content of a paper that is in balance with its surrounding relative humidity is called equilibrium moisture content. No change in the equilibrium moisture content will occur until the surrounding relative humidity is changed.

Exposure to a higher surrounding relative humidity will cause paper to absorb moisture until a new equilibrium is reached. Likewise, a decrease in surrounding relative humidity will cause a loss of moisture until moisture content equilibrates to the lower relative humidity. If relative humidity is in the range of 20–65%, a 10% change will generally cause about a 1% change in a paper's equilibrium moisture content. Temperature changes alone have little effect on the equilibrium moisture content for a constant relative humidity. The graphic relationship of percent moisture content and percent relative humidity for any given paper is shown by its moisture equilibrium curve.

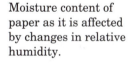

Moisture content of paper as it is affected by changes in relative humidity.

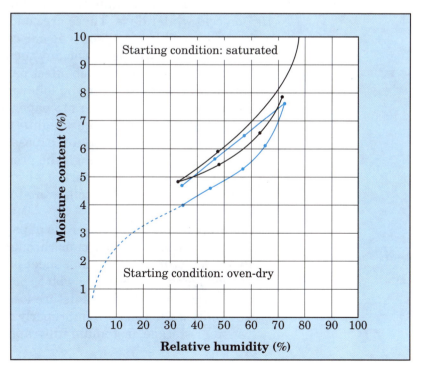

The equilibrium moisture content for any given paper can be lowered by conditioning the paper to its environment, which can be done by starting at a low relative humidity and progressively conditioning to higher relative humidities. This difference, or lag, in moisture content, as shown by the ascending and descending curves for relative humidity and representing opposite starting points in conditioning history, is called **hysteresis.** Hysteresis explains why the equilibrium moisture content of a given paper — when conditioned to a specified relative humidity, for example 45% — will differ depending on its previous moisture history.

The papermaker attempts to manufacture paper to a relative humidity that will cause the fewest printer complaints. The printer can help prevent problems by keeping the relative humidity of the pressroom within reasonable limits. For the finest work on sheetfed papers, GATF recommends 45±2% RH.

For sheetfed printing, it is sometimes necessary to determine, before printing, if the paper is in humidity balance with the pressroom. The detailed procedure for determining the equilibrium relative humidity of paper and paperboard is described in TAPPI T 502. In lithographic sheetfed pressrooms that are not humidity-controlled, the relative humidity may vary from over 80% in humid summer weather to as low as 10% on cold winter days. These are conditions that no papermaker can possibly meet, since no one can predict what the relative humidity will be on the day the paper is printed.

The moisture content of web offset papers is less critical than that for sheet papers in the following respects:

- Air generally has less access to paper in roll form than to paper in sheet form. Rolls are tightly wound and only their ends and outermost wraps are exposed.
- Since rolls seldom go through the press more than once, they are not subject to distortions from wavy or tight edges that might develop if the rolls were to stand between printings.
- The proper time to unwrap rolls of paper is just prior to printing. Since roll paper runs through the press rapidly (two to four times faster than sheet papers), little time is allowed for the edges of the web to pick up or lose moisture and produce distortions. Moisture loss and distortions will occur only if the rolls are improperly protected during transit or storage, or remain unwrapped too long before printing.

- The paper web is under tension during its entire travel through the press.
- Paper traveling through a web press at high speed does not have time to acclimate to pressroom humidity.
- Paper that undergoes heatset drying will leave the press with a moisture content that is lower than its original amount.
- The moisture content of coated papers for web printing is dictated by the level needed to avoid blistering.

Water Resistance   Papers that are unsized and absorb water rapidly are called **waterleaf.** Examples of waterleaf paper are blotting, filter, toweling, and saturating papers. Papers that have a low degree of internal sizing are termed **slack-sized.** Those having a high degree of internal sizing are identified as **hard-sized.** In addition to being internally sized, many papers are also externally sized, or surface-sized.

The purpose of internal sizing is to hinder or retard the penetration of water or other fluids into paper. Internal sizing gives paper wet strength and increases its resistance to the penetration of oil or printing inks but does not make it waterproof. Internal sizing is added to the papermaking furnish before it reaches the paper machine. It usually consists of an alkaline-dispersed rosin introduced into the furnish during stock preparation, followed by the addition of papermaker's alum, which helps the rosin sizing attach to, or "set" on, the fibers. As the paper dries on the paper machine, the internal sizing gives it a resistance to water penetration.

Papers must be hard-sized to minimize water absorption from repeated exposure to the press dampening system. Too much water absorption weakens paper surfaces and causes picking, changes in dimension, and, possibly, excessive curl. Bond, ledger, and other writing papers must be sized so that ink from fountain pens will not feather. A proper degree of internal sizing is required to control the penetration of adhesives in the manufacture of envelopes, boxes, and paper bags, and in labeling and packaging operations. Water repellency is achieved by using wax emulsions.

External, or surface, sizing differs from internal sizing in its application and purposes. Surface sizing normally consists of a heated starch solution applied to a partially dried web by a paper machine size press. Sizing is forced into the two sides of the paper as it passes through the nip of two size press rolls. Surface sizing penetrates below the paper's surface to some extent and contributes little water resistance. One of its purposes is to cement, or seal down, surface fibers and thus increase the surface strength of the paper. The benefits of surface sizing are greater ink holdout, added stiffness, improved erasability, scuff resistance, and increased bursting strength, tensile strength, and folding endurance.

The degree of sizing, both internal and external, varies considerably among the many different papers and paperboards, depending on the individual requirements for their printing, converting, and end use. Letterpress printing does not require hard-sized papers, although they may be sized for other reasons. Newsprint is not surface-sized since it must absorb ink instantly during its high-speed printing. Uncoated offset papers, bonds, bristols, and writing, cover, index, and ledger papers are examples of papers that are sized both internally and at their surfaces. Surface-sizing materials other than starch, or in conjunction with starch, are used for requirements like high water repellency or oil and grease resistance.

The numerous methods used to measure the resistance of paper and paperboard to water and other fluids may be classified into three groups. One group measures the reaction or resistance to water at the paper's surface. In the simple pen-and-ink **feathering test,** lines are drawn on the paper's surface using a steel pen and a water-based writing ink. The degree or absence of feathering, or spreading, of the inked line indicates whether the paper is adequately sized — for example, for writing and ruling applications. This test should be applied to each side of the paper.

Another test in this group is the **contact angle method** (TAPPI T 458), which quantitatively measures the resistance of a paper's surface to wetting. It is based on the principle that the advancing angle of contact between water or writing inks and the paper's surface is a measure of its wettability by these fluids. The contact angle is the angle between the horizontal, or the paper's surface, and a line tangent to the curvature of

Surface wettability of paper as determined by the contact angle method. Water has different angles with different paper surfaces.

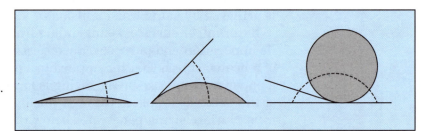

the liquid drop at the point where it contacts the paper's surface. In determining the contact angle, a drop of liquid is carefully placed on the paper's surface. After a short time, the contact angle of the drop is measured by projecting its magnified image on a screen. If the contact angle is close to zero, the drop will have spread over the paper's surface. If it is between zero and 90°, the paper will be only partially wetted. If the angle is greater than 90°, there will be little or no wetting and the drop will maintain its original shape. Under these conditions, the fluid will "bead" on the paper surface.

Other size-test methods measure the time that it takes liquids to partially or completely penetrate the paper. For the **dry indicator method** (TAPPI T 433), an indicator powder containing a water-sensitive blue dye is finely sprinkled on a test specimen of the paper. The opposite side of the specimen is then brought into contact with water by floating the specimen on the water's surface. The measured time interval between the instant of water contact and the development of a pronounced, visual color change by the indicator powder is the time required for water to pass through the paper. This method is useful for moderately sized papers having a reading of 30 seconds or less. Another test used for moderately sized papers is the **ink flotation method** (TAPPI UM 481). This method floats a paper specimen on a dark-colored writing ink. The time required for the ink to penetrate the paper and visually appear on its opposite side is a measure of the degree of internal sizing. Another method, described by TAPPI T 530, allows a water dye solution to penetrate the paper from one of its sides in a manner similar to the ink flotation method. The dye's appearance on the opposite side is determined by the drop in reflection of the paper's surface to a predetermined percentage of its original reflectance, as determined by a photometer. This test removes the human judgment factor of the endpoint of the test and is used for papers having widely differing degrees of sizing.

A further method of measuring the time for water penetration is the **curl test method** (TAPPI T 466). A test sample is cut to a prescribed shape and floated on water. The sample will continue to curl away from its wetted side until the water has penetrated approximately halfway through the paper's thickness. Further penetration will then cause the sample to reverse its movement. The time from water contact until the sample reaches its maximum curl is a measure of water resistance.

Curl test method for measuring relative degree of sizing in accordance with TAPPI T 466. Time is recorded from the instant water contacts the bottom of a specially cut specimen until its unrestrained end curls to its maximum angle.

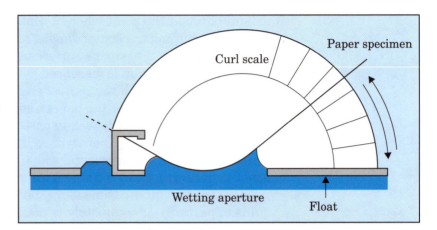

Additional sizing tests are based on the amount of water a prescribed area of paper can absorb in a given time. For the **Cobb size test** (TAPPI T 441), a test specimen of given dimensions is first weighed and then clamped between a metal ring or shallow cylinder and a rubber backing to form a watertight seal.

An apparatus (Cobb) for testing the water absorbency of certain papers and paperboard in accordance with TAPPI T 441.

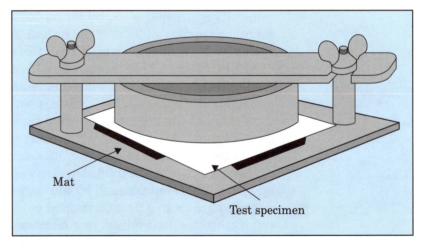

The ring is then filled with a given volume of water, thereby exposing the upward side of the test sample to water absorption. At the expiration of a specified time, the water is quickly removed from the ring, and the test sample is removed from the apparatus. Excess water is blotted from the exposed side, and the sample is weighed again. Its gain in weight, expressed as grams per square meter, is reported as water absorbency. The Cobb size test is used for paper and paperboard.

The overall sizing of hard-sized paperboards, which involves their resistance to water absorption through both their cut edges and their faces, is measured by the **water immersion method** (TAPPI T 491). A test sample of a specified size is first weighed and then submerged in water at a stated temperature and for a given time. After this time has elapsed, the specimen is withdrawn from the water, blotted to remove excess water, and again weighed. Its increase in weight is reported as its water immersion number.

Water Absorption

The relationship of paper to water in either its liquid or vapor state is important for many paper applications. The efficiency of towels, tissues, and saturating papers in absorbing water is determined by the time they need to completely absorb a given quantity of water (TAPPI T 432). The water absorbency of paperboard is determined by TAPPI UM 596. Paperboard, which may be thoroughly wetted by water during use, is tested for its resistance to water absorption at its faces and edges by a water immersion test (TAPPI T 491).

To have the weathering resistance necessary for outdoor signs, paper or paperboard may need to be water-repellent. Water-repellent papers have surface treatments that shed water. Water repellency is measured by the manner and time in which applied water continues to form beads on the surface (TAPPI UM 579). The paper and paperboard used for certain packaging applications must protect the contents from a gain or loss in moisture. Substances such as sugar and salt will absorb moisture, whereas others will lose moisture and deteriorate unless they are protected. If moisture has access to products like chemicals and metal parts, the moisture can be harmful. Packaging materials must therefore act as a barrier to water vapor transmission. The **water vapor transmission rate** of a packaging material is the weight of water, in grams, transmitted from one of its sides to the other for a 1-m^2 area during a one-day period, under prescribed conditions. These conditions include temperature and a difference in water vapor pressure or relative humidity between the material's two sides. The method for this measurement, described in TAPPI T 523 and UM 590, involves placing the packaging materials between a very high relative humidity chamber and a dry chamber. The water transmission rate is determined, with a humidity sensor, by the rate of humidity change in the dry chamber as water vapor is transmitted from the higher humidity chamber through the barrier material. To more closely simulate usage conditions, this test may be performed at various temperatures and for various relative humidity differences between the two sides of the barrier material.

The resistance of paper to water vapor is not determined by internal sizing as is its resistance to liquid water. Resistance to water vapor transmission is obtained by coating or laminating paper or paperboard with a continuous-barrier film such as wax, plastic, asphalt, or aluminum foil.

Wet Strength

Wet strength is the tensile strength of paper after it has been completely saturated with water. It is expressed as the percent ratio of wet-to-dry tensile breaking strength for each direction. With the exception of genuine vegetable parchment, normal papers retain only a small percent of their dry tensile strength after being wetted. Wet-strength paper is made by incorporating specific additives in the paper furnish that enables it to retain a substantial percentage of fiber-to-fiber bond strength after being soaked in water. Without such treatment, the fiber-to-fiber bonds in normal papers are dissolved by water. Wet strength is required for printed papers that must withstand weathering, water immersion, or contact with water—for example, labels, maps, charts, posters, tags, toweling, and wipes.

Humidity

Water vapor is always present in the atmosphere. Compared to liquid water, water vapor is a dynamic force that is constantly entering and leaving organic materials such as paper and influencing their behavior. The weight of water vapor contained in a volume of air is known as **absolute humidity,** expressed in pounds of water per pound of dry air. The atmosphere's capacity for holding water vapor at any particular temperature is limited. When that maximum amount of water is present, the air or atmosphere is said to be saturated. If air is cooled, its capacity to hold water vapor decreases; if the air was saturated before the reduction in temperature, some of the water vapor will condense into liquid water, in the form of fog, dew, or rain. The temperature at which air becomes saturated with water vapor is called its **dew point.** The dew point varies according to the absolute humidity of the air. As the temperature of air rises, its capacity for holding water vapor increases.

Relative humidity, the ratio of the actual vapor content of air to the maximum amount of vapor that air contains when it is saturated with water vapor, might be considered an index of the moistening power of air. As the relative humidity of air increases, the water vapor pressure increases. Thus, exposed paper that has a lower relative humidity than air will gain moisture from it. Likewise, as the relative humidity of the air decreases, its water vapor pressure decreases. Exposed paper with a higher relative humidity than the air will therefore lose moisture.

Paper, when exposed to the atmosphere, will adjust its moisture content to the air's value as long as the relative humidity and temperature of the air remain constant. This value is called the equilibrium moisture content for the ambient relative humidity and temperature. The relative humidity of paper and air are said to be in equilibrium when the paper neither gains moisture from nor loses it to the atmosphere.

The magnitude of moisture exchange with the atmosphere that occurs when paper adjusts to different relative humidities can be illustrated by the following example. A 2,000-lb. (909-kg) skid of paper is in balance with an atmosphere of 50% relative humidity with a moisture content of 6%. The paper is conditioned to an atmosphere of 10% relative humidity. For every 10% change in equilibrium relative humidity, the paper will lose or gain 1% moisture. In this example, the relative humidity goes from 50% to 10%, causing the paper to lose 4% moisture. The total moisture loss to the atmosphere is 9.6 gal. (0.04 × 2,000 = 80 lb.) or 43.6 l (29.8 kg) of water.

Hygrometry

Hygrometry refers to the measurement of humidity. Mechanical hygrometers that use hair, nylon, paper, or membranes whose dimensions change when exposed to different relative humidities are not very sensitive or accurate. A **psychrometer** uses a wet-bulb thermometer and a dry-bulb thermometer and psychrometric tables to measure relative humidity. A sling psychrometer gives accurate readings only if its thermometers are accurately graduated and used in accordance with exacting techniques. Without proper maintenance and procedures, wet-dry bulb hygrometers can give erroneous and misleading results.

Electronic hygrometers, on the other hand, are highly sensitive, accurate, and dependable. They are widely used for indicating and recording relative humidity and temperature. An accurate recording hygrometer is a valuable instrument for the pressroom. It dependably records atmospheric changes and the performance of air-conditioning equipment, and it can help to diagnose paper problems.

Optical Properties for Paper

Brightness

The brightness of paper is commonly indicated by a value called its TAPPI brightness, which is described in TAPPI T 452. The instrument used for measuring brightness by this method was developed by the Institute of Paper Chemistry, now known as the Institute of Paper Science and Technology (IPST). A pad of the paper to be tested is illuminated at a 45° angle and the reflected light is filtered so that only the blue light at 457 nm falls on the instrument's light sensor. The TAPPI brightness tester is sensitive to surface characteristics and requires that the grain direction of the test sample be consistently oriented in the prescribed direction during testing.

The ISO brightness tester, widely used in Europe and Canada, illuminates a large area of the paper with diffused light, which makes its measurement almost independent of the surface characteristics and grain direction of the paper.

While bleaching is used to make pulps whiter and brighter, fillers are also used to increase the brightness of paper. Fillers with high brightness, such as calcium carbonate and titanium dioxide, are most effective for increasing paper brightness.

The Technibrite Micro S-5 measures brightness, opacity, color, and fluorescence in accordance with TAPPI Official Test Methods.
Courtesy Technidyne Corporation.

The Color Touch Spectrophotometer measures ISO brightness as well as opacity, color, fluorescence, whiteness, and residual ink measurement. *Courtesy Technidyne Corporation.*

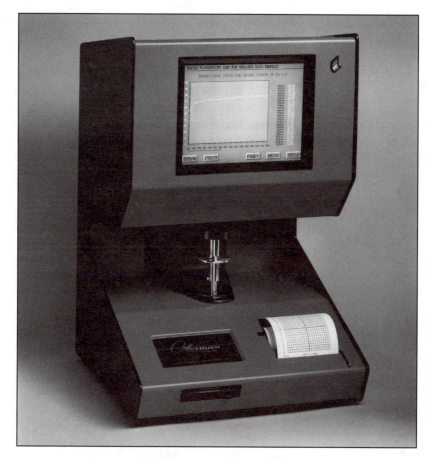

Optical brighteners or fluorescent dyes enhance the brightness of groundwood-free papers considerably because they emit blue-violet visible light when activated by the invisible ultraviolet light of their surrounding illumination. Paper brightnesses as high as 90 or greater are obtained with optical brighteners. The shade matching of fluorescent and non-fluorescent papers under all conditions of illumination is not possible. Optical brighteners are less effective in lignin-content papers such as newsprint and groundwood printing papers. There are instruments that are capable of measuring the amount of fluorescence in paper.

Unbleached chemical fibers produce papers having high light absorbency giving them high opacity but low brightness. Bleaching will reduce the light-absorbing material from the pulp, giving it more brightness, but bleaching also reduces opacity. Fillers and pigments must be added to the paper mix or furnish to achieve desired opacity when fibers are bleached to attain high brightness.

Color

Color measurement has evolved from experiments that determine the specific way in which human observers respond to the spectral distribution of light for the color spectrum. The scientific basis for color measurement is the existence of three different color response mechanisms in the human eye, one for each of the primary colors: red, blue, and green. The basis for all instrumental color measurements is composite data obtained from many observers who visually matched the colored lights of the individual wavelengths throughout the spectrum by adding together lights from three colored primaries: red, blue, and green.

The composite data from this color-matching panel have been mathematically transformed into three numbers called the tristimulus values, designated as X, Y, and Z. The values X, Y, and Z are used to define a color in terms of its primaries: simulating red, green, and blue. All color scales are based on the CIE (Commission Internationale de l'Eclairage, or in English, International Commission on Illumination) Standard Observer data, referred to as the CIE Standard Observer, or the normal eye.

Color scales generally used for the color measurement of white or colored papers are the CIE X, Y, Z tristimulus values and the Hunter L,a,b values, developed by Dr. Richard Hunter. The L,a,b scales are widely used since they can be easily applied and related to color recognition. On these three-dimensional scales, L denotes luminosity, or the degree of lightness from blackness to perfect white; a measures redness when plus, grayness when zero, and greenness when minus; and b measures yellowness when plus, grayness

The three-dimensional Hunter L,a,b, scales. *Courtesy Hunter Associates Laboratory, Inc.*

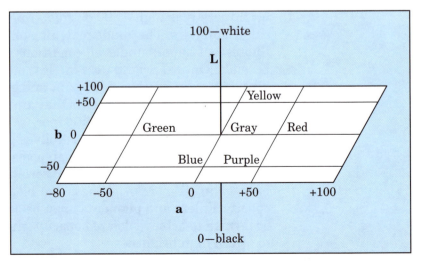

when zero, and blueness when minus. These L,a,b scales measure color as perceived in what are called opponent-color systems: black-white, red-green, and yellow-blue. An observer sees color or shades of white in terms of redness or greenness, and yellowness or blueness.

Yellowness is the result of additions of equal amounts of red and green signals. Whiteness and grayness are the results of additions of red, green, and blue signals. Another set of color dimensions is known by the terms hue (H), saturation (S), and lightness (L).

In 1976, the CIE adopted the so-called CIELab L*a*b* scales. These scales, which are enjoying widespread use because of their international recognition, are directionally similar to the Hunter L,a,b scales, but quantitatively different. The color of paper as measured by Hunter L,a,b colorimetry is described in TAPPI T 524.

A **spectrophotometer** measures the color of a paper by giving wavelength-by-wavelength analyses of its reflected light.

The SPECTRO/plus is a spectrophotometer for doing color and color difference measurements, 60° gloss, as well as many density functions. *Courtesy Technidyne Corporation.*

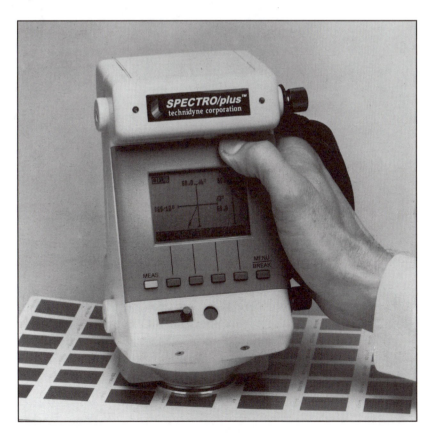

The spectral reflectivity of paper is expressed as a curve of its reflectivity, plotted against various individual wavelengths of its illumination, extending over the visible spectrum. Reflectivity for each individual wavelength is expressed as a percentage ratio of the sample to that of an ideal white reflectance standard. The spectral reflectance curve provides a permanent color record of a paper.

Spectrophotometric curves showing typical reflectance characteristics of black, gray, white, and colored objects.
Adapted from The Measurement of Appearance *(© 1987) with permission of John Wiley & Sons, Inc.*

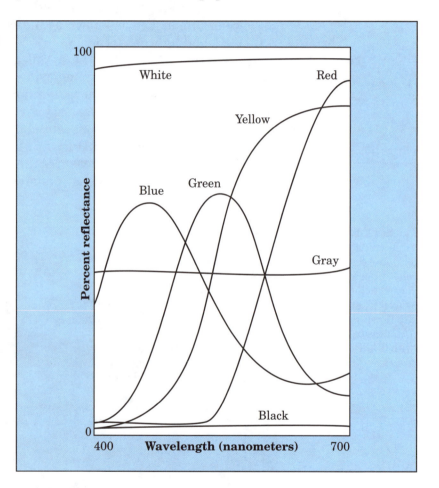

Color measurement with a spectrophotometer is a highly technical procedure and has until recently been too cumbersome for routine color control. This instrument's measurement is useful where color formulation is involved and where it becomes necessary to determine if two samples having the same color will match under all types of illumination. TAPPI T 442 contains detailed information on spectrophotometric measurement.

Gloss

Gloss is that attribute of a paper surface that causes it to be shiny or lustrous. As a paper surface approaches optical flatness through calendering or other surface treatment, light rays striking it are reflected primarily as parallel rays—a mirrorlike action known as **specular reflection.** A matte paper surface, or one having a very low gloss, reflects much of the incident light diffusely: that is, reflected rays are scattered in all directions. When specular reflection appreciably exceeds diffuse reflection for a particular viewing angle, the paper appears to be shiny or lustrous. Because specular gloss is a function of surface-reflected light, it is not affected by color.

Paper gloss is expressed as a ratio of reflected to incident light. It is referenced to a gloss standard such as a polished black glass, which measures close to 100 gloss units on a glossmeter scale. A glossmeter uses a photocell to measure the relative amount of incident light that is reflected from a paper sample. Because the gloss of paper may differ with direction, gloss readings are taken in both the machine and cross-machine directions. Usually the average gloss value for the two directions is reported for each side of the paper. For coated printing papers, gloss is measured at 75° from the perpendicular, or 15° from the plane of the paper, as prescribed

Glossmeter Model T480, which measures 75° gloss in accordance with TAPPI T 480. *Courtesy Technidyne Corporation.*

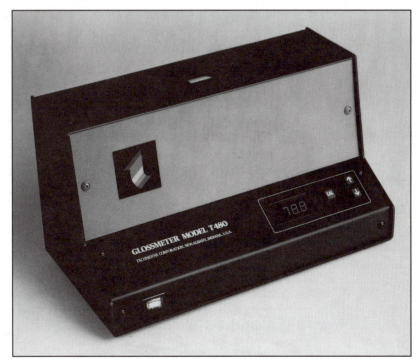

in TAPPI T 480. Gloss values for supercalendered papers will range from approximately 60 to 80 gloss units.

Glossmeter readings on matte-coated papers range from a few units to about 20 units. Dull-finish enamel papers are supercalendered to a gloss range of about 20–40 units, depending on their type and grade level. Very glossy papers—including cast-coated, highly varnished, lacquered, and waxed papers and high-gloss ink films—are preferably measured at 20° from the perpendicular or at 70° from the plane of the paper. Higher paper gloss increases the gloss of printed ink films and enhances the brilliance and color intensity of printing. The gloss of an ink film can also be affected by paper absorbency and ink holdout. Paper absorbency has less influence on the printed ink gloss of heatset inks because of their formulation and almost instant drying capability. Many printing applications require high paper gloss; other applications—for example, for reading—require low gloss to avoid eye strain.

The gloss of a paper affects the color of a print because it affects the way light is reflected through the ink. Variations in gloss must be kept to a minimum by the papermaker if the color printing is to remain uniform throughout a job.

Opacity

Opacity is measured by the TAPPI, or **contrast ratio,** method. This test uses the ratio of the diffuse reflectance of a single sheet of paper when backed by a black, light-absorbing surface to its reflectance when backed by a white, highly reflective surface. Light transmitted through a paper that is backed by a black surface will be absorbed by the black surface; when transmitted through that paper backed with the white reflecting surface, it will be reflected back. The total reflectance from the measured side of the paper will thus be greater with a white backing, because of the added light portion being transmitted back through it (for greater details, see TAPPI T 425). The opacity of papers ranges from a few percent for transparent papers to 100% for opaque papers. Normally, papers are required to have the maximum percent opacity that is consistent with cost and other paper properties.

Diffuse opacity (previously known as printing opacity) differs from contrast ratio opacity in that it replaces its white reflecting surface with a thick stack of the paper being tested. This method of measuring opacity is described in TAPPI T 519.

Opacimeter (Model
BLN-3) measures and
gives a digital readout
of contrast opacity in
accordance with
TAPPI T 425.
*Courtesy Technidyne
Corporation.*

Mechanical Properties

Bursting Strength

The **bursting strength** of paper or paperboard is defined as
the hydrostatic pressure required to rupture it when uniformly distributed and increasing pressure (at a constant rate)
is applied to one of its sides. Bursting strength is related to
tensile strength and stretch and is used as a measurement of
tensile properties. Bursting strength may be considered a
general indicator of toughness and stamina for some paper
requirements and is associated with snap and hardness. It
has no relationship to tearing strength and has little value
for printing papers. Bursting strength can be significant for
specific end-use requirements such as bags, envelopes, and
packaging papers. It is an important specification for linerboard and cartons, which must have a minimum bursting
strength to comply with shipping requirements.

Bursting strength increases with increased refining and
with the addition of surface sizing. It is influenced by the
fiber and filler composition of paper. Longer fibers tend to

TMI Monitor/Burst-200™, which is designed for testing papers and other materials with a burst strength of up to 200 psi (1,380 kPa). *Courtesy Testing Machines Inc.*

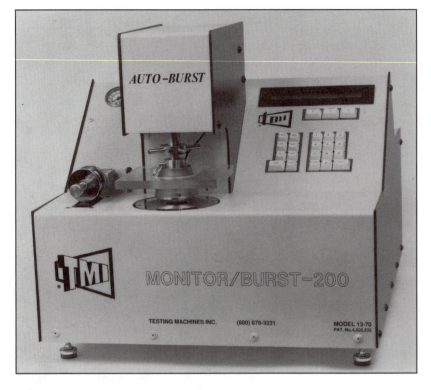

increase bursting strength. Increasing the percentage of filler decreases bursting strength.

Bursting strength is commonly measured with the Mullen-type tester, the procedure being frequently termed the Mullen or Mullen test. TAPPI T 403 provides details for this test.

Mullen tester used internationally for measuring the bursting strength of paper and paperboard. *Courtesy Mullen® Testers.*

TAPPI T 807 is used for paperboard and linerboard, and TAPPI T 810 for corrugated and solid fiberboard.

For the Mullen test, a test sample is firmly held between two annular clamps so that it will not slip between their faces as it is subjected to an increasing pressure by an expanding rubber diaphragm. The maximum hydraulic pressure inflating the diaphragm at the instant of sample rupture is a measurement of bursting strength. It is expressed as pounds per square inch or simply as "points" of burst. Bursting strength may be expressed as kilopascals in the International System of Units (the SI System). Bursting strength may be reported as the average for a number of tests for each side, or as the average for tests done on both sides of the paper.

Folding

Paper folding endurance, which is more sensitive to manufacturing conditions and the environment in which it is used than other strength properties, is very responsive to refining and to the papermaking furnish. Increased refining increases folding endurance. Long, pliable fibers and those that intermesh and bond to a greater degree with increased refining, like cotton fibers, give high folding endurance. Surface-sizing, coatings, and fillers decrease folding endurance. Folding endurance is greatly influenced by moisture content and relative humidity. As paper loses moisture, its fibers become less pliable and folding endurance decreases significantly. As basis weight or grammage is increased for any given paper, folding endurance increases up to a maximum, then decreases with further increases in basis weight. The basis weight for maximum folding endurance differs among papers.

Papers have a wide range of folding endurance, depending on their type and end use. Folding endurance is a good indicator of the permanence and durability of paper. Papers that are permanent and durable must have a high folding endurance and must retain a high percentage of their original fold as they age. Examples of products requiring good folding endurance are envelopes, covers, permanent records, maps, and charts. Folding endurance is used to study the aging of paper because folding resistance decreases rapidly as paper ages.

The ability to withstand repeated folding and handling, a requirement for durability, is best indicated by the folding endurance test. Folding endurance is the number of folds a paper will withstand before breaking under tension under

Schopper folding
endurance tester for
use in accordance with
TAPPI T 423.
*Courtesy Testing
Machines Inc.*

MIT folding endurance
tester for use in accor-
dance with TAPPI
T 511.
*Courtesy Testing
Machines Inc.*

specified conditions. It is measured both with and across the grain. Generally, paper has a greater folding endurance when folded against the grain. Folding endurance is measured by two methods. In the Schopper method (TAPPI T 423), a strip of paper is held under tension while a slotted reciprocating blade catches the strip in its middle and folds it back and forth between four rollers, folding it first toward one side, then toward the other side. The number of double folds the paper withstands before breaking is its folding endurance.

In the MIT method (TAPPI T 511), a strip of paper is clamped under tension between a spring-loaded jaw and an oscillating folding head. As the folding head oscillates an exact number of degrees on each side of its starting position, the paper is alternately folded toward each of its two sides. Folding endurance is the number of folds the paper undergoes before breaking at its fold line. The average result for a number of double folds endured is reported for both the machine and cross-machine directions. Although both methods measure folding endurance, there is no fixed correlation between their readings. The MIT method is faster and more versatile since different tensions can be used for very weak and very strong papers and a greater range of thicknesses can be tested.

Stiffness

The two properties having the greatest influence on stiffness are thickness and basis weight, or grammage. Theoretically, the stiffness of any given paper varies as the cube of its thickness, which means that if its thickness were doubled, its stiffness would increase eight times.

All papers are stiffer when flexed (bent) across their grain than when flexed with, or around, their grain direction.

The ratio of stiffness in the cross-machine direction (CD) to stiffness in the machine direction (MD) averages two to one for papers made on a fourdrinier machine, and three to one for those made on a cylinder machine. For this reason, duplicator and office machine papers are fed into the machine in the grain direction. The increased stiffness helps in the feeding and delivery of the paper.

Up to a certain point, stiffness increases as refining increases fiber bonding. As with many other physical properties, excessive refining will ultimately reduce stiffness. Stiffness is affected by the type of paper pulp used, decreases as the filler content of paper increases, and decreases as the moisture content and relative humidity increase. Stiffness is also

Flex test for paper grain. Since paper is stiffer across its grain, two strips of the same width cut at right angles from a sheet can show grain direction.

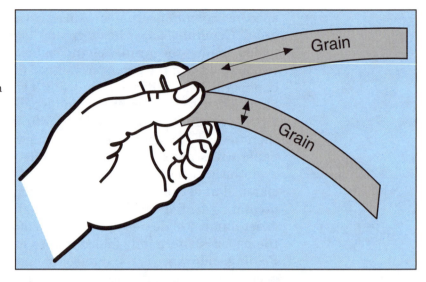

reduced by the calendering of paper. The interrelationship of stiffness, grain direction, and runnability is explained in the discussion on grain direction, which follows in this chapter. Adequate stiffness is essential for file folders, index cards, and posters, which must support their own weight, and for the rapid transporting of tab cards, checks, and documents through their processing equipment. High stiffness is important for paperboard used to make cartons and containers. Low stiffness is required for paper tissue, toweling, and napkins, for the easy opening and turning of pages in a book, and for music paper.

Stiffness is measured in arbitrary units, as determined by several different types of testing equipment. Commonly used are the Taber, Clark, and Gurley stiffness testers, each with its own unit of measurement. For details see TAPPI T 451, T 489, and T 543.

Tearing Resistance

Tearing resistance is an important property for many paper applications and is widely used for strength measurement. High tearing resistance is required for durable papers such as cover, bristol, tag, kraft wrapping, and bond, as well as for maps, envelopes, and file folders. High tearing resistance may work against printability since it can result in a wilder formation and reduced surface levelness. The need for tearing resistance may have to be balanced between end-use demands and printability. Tearing resistance depends on fiber length and strength. Longer fibers give greater tearing resistance, and some fibers produce greater resistance to tearing than do others. Greater fiber-to-fiber bonding from added refining increases tearing resistance. However, added refining that results in fiber cutting and a reduction of fiber length will reduce tearing resistance even though fiber-to-fiber bond strength increases. The addition of fillers reduces tearing resistance.

Tear resistance is the amount of work required to tear paper through a fixed distance after the tear has been started. One or more samples cut to a specified size are torn together through a fixed distance by a downward-swinging pendulum.

The work required to tear paper determines the distance the pendulum swings and, in turn, the indicated tearing resistance in grams. Tearing resistance determined in this manner is described in TAPPI T 414 and TAPPI T 496. A number of measurements and their average are reported for both the machine and cross-machine directions. Paper usually has a greater tearing resistance when torn against its grain or with its line of tear perpendicular to the grain direction.

The **edge tearing resistance** of paper, which differs from its internal tearing resistance, is measured with a tensile tester by folding a paper strip around a thin steel beam having a V-shaped notch. When tension is applied to the folded strip, it will be simultaneously torn at its two edges, which bear against the V-shaped beam. This method is described in TAPPI T 470. Edge tearing resistance is a significant property for newsprint and lightweight papers that are subjected to the high stresses that lead to web breaks.

Tensile Strength

Tensile strength and its associated properties are of fundamental importance both to the papermaker and the printer. In many packaging applications, tensile strength is an indicator of durability for papers like wrapping, bag, creping, gummed tape, cable wrap, and twisting. It has significance in relating to the stresses applied to paper as it is pulled through sheetfed presses by the grippers, to web travel, to breaks in printing and converting, and to the deleaving and perforation strength of business forms. The tensile strength of paper is of little importance with sheetfed papers. Web breaks are related more to basis weight and tearing strength than to tensile strength.

Tensile breaking strength is the maximum tensile stress that paper will withstand before breaking under prescribed conditions. As paper undergoes tensile stress, it elongates, or stretches. Elongation, as measured during a tensile test, is the maximum stretching that the paper undergoes before it breaks under tension. All papers have higher tensile strength in their machine, or grain, direction and greater elongation across their grain when subjected to tensile stress.

Tensile breaking strength and elongation are measured with either of two types of testers. The pendulum type of tester for TAPPI T 404 uses two jaws to gradually apply increasing tension to a paper strip of specified width and length. One jaw is moved downward and the other swings a pendulum away from its starting position, by the pulling force of the paper strip. As the pendulum is pulled upward, increased tension is applied to the paper strip until it breaks. A number of strips are tested and their values averaged for each direction. Tensile breaking strength may be reported in pounds per inch-width strip, or kilonewtons per meter.

The second type of tester strains, or elongates, the paper at a constant rate between a fixed lower clamp and an upper one that moves upward at a constant rate, as described in TAPPI T 494.

Tensile strength is influenced by refining, wet-pressing on the paper machine, fiber length, furnish, basis weight, and moisture content. Increased refining, greater wet-pressing, higher basis weight, and increased fiber length raise tensile strength. Increasing the percentage of filler lowers tensile strength.

Wet tensile breaking strength, described in TAPPI T 456, is used to determine wet strength. Tensile strength is measured after the test sample has been thoroughly saturated with water. Wet strength is reported as the percent ratio of wet-to-dry tensile breaking strength for each direction.

Tensile energy absorption (TEA) is a measure of the energy-absorbing capacity of paper and refers to its ability to withstand shock when it is subjected to sudden high tension. Examples are the dropping and handling of filled paper bags without their bursting open, and the sudden acceleration of paper web speed during printing and converting. Tensile energy absorption is measured as work, which is force times distance. A tensile tester measures this as the tensile force applied to paper, plotted against its elongation up to its breaking point. The area under the tensile force-elongation curve mathematically gives tensile energy absorption, which is measured in each direction of the paper (see TAPPI T 494).

Tensile energy absorption is a good index of paper toughness for bags, containers, plastic bottle labels, and mailing wrappers. Extensible papers are manufactured to undergo a much higher degree of stretching under sudden tension than ordinary papers.

A tensile stress-strain curve. The tensile energy absorption of paper is represented by the shaded area under this curve. It is calculated for each of the principal directions of the paper in accordance with TAPPI T 494.

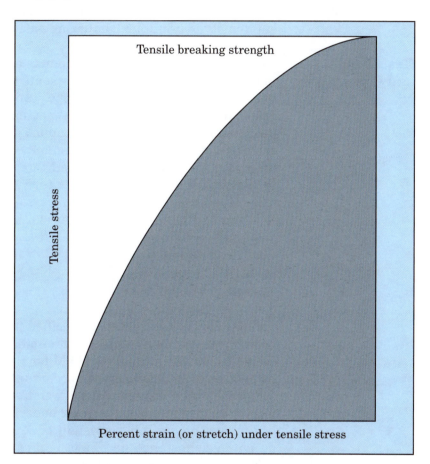

Tensile breaking strength

Tensile stress

Percent strain (or stretch) under tensile stress

Apparent Density The apparent density of paper, or its weight per unit volume, is a fundamental property. In the metric system, it is expressed as grammage per cubic centimeter, and is calculated as follows:

Apparent density (grams per cubic centimeter) =

$$\frac{\text{Weight in grams per square meter} \times 0.00001}{\text{Single-sheet thickness in millimeters}}$$

Apparent density may also be calculated by dividing the basis weight in pounds by the single-sheet thickness in thousandths of an inch. Its value, however, will depend on the basic ream size used. Conversion to a common ream size is required when different basic sizes are involved.

Apparent density influences the mechanical, physical, optical, and electrical properties of paper and relates to its structure as determined by its furnish and manufacturing conditions. A common, fundamental paper property, apparent density is useful for comparing various types of paper.

Basis Weight and Grammage

Basis weight is the weight in pounds of a ream of paper cut to its basic size in inches. It represents the weight for a given unit area. With few exceptions, the standard ream quantity is 500 sheets. **Basic size** is the sheet size in inches that has been adapted through practice and usage. It differs for various types of paper. The most commonly used basic sizes, their metric equivalents, and their total 500-sheet ream area in square feet are as follows:

U.S.	Metric	Square Feet	Paper Type
17×22 in.	432×559 mm	1,300	Bond and Writing
20×26 in.	508×660 mm	1,805	Covers
24×36 in.	610×914 mm	3,000	Newsprint and Wrapping
25×38 in.	635×965 mm	3,300	Book Papers

Basis weight is sometimes specified per 1,000 sheets. A book paper having a basis weight of 50 lb. is designated as 25×38—50(500) or 25×38—100M for a ream or 1,000 sheets, respectively. The term **substance** or **substance number** is sometimes used instead of basis weight to designate the weight of bond and other writing papers. For example, a bond paper having a basis weight of 20 lb. (75 g/m^2) is also designated substance 20. The weight of paperboard is expressed as pounds per 1,000 sq. ft.

Nominal weight is the basis weight for ordering and specifying paper and the basis weight to which it is made. The actual basis weight may vary from the nominal weight due to the variability of the papermaking process. Basis weight is also affected by moisture content and will increase as paper gains moisture and decrease as it loses moisture.

The weight of all papers and paperboards in the metric system is designated as **grammage.** Grammage is the weight in grams for a single sheet of paper having an area (per side) of 1 m^2. There are approximately 454 g in 1 lb., and 1 m equals 39.37 in. When expressed as grammage, the weight relationship of all types of papers is instantly apparent. There is no need to memorize or refer to a table of equivalent weights in order to compare papers of different basic sizes, as is required for the English system of units. Basis weights can be quickly converted to the metric system, or vice versa, by conversion factors.

The basis weight of paper is commonly measured by weighing a single sheet on a basis weight scale that is designed and graduated to indicate the weight in pounds for 500 sheets of the size weighed. For accuracy, large-size sheets should be weighed on a sensitive basis weight scale. Portable scales that weigh a very small sample are not very accurate. Weighing a single small sample or a single large-size sample can give an erroneous indication of the average basis weight for a manufacturing run or lot of paper. Samples should be taken from different locations throughout a lot of paper to determine the paper's average basis weight.

During paper manufacturing, basis weight measurements are made at a specified frequency and in accordance with a proper sampling plan that includes samples from specified locations across the paper machine. The proper procedure for measuring basis weight is described in TAPPI T 410.

TMI Monitor/Basis Weight™, a fully automated device that enables the operator to enter any specimen size and report it in any trade size with any number of sheets in the ream. Conforms to TAPPI T 410. *Courtesy Testing Machines Inc.*

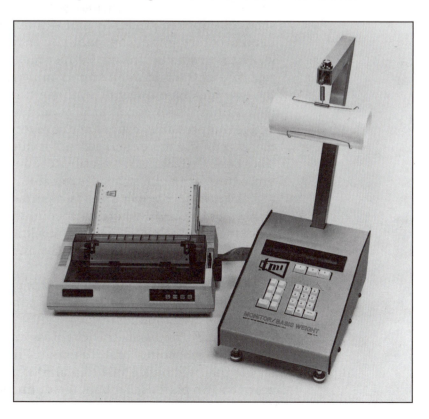

In sheetfed printing, the number of impressions is determined by the number of sheets ordered and run. A variation in basis weight does not alter the number of sheets. In web printing, however, the number of impressions or signatures realized from an order depends on the surface area of a roll of paper. For example, a roll of paper with a nominal weight of 50 lb. will have 2% less printing area if its average weight is 51 lb. Likewise, it will have 2% more printing area if the average basis weight is 49 lb. In one case, the printer will realize 2% more signatures; in the other case, the number of signatures will be under count by 2%. The total printable area of a given roll of paper is more accurately calculated from the total roll length or footage. The number of impressions or net printing area can be estimated for a given press cutoff length and total roll footage, after making allowances for normal prepress and press waste. Some paper manufacturers indicate the footage on their rolls for this purpose.

Caliper and Bulk

The thickness of paper and paperboard is commonly described as **caliper,** which is the perpendicular distance between the two surfaces of a single sheet, as measured with a micrometer. Because paper is compressible, the micrometer measurement should be applied gradually and without impact. For maximum accuracy, either the manually or motor-operated dead-weight micrometer is used. Caliper measurements may be reported as the minimum or maximum readings, as well as the average of a number of readings taken for a sample of paper. Since paper varies in thickness from point to point and is compressible, the caliper of several sheets may be measured for a more representative value of its average thickness. TAPPI T 411 describes the instrumentation and procedure for thickness measurement.

Thickness in English units is reported in thousandths of an inch or in points, where each point equals one thousandth of an inch. In the metric system, thickness is expressed in millimeters or micrometers (one thousandth and one millionth of a meter, respectively).

The **bulking number** and pages per inch (ppi) are used when manufacturing and specifying paper thickness for book production. The bulking number (TAPPI T 500) is measured in a manner simulating the compression applied to a book during its "smashing" and "casing in." It is the number of sheets that will bulk 1 in. (25.4 mm) after being placed between two platens of a bulk tester and subjected to a pres-

TMI precision microm-
eter. Conforms to
TAPPI T 441.
*Courtesy Testing
Machines Inc.*

sure of 36 lb./in.^{2} for 30 sec. To be more practical, the bulking
number is multiplied by two to give pages per inch since each
sheet in a book represents two pages. "Smashed" bulk, which
is significant during book manufacturing, may not be the
same as that calculated from the thickness of a single sheet
or several sheets of paper, because of the nesting, or packing,
effect when a stack of sheets is compressed.

The **bulking index** is used to compare the bulk of different papers having the same basic size with different basis
weights. Bulking index is the thickness per pound of basis
weight and is calculated by dividing a paper's single-sheet
thickness by its basis weight. Bulking index differs widely

among papers and is dependent on the type of fibers used, the percentage of filler, degree of refining, degree of wet-pressing on the paper machine, and the extent of calendering. Additional refining, greater wet-pressing, increased filler content, and calendering reduce the bulking index.

Control of paper thickness and profile across the paper machine web is a critical requirement for manufacturing rolls that will have good runnability for webfed printing presses and converting equipment. Variations in thickness profile when superimposed onto the thousands of layers or wraps of paper in a roll will produce tight bands that stretch the paper beyond its elastic limit. The result is rolls that unwind with uneven tension. Close control of thickness is required for many converting applications like high-speed envelope manufacturing and the manufacture of business forms. There is also a minimum thickness requirement for first-class mailing. The packaging of paper products like envelopes, cards, and business forms demands constant thickness so that a chosen number of items will occupy the designated volume of the container. Papers for book manufacturing must have consistent bulk from run to run and within a run. Thickness consideration is important as it relates to the capability or limitations of printing presses.

Curl and Sheet Flatness

A basic cause of curl is the difference in fiber orientation and the fibrous and nonfibrous composition of the wire and felt sides of paper made on a fourdrinier machine. Because moisture causes paper to expand, the sheet curls away from the side that is wetted. Upon drying, the sheet sometimes curls toward the wetted side, causing a problem known as reverse curl. With changes in moisture content, differences in the fiber orientation and structure of the sheet can account for different degrees of expansion or contraction between the two sides. Because of these structural differences, paper will normally curl toward its wire side with the axis of curl parallel to its grain when moisture loss and a lowering of relative humidity occur. With moisture gain, or exposure to a high relative humidity, paper tends to curl toward its felt side. Other involved stresses or causes also may prevent paper from curling in this manner.

As paper is dried during manufacturing, it undergoes various stresses due to shrinkage and tension. Drying must be controlled so that residual stresses are minimal and are balanced for sheet flatness. Papers that have been highly refined will have a greater tendency to curl with changes in relative humidity. As papers are made more porous and less dense, they are less prone to curl. The addition of fillers also tends to reduce curl. Lightweight papers may exhibit greater curling tendency since they are less stiff and offer less resistance to the forces that produce curl.

Papers that have two vastly different sides, like label papers and gummed papers that are coated on one side only, are treated by the papermaker to minimize their inherent tendency to curl. In addition to structural causes, curl can be caused by roll or reel set. Once paper has been kept in roll form for a period of time, its curved condition becomes permanently set and a cross-grain curl results after sheeting. Roll set curl becomes greater near the roll core, and is more pronounced in heavier, stiffer papers. It is therefore often found in paperboard, occasionally in cover stock, but rarely in book papers. Decurling bars are used to break roll set curl during sheeting.

Tests for curl usually consist of measuring the degree of curl of samples taken from various positions across the paper machine. These tests are conducted after the samples have been exposed to relative humidities and temperatures that simulate the environment under which the paper will be printed or used. Test samples are cut to small sizes, since curl is generally more evident when paper is cut into small-size sheets. The degree of curl may be determined with templates having various degrees of curvature or by the extent (vertical rise) to which a curled sample departs from a flat plane on which it rests. Curl is checked to determine the side to which it curls and whether it occurs with the grain, across the grain, or diagonally to the grain direction for various relative humidities or temperatures. Curl, which can cause serious runnability problems with sheet paper, is generally more evident at low relative humidities.

Dimensional Stability

Dimensional changes that result from changes in moisture content and relative humidity or from applied stresses can interfere with runnability. Papers that are subjected to tensile stresses will stretch and recover if the stretch has not exceeded the elastic limits of the paper. This stretching can occur on sheetfed offset presses where excessive stresses result when paper is pulled from a blanket with heavily inked solids. These stresses can permanently stretch the paper and cause curl, tail-end hook, or waffling.

Paper is **viscoelastic,** which means it can be stretched up to a point. During printing, paper is stretched as the sheet is peeled off the blanket, particularly when solids are being printed, and because of the rolling squeeze-pressure of the offset impression. This mechanical stretching is usually not a problem in web printing because normally the paper is sufficiently strong in its stronger grain direction (direction of web travel) that little or no permanent stretch occurs. In sheetfed printing, however, when stresses are applied to cross-grain paper, the paper can be permanently deformed if its elastic limits are exceeded. This is most likely to occur when printing multiple colors and solids on lightweight papers. If all the sheets stretch to the same degree there is usually no problem, since the length of the printed impression can be controlled by adjusting the plate and blanket packing. But if the paper varies in stretch from sheet to sheet, as might result from multiple-roll sheeting, the colors may register on some sheets but not on others. This problem is called sheet-to-sheet misregister. It usually occurs when a large part of the coverage of one or more colors consists of solids, and the press operator has no way to compensate for it.

Embossing, or "waffling," is caused by a permanent mechanical stretching or deformation of sheet papers. It is usually most noticeable when bands of solid color extend the length of the sheets, parallel to the grain. The pull of the ink, as the paper is peeled from the blanket, stretches the paper in the solid areas, while the rest of the sheet remains unstretched. Since tension is applied when the solid areas are bent as they are peeled off the blanket, the stretched areas curl and stand up in relief.

Embossing is seldom, if ever, a problem in web offset printing because the direction of paper travel through a web press is always in its grain direction. Also, the constant tension of the web allows far less blanket wrap than does sheetfed printing and prevents the sharp angle of peeloff that causes embossing and tail-end curl. To avoid permanent mechanical stretch in sheetfed offset printing, a paper should have good strength in its cross-grain direction.

Producing continuous business forms requires a high degree of dimensional stability. To maintain their "lengths," or "throws," and the alignment of their sprocket holes for collating, individual webs must not grow or shrink after printing. Close registration, when required between binding, folding, and diecutting, allows for few dimensional changes.

Grain Direction

Paper fibers, as they flow onto the paper machine wire, align themselves in the direction of flow. This alignment of fibers, parallel to the direction that the paper machine wire is traveling, is referred to as **machine direction,** or MD. The direction across the web, or from side to side on the paper machine, is called **cross-machine direction,** or CD. The percentage of fibers to water, as they flow from the headbox to the paper machine wire, is approximately 99.5% water and 0.5% fibers. At the other end, or dry end, of the paper machine, the percentage of fibers to water is approximately 4% water and 96% fiber. This loss of water causes the fibers to shrink. The paper web, however, as it progresses through the paper machine, is constrained in the machine direction but is not constrained in the cross-machine direction. This causes a greater amount of shrinkage from edge to edge of the web and creates stresses that produce paper grain.

Paper in roll form will always have grain that is in the direction of the wrap. Grain in sheeted paper is referred to as being **grain-long** or long-grain when the grain runs in the direction of the long dimension of the paper. It is known as **short-grain** when the grain is parallel to the short dimension of the paper.

Grain direction is important for runnability and end-use performance. While long-grain sheet paper is required from a printing register standpoint, short-grain paper may be preferred for greater stiffness, better blanket release, and a

Effect of grain direction on paper properties.

Grain Property	In the grain direction	Across direction
Tear strength is generally	—-	Greater
Tensile strength is always	Greater	—-
Stretch under tension is always	—-	Greater
Folding endurance is generally	—-	Greater
Paper folds	More easily, with less tendency to crack	—-
Tensile strength at fold is	—-	Greater
Stiffness and resistance to bending is always	—-	Greater
Expansion or contraction with change in relative humidity is always	—-	Greater

lesser tendency to develop embossing, curl, waffling, or tail-end hook. This is particularly true for lightweight papers. For proper feeding on small offset presses and duplicating equipment, grain should be parallel to the direction of sheet travel to minimize its rolling up or curling from a lack of stiffness, and its pickup of press moisture or water-containing fluids. The grain direction of heavyweight papers may have to be put parallel to the press cylinder axis to provide better conformance to the curvature of the cylinders.

For book manufacturing, the grain direction should parallel the bound edge of the book. Grain perpendicular to the bound edge can cause buckling and distortions at the spine and make the pages stiffer and more difficult to turn. Paper used in ring or other loose-leaf binders will have greater strength and stiffness for turning if grain is perpendicular to its binding edge.

Paper will fold more easily and have less tendency to crack when folded with the grain. Strength at the fold, however, will be greater when paper is folded across the grain, since tensile strength is always greater in the grain direction. For right-angle folds, the more difficult fold should be made with the grain. Scoring is required as basis weight increases and, in many instances, when paper is folded across the grain.

Grain and its relationship to stiffness is important for many end-use requirements. Grain direction should be perpendicular to the supporting edge of display cards, posters, file folders, and index cards to minimize sagging. Letterheads should have long grain for greater stiffness. Checks and documents processed on high-speed equipment should have grain perpendicular to their advancing edge.

The grain direction for printing register may be opposite to that required for runnability, the bindery, and other considerations, in which case the papermaker must decide which requirement will dictate grain direction.

The grain direction of paper may be determined by any of the following methods:

- Float a square piece of paper or paperboard on water, or simply moisten one of its sides. It will curl away from its wetted side, and the axis of curl will be parallel to its grain direction.
- Cut two ½×6-in. (13×150-mm) strips of paperboard from the sheet at right angles to each other and parallel to its edges. Lay one strip on the other, making sure they are aligned at one end. Grasp this end with thumb and forefinger and

hold the strips so that they are free to bend under their own weight. Repeat by placing the bottom strip on top. The strip having short grain will bend more and fall away from the other strip when placed on the bottom, since paper has less stiffness when it is flexed, or bent around, its grain direction. The grain direction so determined is then referenced to the sheet from which the strips were cut, to indicate the sheet's grain direction.

- A bursting test, as described in TAPPI T 403, will indicate the grain direction. The sheet's principal line of rupture will be perpendicular to its grain direction.
- A tensile test, performed in accordance with TAPPI T 404, will indicate the grain direction.

Bursting test for paper grain. The long continuous fracture line of the bursting test is perpendicular to the grain.

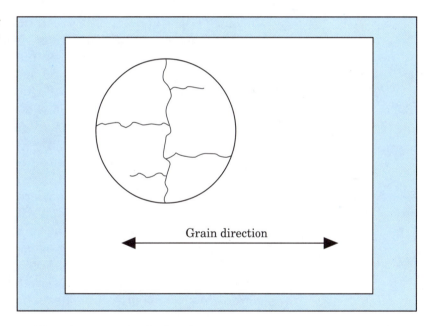

Grain direction

The above methods for determining grain direction are described in TAPPI T 409.

The combined effect of grain direction and changes in moisture content on dimensional stability are important during printing. Sheet paper for offset printing is almost always specified to be long-grain so its grain will be in the long direction of the sheets and parallel to the axis of the press cylinders. Trying to register on short-grain sheets when two or more passes through the press are involved often can be disastrous for some of the following reasons:

- There are fewer overall dimensional changes if the direction of greater stretch or shrinkage with moisture changes —

that is, the cross-grain direction — is in the shorter sheet direction. Long-grain paper will minimize the overall dimensional change, whereas short-grain paper will maximize dimensional change.

- The offset printing plate is one piece and the printing impression cannot be lengthened or shortened sideways (across the press) if the paper changes its dimensions in that direction. On the other hand, dimensional change in the paper in the direction of feeding can be compensated for by shifting the cylinder packing from plate to blanket, or vice versa. Consequently, long-grain paper will minimize its dimensional change in the direction across the press for which no compensation can be made for register.

- When wavy edges develop due to moisture absorption at the outer edges of a pile, the greater degree of waviness will be in the cross-grain direction, since the paper has a greater hygroexpansivity in this direction. Long-grain paper will cause this greater waviness to be in the running, or around-the-cylinder, direction, where it will have a better chance of ironing out back to the trailing edge without producing misregister and wrinkling.

Short-grain paper is sometimes specified for black-and-white or single-color work when it is required for a more economical layout, for bindery considerations, and when register and wrinkling are not problems. Short-grain paper is also sometimes specified for multicolor work on multicolor presses where there are heavy, all-over printed solids, and for light-basis-weight papers. Since paper is stiffer and stretches less in its machine direction than in its cross-machine direction, short-grain sheets have less tendency to acquire tail-end hook and to curl, emboss, or waffle.

Paper for duplicator presses is usually cut grain-long but printed grain-short (that is, the grain direction is perpendicular to printing cylinders) because register is of no consequence in one-color work, and the paper is stiffer and therefore feeds better into the press.

The printer and papermaker alike should note that they use the terms "grain-short" differently. The papermaker relates grain direction to the machine direction; the printer relates grain direction to the cylinders of the press. It is therefore possible, as with duplicator presses, to take paper that is cut grain-long and to print it grain-short. With most commercial sheetfed presses, the paper is cut and printed grain-long.

Roll-to-sheetfed presses are those in which the web is cut into sheets for feeding directly into the press. If the cut sheet is advanced to the press in the same direction it leaves the cutter, it will be printed grain-short. Because of the problems of printing short-grain paper, roll-to-sheetfed equipment has been designed with the roll and sheeter at right angles to the movement of paper through the press. The paper is unwound and sheeted at right angles to the press, so that it enters the press as long-grain paper.

Interdependence of Basis Weight (or Grammage), Caliper, and Finish

For any given uncoated paper, a three-way relationship exists for its basis weight, or grammage, and its caliper and finish. None of these three properties can be changed without altering at least one of the other two. If basis weight is to be reduced and caliper is to remain unchanged, then the fibrous structure must become more porous so that fewer fibers maintain the same caliper per unit area. This results in a paper with a rougher finish. Likewise, if the caliper of a

Interdependence of basis weight (or grammage), finish, and caliper in uncoated paper. For any given uncoated paper, a three-way relationship exists between its basis weight (or grammage) and its caliper and finish.

Finish remains constant and basis weight changes:

Basis weight	Caliper	Porosity	Ink absorbency
Increases	Increases	Relatively unchanged	Relatively unchanged
Decreases	Decreases	Relatively unchanged	Relatively unchanged

Caliper remains constant and basis weight changes:

Basis weight	Finish	Porosity	Ink absorbency
Increases	Becomes smoother	Decreases	Decreases
Decreases	Becomes rougher	Increases	Increases

Basis weight remains constant and caliper changes:

Caliper	Finish	Porosity	Ink absorbency
Increases	Becomes rougher	Increases	Increases
Decreases	Becomes smoother	Decreases	Decreases

given paper cannot be changed and its finish is to be made smoother, then its basis weight must be increased to maintain its caliper as it is calendered to a higher finish and becomes denser.

The **hygroexpansivity** of paper is the percentage of elongation or shrinkage caused by a given change in its surrounding relative humidity or its moisture content. The hygroscopic properties of paper and board are important to printers doing color work on sheetfed presses, where the stock must pass through the press two or more times in printing one side. If the paper expands or shrinks between printings, good register is difficult or impossible to obtain. Hygroexpansivity is an important factor in the manufacture of charts and maps requiring hairline register.

Hygroexpansivity is generally measured by placing suspended paper strips of a known length under light tension in a cabinet through which conditioned air is circulated. After the paper strips have had time to acclimate to the relative humidity of the circulating air, their length is carefully measured. The test is usually conducted by starting with a lower relative humidity, then increasing it to a desired higher value. The elongation of the paper for each of its grain and cross-grain directions is reported as a percent of its original dimension. This method, TAPPI UM 549, is time-consuming and not suitable for routine measurement.

Abrasion Resistance

The resistance of paper or paperboard to wet or dry abrasion is significant for packaging uses. Abrasion resistance is also important for erasability on typing and writing papers. Resistance to abrasion is measured as a sample's loss in weight after it has turned a specified number of revolutions on a supporting turntable with abrasive wheels resting on its top surface under a specified loading. This test, described in TAPPI T 476, is used for either dry or wet abrasion.

The Gavarti Comprehensive Abrasion Tester is used to test printed paper and paperboard for abrasion damage. The Sutherland ink-rub tester evaluates the scuffing or rubbing resistance of printed ink films on paper or paperboard, as described in TAPPI UM 487.

A paper coating's resistance to rubbing off when wet may be measured in various ways, one of which is given in TAPPI UM 462, where the coating is subjected to rubbing under controlled conditions of pressure and wetting.

Frictional Resistance

Friction is the resisting force that arises when one material slides over itself or another material. **Static friction** is the resisting force that exists before sliding takes place. Once sliding has taken place, the force resisting its continuation is called **kinetic friction.** The frictional resistance of paper is not normally a significant property during printing. Greater frictional resistance, which prevents paper sheets from sliding easily over each other or over other surfaces, may be a cause of greater static buildup.

Frictional resistance is important for paper and paperboard in that it relates to the slippage and skidding of cartons, shopping bags, and containers during handling and storage. Antiskid surface treatments of paper and paperboard are used to increase their frictional resistance and reduce slippage. The frictional resistance of a surface is indicated by its coefficient of friction, as measured by friction or slip testing equipment. TAPPI T 503 and T 542 are used to determine the static friction of shipping and packaging papers. T 815 and T 816 are used to determine the static friction of paperboard.

Adhesion to Surface

The ability of paper and paperboard to stick to their own or other surfaces by means of adhesives is important for specific converting and end-use requirements. Paper labels and tapes must adhere to various surfaces, including canvas, metal, glass, and plastics. The various types of adhesive-coated papers are pressure-sensitive, heat-activated, and remoistenable. A coated paper must be able to accept hot-melt adhesives and form a strong bond if it is to be used with adhesive binding.

The **glueability** of paperboard is an important property for carton packaging. Glueability refers to the speed and bond strength that develops when the two surfaces of a paperboard are joined with an adhesive. It assesses the ability of the flaps of a folded carton to remain bonded after cartons are filled and glued. Methods for measuring glueability are given in TAPPI UM 512, 559, and 564.

Compliance with Governmental and Packaging Requirements

Paper and paperboard used for packaging edible products and drugs may have to comply with regulations stipulated by governmental agencies like the Food and Drug Administration. Odors emanating from paper may be objectionable if the paper is used for packaging food or drugs. TAPPI T 483 describes an elaborate procedure using a panel of observers to detect objectionable odors in printed packaging materials.

When used as wrapping or as interleaves between silver and ferrous metals, papers must be chemically neutral and contain no corrosion-producing chemicals like sulfur.

Flame Resistance

Flame-resistant papers contain flame-retardant chemicals that prevent a flame from spreading should the paper be ignited. Such papers are not flameproof or fireproof, as they are sometimes called. Paper, when used for drapes, curtains, gowns, tablecloths, hats, streamers, and entertainment products, may be required by public ordinances to be flame-resistant. Flame resistance is measured in accordance with TAPPI T 461 as the time in seconds a paper continues to glow and by the length of its charred portion after it has been removed from the flame of a burner and ceases to flame.

Lightfastness

Lightfastness is the resistance of a paper to fading or yellowing upon exposure to light. The property depends on the fibrous and chemical composition of the paper. Lignin, which constitutes a substantial part of groundwood pulps, is light-sensitive. It quickly darkens and turns yellow when exposed to sunlight or other light in the ultraviolet region of the spectrum. Even a small percentage of groundwood or high lignin-containing fiber in paper will greatly reduce its lightfastness. Papers used for outdoor applications such as posters, banners, and signs and for indoor use under prolonged exposure to fluorescent lighting (permanent records and packaging) should have a high degree of lightfastness. To prevent fading or yellowing, these papers are made with fully bleached fibers and with fast-to-light dyes or pigments.

No paper is perfectly lightfast. Lightfastness is a relative property and is difficult to measure under the varying and uncontrollable condition of exposure to natural daylight. The relative fading resistance of papers is determined in an accelerated and reproducible manner by exposing them for selected time periods to a light radiation of constant intensity and composition that simulates a chosen natural daylight standard. TAPPI UM 461 describes the procedure, which makes use of the Fade-Ometer®.

Permanence and Durability

The permanence of paper is its ability to resist change in one or more of its properties during its storage and aging. Permanence is a relative property and depends on the chemical composition of the paper and its environment. For maximum permanence, paper should be made with bleached cellulose

Ci4000 Weather-Ometer® used for accelerated weathering and lightfastness test requirements. *Courtesy Atlas Electric Devices Co.*

fibers of high purity and should have a pH of 7 or somewhat higher; that is, it should be on the slightly alkaline side.

The relative permanence of paper is indicated in two ways. One is a measurement of its brightness loss and its yellowing tendency after artificial aging. The second and more important measurement is the percentage of its original strength retained after artificial aging. Folding endurance is very sensitive to the effects of aging and is used to indicate the weakening and embrittlement of paper. Tear resistance may also be used to measure strength loss. Since long-term, natural aging is not possible, accelerated aging methods are used. The dry method ages the paper at a temperature of 220°F (105°C) in a dry oven for a specified time. TAPPI T 453 describes a procedure for aging in this manner. Since it has been determined that the degradation of cellulose is very sensitive to moisture, it is believed that the moist accelerated aging method correlates more accurately with natural aging. TAPPI T 544 describes the procedure for moist accelerated aging at a temperature of 195°F (90°C) and 25% relative humidity.

One of the properties that critically influences the permanence of paper is pH. Low pH will shorten a paper's life and reduce its color permanence. For maximum permanency, paper should have a pH close to 7, or preferably slightly above 7, with an alkaline reserve to resist the detrimental effects of an acidic environment. For this reason, specifications for archival papers may include a minimum pH value and an alkaline reserve. Research studies show that the presence of sulfate ions from papermaker's alum shortens a paper's life by lowering its pH. Papers used for electrical applications like condenser tissue and cable wrapping must be chemically neutral — without traces of acidity or alkalinity — to meet rigid dielectric requirements.

Durability, as distinguished from permanence, indicates the extent to which paper will retain its properties with continued use or, more practically, its degree of deterioration with use and handling. Papers may be either permanent or durable or both permanent and durable. Sanitary papers made from pure cellulose are permanent but not durable. Unbleached kraft paper used for bags or cartons is durable but not permanent. High-quality bond ledger and bristols made from purified wood or cotton fibers and having a neutral to slightly alkaline pH are considered permanent and durable.

Papers that come into contact with alkaline products like soaps and adhesives should not stain or discolor. This restriction applies to both white and colored papers. Such papers should not contain mechanical pulps or dyes that are sensitive to alkalis. TAPPI UM 585 describes a measurement of alkali-staining resistance. Paper may have to resist the penetration of blood, oils, and grease associated with the packaging of products like food and machine parts. Special test methods are used to measure the penetration resistance of the substance involved.

9   The Manufacture of Paper

Fibrous Raw Materials

Wood is the major source of fibrous papermaking raw materials — about 95% worldwide and about 99% in North America. The remainder of fibrous raw materials are derived from recycled papers; from plants such as sugarcane, bamboo, hemp, cotton, and flax; and from synthetic fibers.

Trees are classified botanically into two main groups: the coniferous (cone-bearing), or softwood, group (redwood, spruce, pine, fir, larch, cedar, and hemlock) and the deciduous, or hardwood, group (birch, beech, maple, oak, poplar, gum, elm, aspen, and cottonwood).

The size and shape of wood fibers vary considerably from tree to tree and within a given tree. On the average, softwood trees have a fiber length of about ⅛ in. (3 mm), whereas the hardwood trees have a much shorter fiber length, about 0.04 in. (1 mm). The differences in the length and structure of fibers produced by softwood and hardwood trees have an important influence on their papermaking characteristics.

The various forms of wood used in papermaking — such as roundwood, logs, chips, sawdust, and shavings — are known as pulpwood. Although pulpwood once consisted entirely of roundwood cut from the tree, today a substantial portion comes from sawmill and logging residues. By 1986, the United States was obtaining more than 30% of its papermaking fibers from wood waste residuals like slabs, edgings, sawdust, and fines from lumber manufacturing. Whole-tree utilization, whereby the tree is cut at its base or ground level and its entire foliage, branches, and trunk are converted into chips at the harvesting site, also provides an efficient use of wood. As the technology for processing wood improves, whole-tree chipping will increase, relieving some of the pressure on fiber sources for the future.

Softwood *(left)* and hardwood kraft fibers before beating, magnified 90×.
Courtesy Institute of Paper Science and Technology.

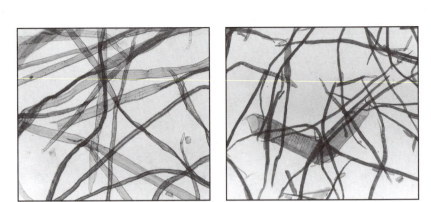

The importance of a sufficient pulpwood supply to support the future needs of the paper industry is recognized in scientific professional forestry practices. These practices include the harvesting of more pulpwood from available acreage, using forest genetics to obtain a higher yield per growing area with faster-maturing, superior pulpwood trees; developing new tree species more resistant to diseases and insects; and planting trees that are best suited to thrive in specific sites and climatic conditions.

Most of the world's pulpwood is supplied by North America, Finland, and the Scandinavian countries. In the future, the tropical woods of South America and Africa may also become a source of pulpwood. A very fast growing species of the eucalyptus tree, indigenous to Australia, is now being

Ground-level hydraulic shear, permitting whole-tree utilization when converting into chips at the harvesting site.
Courtesy Glatfelter Pulpwood Co.

successfully grown for pulpwood in climatically favorable regions of South America, Africa, and Southern Europe.

Another source of fibrous raw material is secondary or recycled fibers. The paper industry in the United States obtains about 25% of its fibrous materials from the recycling of wastepapers. Most of this recycled wastepaper is used to manufacture paperboard, with a lesser percentage used for manufacturing fine white printing and writing papers.

Although nonwood plants represent a minor source of fibrous material in wood-rich countries, they are important for manufacturing specialty papers. Many wood-deficient countries rely heavily on nonwood plant fibers for papermaking. Nonwood sources originate from such annual crop plants as sugarcane, which is grown in most tropical and subtropical regions. After the cane is ground for its sugar juices, a fibrous residue called **bagasse** remains. Before chemical pulping, bagasse undergoes a depithing treatment to isolate its fibers. In some parts of the world, cereal grain straws — wheat, oat, rye, barley, and less commonly, rice — are sources of papermaking fiber. **Esparto,** a grass that grows wild in North Africa and southern Spain, has long been used in England for papermaking fiber. **Bamboos,** which are wood plants of the grass family that grow in tropical regions, represent an important fiber source for some countries.

Certain plant fibers that are used for making exceptionally strong papers are derived from pulping their by-products, or from cellulosic raw materials that have outlived their usefulness. Examples are **manila hemp** or **sisal hemp,** which is derived from used ropes and cordage, and **jute,** a fiber derived from burlap cuttings.

Cotton and linen fibers have long been used to make papers. Sources of cotton fibers are cuttings, threads, and waste from textile manufacturing; raw cotton; and **cotton linters.** Cotton linters are the short, seed-hair fibers remaining on cotton seeds after the staple — long-fibered cotton — has been removed by ginning. Cotton fibers are longer than wood fibers and are flat and twisted. These properties, as well as the high degree of pure cellulose, make cotton fibers unexcelled for manufacturing high-quality, fine-textured, durable writing papers. **Flax tow** is the source of linen fibers used for manufacturing cigarette, bible, carbonizing, and other high-quality specialty papers.

Kenaf, an annual agricultural plant native to India, has been used to make newsprint and is the subject of research as a future potential fiber source in the southern regions of the United States.

To a very limited extent, synthetic fibers are used alone or in combination with cellulose fibers for manufacturing papers having specific characteristics unobtainable with cellulose fibers alone. The drawbacks of synthetic fibers are their high cost, their dependency on nonrenewable raw materials like petroleum, and the fact that they are not biodegradable or generally recyclable.

The Manufacture of Pulp

There are two fundamental steps in papermaking. First, the fibrous raw material, or cellulose, from pulpwood, nonwood fibers, or recycled papers is converted into **pulp,** a mass of fibers suitable for papermaking. Second, the pulp, or fibrous material, is interwoven and bonded into a structure known as paper.

The key substance in papermaking pulp is cellulose, a complex polymer made up of the chemical elements carbon, hydrogen, and oxygen. Cellulose is composed of a large number of relatively simple, repeating units having the empirical formula $C_6H_{10}O_5$. The chemical structure of cellulose in plants, and other constituents with which it is associated, is an ongoing subject of fundamental research.

Cellulose has many desirable properties for papermaking: it is abundant and replenishable; it can be easily harvested and transported to its usage site; and, in its fibrous form, it has very high tensile strength and a great affinity for water. These last two characteristics are needed to bond fibers strongly together into the network we know as paper. While cellulose fibers can be changed mechanically and chemically in the presence of water, they resist change or degradation by many chemicals. Because of this unique characteristic, it is possible to isolate cellulose fibers from plants and to purify them for papermaking. Cellulose is found in the woody structure of trees, which consists of about 50% cellulose by weight; in nonwood plants such as cotton, whose fibers are over 98% cellulose; and in recycled papers.

Wood, which consists of the three complex organic constituents **cellulose, hemicellulose,** and **lignin,** is made up of multilayers of cellulose fibers bound together by lignin. Papermaking fibers, or pulp, may be obtained from wood by three basic methods: mechanical pulping; chemical pulping, which liberates the cellulose fibers from their lignin bonding material; and semimechanical pulping (a combination of mechanical and chemical treatments). Each method produces pulp having different characteristics. Used alone or in combination, these methods produce the vast numbers of papers and paperboards available. Modifications of these methods are used to tailor-make pulps for very specific needs.

Pulpwood debarking and preparation. The pulping process begins with pulpwood, which comes in various forms: roundwood, chips, sawdust, shavings, slabs, and edgings. Roundwood is usually debarked before being sent to the pulp mill because bark has little or no fiber value, contributes to dirt, consumes wood-digesting chemicals, and lowers pulp quality. (Nevertheless, whole-tree chipping is an important and growing practice.) Several methods are used to remove bark from pulpwood logs. A common method is to process them in a drum-type barker — a large, inclined cylindrical steel drum. Pulpwood logs enter at one end, are forced to travel through the rotating drum, and are discharged at its opposite end. The pounding and abrasive action of the tumbling logs tears loose their bark. In the western regions of North America, pulpwood logs from tall, large-diameter trees are barked hydraulically. High-pressure water jets, impinging on a rotating log, peel away its bark. The leftover bark is used as an auxiliary fuel or as a mulching material.

Debarked roundwood can be sent directly to the pulp grinders. When used with other pulping methods, it must be converted into chips or another suitable form for conveying

A barking drum. Logs enter drum, are debarked by impact, compression, and shear forces, and are continuously discharged. *Courtesy S.W. Hooper Co.*

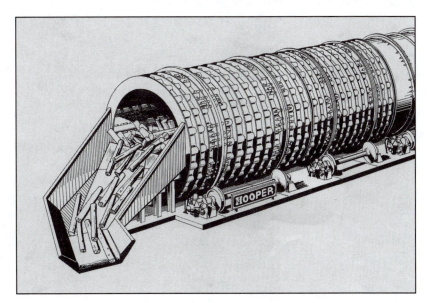

Hydraulic barking.
Tall, large-diameter
trees are debarked by
jets of high-pressure
water (1,300 lb./sq.in.).
*Courtesy Georgia-
Pacific Corp.*

to refiners or digesters. This is done in order to permit a
rapid, uniform penetration of the digesting chemical into the
wood. Normally, the multiple-knife disk-type chipper is used.
This chipper consists of a heavy steel disk with knives protruding from its surface. As the disk rotates at high speed,
pulpwood logs are fed into the chipper with their ends
directed into the path of the rotating knives. The cutting or
shearing action of the knives slices the wood into chips.
Afterwards, the chips are screened for uniform size, and
unwanted material is eliminated.

Pile of chips ready
to be taken to the
digester.
*Courtesy P.H. Glatfelter
Co.*

Chips ready for conversion into chemical pulp. *Courtesy P.H. Glatfelter Co.*

Pulping methods. The first commercial wood pulp was a mechanical pulp, called groundwood. No attempt is made to soften lignin, the cementing material that binds the fibers together, because the grinding itself develops enough heat to accomplish this. **Groundwood** or **mechanical pulp** is produced by forcing pulpwood against a revolving, abrasive grinding stone at atmospheric pressure. Water showers wash away the pulp fibers from the grinding stone and prevent damage to the wood from heat and friction. Wood is pulped into fragments of various shapes and sizes. The chemical composition of the pulp is the same as that of the wood from which it originated.

Advantages of groundwood pulp are its low cost and high yield. One hundred pounds (45 kg) of pulpwood yield from 80 to 95 lb. (41 to 43 kg) of groundwood pulp. This pulp has high

Two-pocket grinder for manufacturing groundwood pulp. Debarked logs are pressed against a revolving pulp stone in the presence of water. *Courtesy Montagne Machine Co.*

Groundwood fibers (enlarged 110×). *Courtesy Institute of Paper Science and Technology.*

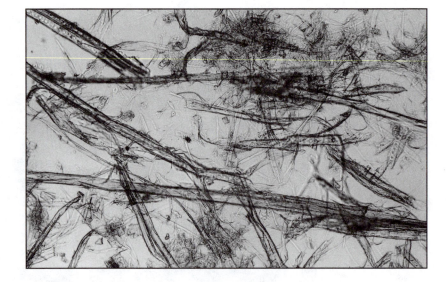

bulk and opacity, as well as excellent printing cushion and ink absorbency. The disadvantages of groundwood are low strength and brightness, lack of permanency, and yellowing with age. Newsprint, which is made from 75% or more mechanical pulp, is a good example of a material that yellows quickly in the presence of light. Another disadvantage of groundwood is its objectionable **shives,** or undefibered fiber bundles, that are torn from the wood during grinding.

Mechanical pulp represents 23% or more of the pulp used in the world. It is used extensively for manufacturing newsprint, coated groundwood printing and publication papers, uncoated groundwood papers for pulp magazines, telephone directories, catalogs, and household papers like towels, tissues, and sanitary papers.

Innovations in pulping technology have made it possible to overcome some of the undesirable properties of groundwood, while maintaining its advantages. One of these developments is called **refiner mechanical pulp,** or **RMP,** produced by passing wood chips through a disk refiner at atmospheric pressure instead of grinding wood against stone. Chips, in the presence of water, are introduced between the grooved surfaces of two disks rotating in opposite directions at high speed (or one rotating and one fixed). This subjects the chips to an intensive mechanical action as they contact refining surfaces and each other. High frictional resistance heats the chips and softens the lignin that binds the fibers, thereby permitting fiber separation with less fiber damage. The resulting refiner mechanical pulp has few shives and has fibers that are more individually separated than groundwood fibers, but contains some debris from fiber bundles. Since RMP is stronger than groundwood, it permits lower use of the more costly chemical pulp. Refiner mechanical pulp also utilizes waste chips and makes wider use of tree species and low-grade wood than does groundwood. Still, it has the high opacity and yield of groundwood.

Most RMP installations have been replaced, however, by another type of pulping operation that produces **thermo-mechanical pulp,** or **TMP.** TMP is produced in a manner similar to RMP except that wood chips are separated into fibers in refiners operated at elevated temperatures and under pressure. In some cases, chips are first preheated in a steaming vessel before passing through refiners. Preheating softens the lignin that binds the cellulose fibers together. Fibers are thereby separated more easily as the softened chips pass through refiners, producing more long fibers and fewer fines. TMP is usually given a second stage or even a third-stage treatment in pressurized or atmospheric discharge refiners for further defiberization and surface development of the fibers. TMP is stronger than RMP and significantly stronger than stone groundwood, reducing or eliminating the use of the more costly chemical pulps that are blended with mechanical pulps for adequate paper strength. TMP has high yield and high opacity. Newsprint made with TMP has better runnability on the press than that made with groundwood. TMP is also used to manufacture coated publication papers.

The latest development in mechanical pulping technology is **CTMP** or **chemi-thermomechanical pulping,** where wood chips are treated with mild chemicals prior to refining. Mild chemical pretreatment improves pulp brightness to some extent and reduces shive content significantly.

Pressurized groundwood, PGW, differs from conventional groundwood because it is produced by grinding wood under elevated pressure. Other mechanical pulping systems are emerging for the production of high-yield, superior mechanical pulps that provide high bulk, good ink absorbency, high opacity, good printability, and the optimum use of local wood species. All mechanical pulps may be bleached to a higher brightness without removing the residual lignin and other constituents that account for their high pulping yield.

Semichemical pulps are produced in two stages. Wood chips are first given a mild chemical cooking to partially

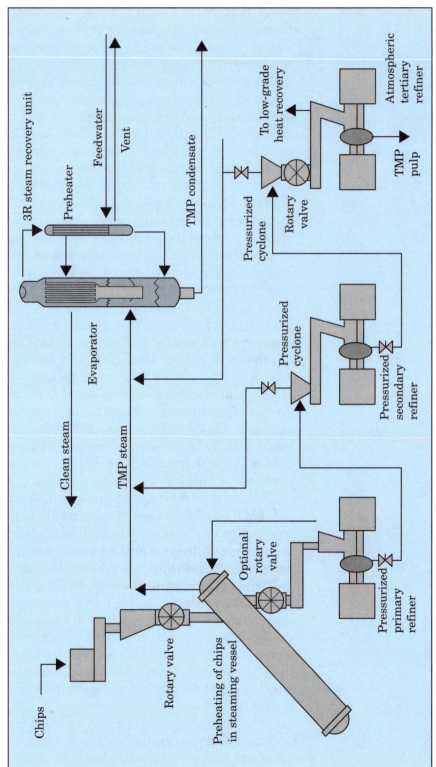

Three-stage TMP system for lightweight coated papers (pressure/pressure/atmospheric refining and heat recovery system). *Courtesy Sprout-Bauer, Inc.*

remove and soften their lignin and to weaken their intercellu-
lar bonds. The most commonly used cooking chemicals are
sodium sulfite with a small amount of alkaline salts, such as
sodium carbonate, bicarbonate, or hydroxide. They provide a
cooking treatment in the near-neutral pH range, and the
result is described as neutral sulfite semichemical pulp. Next,
cooked chips are passed through a disk refiner for fiberizing,
then washed to remove cooking chemicals. Semichemical
pulping converts wood into fibers with little damage to the
fibers. A substantial portion of the lignin in the original wood
is retained, resulting in yields ranging from 60 to 80% of the
original wood, depending on the characteristics of the pulp
and its end use. Semichemical pulping produces the stiff
fibers required to make corrugating board, fiber tubes, cores,
and containers. It is not used for the manufacture of printing
and writing papers.

Chemical pulping is carried out by either an acid or alkaline cooking of wood under heat and pressure. During the
chemical cooking of wood chips and, if present, sawdust, the
lignin and hemicellulose constituents of wood are dissolved to
liberate cellulose fibers from the composite wood structure.
Unbleached chemical pulp still contains some lignin and
hemicellulose associated with the cellulose fibers; bleaching
removes these constituents. Chemical pulps have a much
lower fiber yield than mechanical pulps. Unbleached chemical pulp has a fiber yield ranging from 50 to 55%. Bleaching
would result in a lower fiber yield.

In the **sulfite** process, wood chips are cooked with sulfurous acid and one of its base salts, which may be calcium,
sodium, magnesium, or ammonia. Sulfurous acid is produced
by burning sulfur to form sulfur dioxide gas, then reacting it
with water. Sulfurous acid and limestone are next reacted to
form calcium bisulfite. This combined solution of sulfurous
acid and calcium bisulfite solubilizes lignin during cooking.
The sulfite process is not suitable for pulping woods having a
high resinous content, as do the southern pines of the United
States.

Unbleached sulfite pulp has moderate strength, is soft and
flexible, has a low lignin content, and is easily bleached. It is
used as a supplement to mechanical fibers (for example, in
newsprint). Bleached sulfite pulp has long been used to make
white printing and writing papers.

The sulfite process was the most important chemical pulping process until the mid-1900s. In recent years, pollution

Continuous-chemical pulping system (Kamyr). Steam and mechanically softened chips, fed continuously into the top of the vertical digester, descend through cooking and washing treatments to the bottom outlet. *Courtesy Kamyr, Incorporated.*

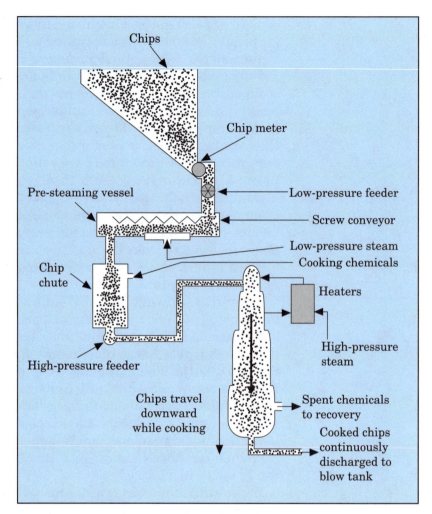

abatement has become more stringent, requiring the recovery of polluting substances. Since it is impractical to recover calcium-base sulfite liquors and thereby reduce the pollution load of its effluent, other chemical bases have evolved. The sulfite process has been largely replaced by the alkaline pulping process, which uses sodium, magnesium, and ammonia bases adapted to pulpmill chemical recovery systems.

Alkalis have long been used to remove lignin from plants. **Soda** pulp, first produced commercially in 1851, uses caustic soda or lye to digest wood chips. In 1879, a sulfur salt, sodium sulfate (Na_2SO_4), was introduced into the soda pulping system. Surprisingly, a much stronger pulp resulted. This modified process was erroneously called sulfate pulping since it was only discovered later that the active chemical responsible for higher strength was not sodium sulfate, but rather sodium sulfide (Na_2S). The process, still called sulfate, is also (more accurately) described as **kraft,** which in German and Swedish means "strength."

Soda mills were converted to the sulfate, or kraft, process soon after papermakers discovered its advantages: greater pulping adaptability (including almost every known wood species) and the ability to recover chemicals and heat energy by incinerating the waste liquors, which greatly lowers processing costs. The final impetus for the rapid growth of kraft pulping was the discovery of multistage bleaching for the production of high-brightness pulp. Kraft pulping produces a strong pulp needed for operating high-speed presses and converting equipment. Today it is the dominant chemical pulping method.

Since 1950, the older batch method of cooking wood has been replaced by continuous pulping systems, a major development in pulping technology. Compared to the batch system, they provide tighter control of cooking variables by using computers and continuously monitoring operations. A better-quality, more uniform pulp with greater economy results.

In addition to wood, paper can be made from many different plants. Since a hollow tubular, or quill-shaped, fiber is required for papermaking, a plant's suitability as a fibrous source depends largely on the shape of its fibers. The selection of a plant for fibrous raw material is also determined by the dependability of its supply and the costs of its harvesting, transportation, and manufacture into pulp.

Nonwoody plants are generally pulped by modified alkaline methods. Botanically less complex than wood, nonwoody plants provide cellulose more easily during pulping, but their yield of cellulose is less than that of wood. An exception is cotton, which is almost pure cellulose.

Cotton — in the form of linen rags, raw cotton, cotton linters, and cotton textile waste — is used to manufacture high-quality, permanent writing papers. The cotton materials are given prolonged cooking with chemicals such as soda ash, lime, or caustic soda, along with detergents. Next, the cooked fibers are washed extensively and are usually refined simultaneously in a beater-type washer. This treatment thoroughly removes residual chemicals, dirt, and coloring matter, and teases out the long fibers for their subsequent refining and bleaching.

Recycled paper is an important source of papermaking fibrous material. Although considered a contemporary practice, there is evidence that paper recycling was practiced before 1637 by the Chinese. About 26% of all paper and paperboard manufactured in the United States is recycled, and the world average is 30%. The amount of wastepaper recycled depends on the economics of collecting wastepaper, as opposed to the economics of growing trees and pulping them. Collecting wastepaper for recycling is relatively expensive. Pulpwood, on the other hand, is a major farm crop in the United States, and agricultural advances have managed to keep the costs of producing it low while increasing the yield.

The Bleaching of Pulps

Prior to bleaching, the color of wood pulp ranges from cream to dark brown. The color of brown wrapping paper and paper bags is typical of unbleached kraft pulp. Papers are bleached to whiteness for several reasons: printing contrast improves as the whiteness of paper increases; whiter papers are aesthetically desirable; colored papers become more brilliant when made from whiter pulps; bleaching contributes to the chemical stability, purity, and permanence of chemical pulps; and bleaching is necessary for sanitary reasons (for example, in food-packaging papers).

Unbleached chemical pulps contain residual lignin and other extractives. Chemical pulping cannot be continued to the point of complete lignin removal without severe degradation of the cellulose fibers. To produce white pulp, this residual lignin, which is mainly responsible for the dark color, must be removed or altered by bleaching. Bleaching removes or alters lignin without chemical damage to cellulose and may be considered a continuation of pulping.

For years, the paper industry used **calcium hypochlorite,** which is similar to household bleach, to bleach sulfite and soda pulps in a single-stage treatment. This earlier bleaching method was ineffective for bleaching kraft pulp. Multistage bleaching, which made it possible to obtain white kraft pulp, consists of two steps: first, removing lignin and its by-products; second, bleaching after these color-producing substances have been eliminated. During the earlier stages, lignin is progressively removed. Bleaching then removes or decolorizes the remaining substances to expose the inherent whiteness of the cellulose fibers. In the lignin-removal stages, the pulp is treated with chlorine gas, which produces a partial degradation and chlorination of the lignin and causes it to become soluble in water and in a caustic solution. These solubilized by-products are then progressively washed from the pulp. The first stage of bleaching is usually done by using calcium or sodium hypochlorite, which whitens the residual coloring substances by chemical oxidation. By-products of this treatment are also withdrawn by washing. The final bleaching step for kraft pulp normally consists of treating it with **chlorine dioxide,** a gas that rapidly and selectively removes the remaining lignin and produces a clean, bright white pulp.

A typical, five-stage multiple-bleaching sequence would then comprise chlorination with chlorine, alkaline extraction, hypochlorite bleaching, a second alkaline extraction, and, finally a chlorine dioxide treatment. Computer-controlled multistage bleaching produces clean, high-brightness kraft pulp of uniform quality, which is used to make a vast array of paper and paperboard products. Oxygen, which reduces the pollution load of a bleach plant, is being used increasingly during multistage bleaching.

In mechanical pulps, most of the lignin is retained. Since high yield is one of the main advantages of mechanical pulps, it is necessary to prevent undue loss of fiber weight and yield. Bleaching these pulps removes or alters some of their coloring substances without substantially removing the constituents responsible for their dark color. The chemicals commonly used for bleaching mechanical pulps are chemical reducing agents like sodium and zinc hydrosulfite and oxidizing agents like hydrogen and sodium peroxide. While these treatments increase brightness, they do not impart the high brightness of bleached chemical pulps, nor do they produce greater brightness stability or permanency. The whiteness level of pulp is commonly measured with either the TAPPI or the ISO brightness tester. The brightness of bleached pulps ranges from about 82 to over 90, depending upon the end use. Unbleached mechanical pulps will generally range from 57 to 62 G.E. brightness. Bleaching will raise their brightness to the upper 60 to 70 level, depending on the extent of bleaching and the wood species. Mechanical pulps are bleached to make groundwood printing, catalog, directory, converting, and coated base stock.

Nonfibrous Raw Materials

Most paper is made up of more than fibers. It also contains nonfibrous raw materials that are added to impart certain properties or qualities to the finished paper. The papermaker's use of nonfibrous additives accounts for the vast number of different papers having different characteristics and end-use applications.

The major nonfibrous raw materials fall under the term **loading,** or **fillers.** Loading is made up of finely divided, relatively insoluble inorganic materials or minerals — most commonly clay, titanium dioxide, and calcium carbonate — that are incorporated into the papermaking composition prior to sheet formation. The purpose of loading is to modify such characteristics of the finished paper as opacity, brightness, printability, texture, and weight. Loading is also used to impart softness, reduce bulk, increase smoothness, make paper more uniformly receptive to printing inks, and lend greater dimensional stability. The prime reason for loading in printing papers is to increase opacity and brightness, reduce ink strike-through, and decrease the harshness of the fibers.

Fillers for papermaking are required to possess high brightness, good light-scattering properties for increasing opacity, nonabrasiveness, and chemical inertness. **Clay** for papermaking originates from refined natural kaolin clay. **Titanium dioxide** is the most efficient filler for opacifying paper. **Calcium carbonate** is used in alkaline papermaking systems. Examples of lesser-used fillers are hydrated alumina, talc, calcium sulfate, barium sulfate, the natural or synthetic silicas or silicate pigments, and zinc pigments. The percentage of fillers used in printing and writing papers normally ranges from 5 to 30% of the papers' total weight. For some papers, less or no filler is used.

In addition to fillers, other nonfibrous raw materials may be mixed with paper fibers to effect certain results. Rosin and papermakers' alum are used for internal sizing; synthetic sizing materials are used for alkaline-sized papers. Additives like starches, gums, and synthetic polymers are used for improved fiber adhesion, dry strength, and filler retention. Specific additives are used to make papers that must retain a substantial portion of their dry strength after soaking in water. Dyes and colored pigments are added to tint white papers and to produce colored papers. Optical brighteners (dyes) are used to increase the brightness of white papers.

The combination of paper fibers and nonfibrous additives is called the papermaking **furnish** — that is, the composite materials that are formed into a sheet of paper on the paper machine.

Stock Preparation and Refining

Papermaking fibers from the pulpmill are only partially prepared for paper manufacture. If used in this state, they would produce paper having low strength, uncontrollable texture, and a wild, uneven formation. Before being made into paper, therefore, fiber must undergo what has come to be known as **stock preparation.** Stock preparation includes fiber refining and the blending of fibrous and nonfibrous materials into the desired proportions for the papermaking furnish.

At the beginning of the stock preparation process, paper fibers arrive as pulp slushed directly from the pulpmill, as wet laps, or as dried pulp sheets. The fibers must be suspended in water to provide the proper consistency and to permit blending with other additives. Pulpers, which consist of tanks or chests having high-speed rotors with pulping vanes, are used to disintegrate the pulp into a water suspension. The vanes create a violent agitation and turbulence, quickly producing a pulp slurry that can be pumped to subsequent operations.

Refining is the next step in stock preparation. The first mechanical refiner was the **beater,** which is still used as the initial refining step in many smaller-capacity mills. The beater consists of an oval-shaped tank, rounded at both ends

As stock travels around the beater and passes between the beater roll and bed-plate, the fibers undergo refining. *Courtesy Black Clawson Co.*

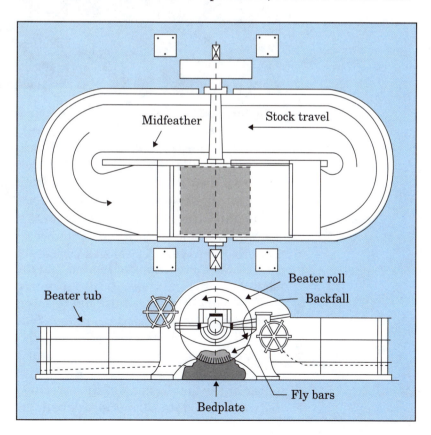

Unbeaten softwood pulp (enlarged 160×). *Courtesy Institute of Paper Science and Technology.*

Beaten softwood pulp (enlarged 160×). *Courtesy Institute of Paper Science and Technology.*

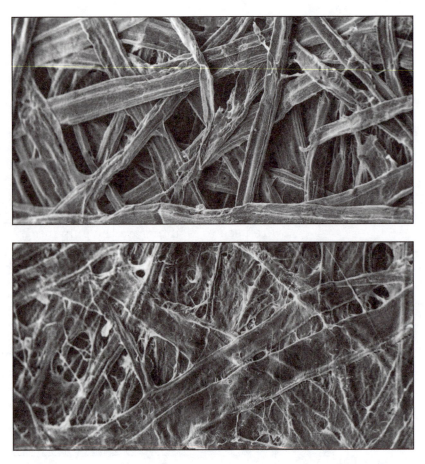

and equipped with a roll fitted with metal bars. This roll rotates over a bedplate having similar rows of metal bars. The action of fibers being drawn between moving bars that contact stationary bars in the presence of water is known as **beating.** Beating subjects fibers to brushing, cutting, fraying, and shortening, and unravels their surfaces to form fine hairs or fibrils resembling the pile on velvet. Fibers become swollen and softened, and their surface area is increased for greater fiber-to-fiber contact and bonding during papermaking. Photomicrographs of beaten and unbeaten pulps vividly show the physical changes fibers undergo during beating.

Following beating, additional refining can be accomplished by a conical-type, or **jordan,** refiner. The jordan refiner consists of a conically shaped rotor, or plug, fitted with longitudinal metal bars rotating on a horizontal shaft and surrounded by a conical shell also fitted with longitudinal bars. Fibers enter at the smaller end of the rotating plug, are swirled between it and its surrounding shell, and are forced to exit

Conical-type refiner (jordan) continuous refiner. Fibers are refined as they pass between the refining bars of the rotating plug and the stationary bars of its surrounding shell. *Courtesy Black Clawson Co.*

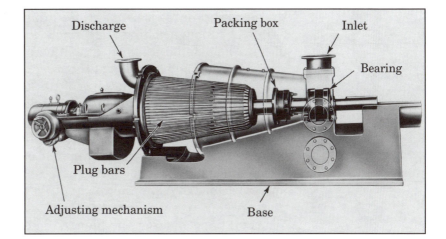

Discharge   Packing box   Inlet

Bearing

Plug bars

Adjusting mechanism   Base

from the larger end by centrifugal force. Fibers are brushed out and cut during jordan refining. After refining, paper fibers can be blended with nonfibrous additives to form the papermaking furnish.

In large production mills, the beater, which refines paper in batches, has been replaced by the disk refiner, which refines continuously. **Disk refiners** have two vertical disks with refining surfaces of various ridged or serrated contours. One disk may rotate while the other remains stationary, or each disk may rotate in a direction opposite to the other. Paper fibers enter at the center opening of one of the disks and are driven out to the periphery of the disk by centrifugal force. The clearance between the disks is adjusted to obtain

Open twin-disk refiner. Fibers advancing from the center to the periphery of the disks are refined by numerous impacts between the raised surfaces of the rotating and stationary disks. *Courtesy Black Clawson Co.*

the desired refining treatment. Refining consists of a combination of rubbing, rolling, dispersion, and cutting of the fibers. The extent and type of refining in disk refiners can be varied by the configuration of their refining surfaces.

Basically, there are two types of stock preparation systems. One is the older batch system, which uses a combination of beater and conical refiners. The other is the newer continuous system, used in large-capacity mills, which consists of disk refining followed by conical refiners. Continuous stock preparation lends itself to the on-line process control of refining and to the use of papermaking additives. Different types of pulp are selectively refined to optimize their individual properties for papermaking and blended in the desired ratio. Likewise, refined fibers are continuously and automatically blended with nonfibrous additives—such as internal sizing, dyes and color pigments, and fillers in the desired ratios—for the papermaking furnish. Furnish to the paper machine may be quickly altered to keep paper within its specifications or when making a grade change.

Refining, which develops the interfiber bonding necessary for papermaking, profoundly affects the characteristics of paper fibers. In the past, papermakers have said that paper is made in the beater, not at the paper machine. In a sense, this remains true for all refining systems, since the ultimate characteristics of a sheet of paper are greatly influenced by stock preparation. For example, blotting and greaseproof papers are directly opposite in their properties, yet both are made from cellulose fibers. Their contrasting properties originate from differences in refining.

Paper Machines

Transforming papermaking furnish into a finished web of paper involves diluting, cleaning, and screening the furnish, then processing it in a paper machine. Following stock preparation, the furnish is diluted to a low fiber consistency. Centrifugal cleaners, employing centrifugal force and a cyclone action, are used to remove small particles of unwanted material such as sand, grit, metallic particles, and plastic from the diluted water suspension of the furnish. The resulting material is then ready to be formed and finished in a paper machine.

There are three basic types of paper machines: the conventional fourdrinier machine, the twin-wire former, and the cylinder machine. All paper machines have three major sections—the wet or forming section, the press section, and the

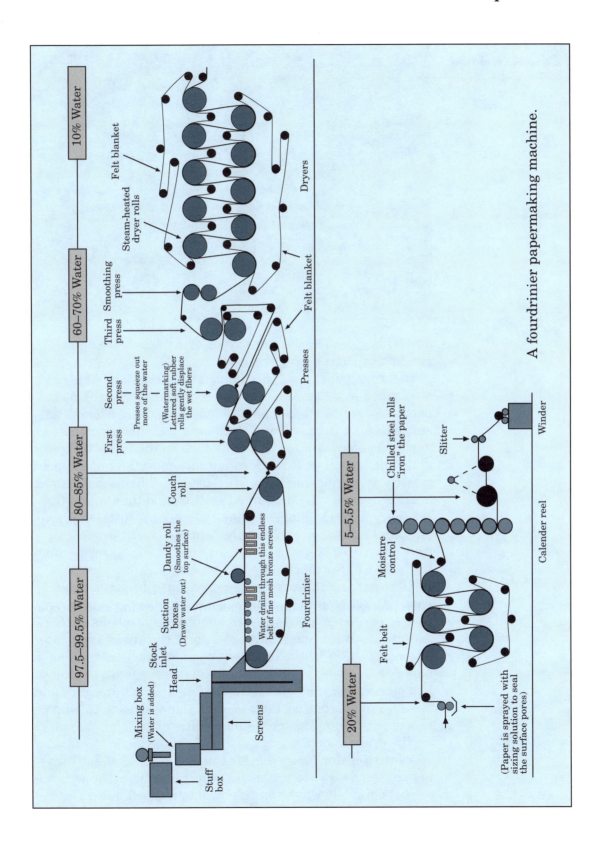

A fourdrinier papermaking machine.

Wet end of a large, high-speed fourdrinier. *Courtesy P.H. Glatfelter Co.*

drying section. The different types of machines are distinguished by their drying sections.

To form a paper web, the cleaned and screened fibers are suspended in water at a very low consistency equivalent to about 1 part fiber to 200 parts water, by weight. This water suspension of papermaking stock enters the paper machine at the headbox, whose function is to keep the fibers dispersed and to deliver them to the forming section at the proper speed relative to the moving wire. The suspended fibers have a natural tendency to clot or clump together, and they retain that tendency until the moment they are woven into a uniform structure on the wire. Since fiber entanglement produces a poor paper web, keeping the fibers separate is a crucial function of the paper machine.

After passing through the headbox, the fiber suspension enters the slice, an adjustable rectangular orifice whose purpose is to deliver across the wire width a continuous sheet of water-suspended fibers having uniform thickness, fiber consistency, and velocity. This process is necessary for making a paper web having uniform profiles of basis weight, thickness, and other properties. As the fibers flow through the slice and increase in speed, they tend to align themselves in the direction of their flow. This pronounced fiber alignment accounts for the grain of paper.

A **fourdrinier** paper machine uses a horizontal, forward-moving, endless wire belt as its forming section. The wire consists of finely woven bronze or plastic mesh. Fibers and water flow onto the wire, with the water draining through the wire because of gravity. Fibers are trapped on the wire and interlace in a random fashion to form a mat. Some fine fibers, fillers, and other additives are lost by their drainage through the wire. As the wire moves forward, more fibers are deposited over the first formed layer, thereby building up a succession of fiber layers. The side of the fiber mat formed in contact with the wire is called the **wire side** of paper. The top side, or the side not in contact with the wire, is designated as the **felt side.** The felt side has more short fibers, fines, and filler than the wire side. Recent engineering developments have significantly reduced this "two-sidedness" characteristic of paper.

The wire is supported by stationary **foils,** which are arc-shaped plastic surfaces, or by turning table rolls over which the moving wire rides. In addition to providing support, they assist in removing water from the underside of the wire by suction. Slower running paper machines may have their wire oscillated at a right angle to the wire movement. This **shake** breaks up fiber flocs and helps the fibers to felt together with a more random orientation for better sheet formation.

Dry end of a large, high-speed fourdrinier. *Courtesy P.H. Glatfelter Co.*

The Sym-Press II press section on a Repap A-1 paper machine.
Courtesy Repap Marketing, Inc.

As the wire continues forward, drainage by gravity and by the action of table roll or foil becomes ineffective. The wire next passes over vacuum boxes that suck water from the newly formed web. A **dandy roll** may be used at this point. It is a turning, hollow, wire-covered roll that rides on the wire, compacting the fibers that are still in a mobile state, and improving formation. A plain-woven wire covering on the dandy roll produces a **wove** finish. **Watermarking** is produced with a raised design in the dandy roll's covering that causes fiber displacement and greater final transparency, seen as a watermark in dried paper. Similarly, a **laid**-marked paper is produced by a watermark design.

The wire reaches the end of its forward journey at the **couch roll.** The couch roll has a perforated shell through which a vacuum is applied for further water removal. At this point, the paper web has about 80–85% water and is sufficiently consolidated for its separation from the returning wire and its transfer to the press section. On high-speed machines, the paper web is lifted from the wire by suction and transferred to a felt for entry to the press section.

The purpose of the press section is to remove as much water as possible from the web by pressing and suction. This process levels out moisture distribution across the web and minimizes the amount that has to be removed, at greater cost, in the drying section. The press section also compacts the paper web and brings fibers into closer contact for better fiber bonding and sheet strength. It smooths the paper and

The Repap A-1 paper machine with a Valmet Syn-Flo headbox. *Courtesy Repap Marketing, Inc.*

has an important influence on the paper's final bulk and finish. High-bulk, antique-finish papers are given little wet pressing, whereas lower-bulk, high-finish papers need a greater degree of wet pressing.

The paper web contains 60–70% water by weight when it leaves the press section. More water is now removed by evaporation in the drying section, which consists of a number of hollow, steam-heated cylinders over which the web passes in a serpentine manner. The felt and wire sides of the web alternately come into direct contact with the hot drying cylinders to produce a balanced drying of the paper from its two sides. As it dries, the web is kept under tension to prevent cockling, distortion, and uncontrolled shrinkage. Paper is dried to the desired moisture level for its end use, which can range from 2 to 8%.

Fundamental physical and chemical changes occur from the time paper is formed until it is dried in its final form. Individual cellulose fibers are very strong in a wet or dry state. The paper web has very little strength at the wet end, but becomes strong as it arrives at the dry end of the paper machine. Wet paper is weak because its fibers are not bonded to each other. As water is removed from the web by pressing and drying, strong cohesive forces bind the fibers at their point of contact. While some strength comes from the

Optireel, which is used
in the reeling process
on paper machines.
*Courtesy Valmet Paper
Machinery, Inc.*

physical interlocking of fibers, far greater strength comes
from the molecular bonds and cohesion of the cellulose fibers.
Water will redissolve these bonds, accounting for the loss of
strength in wetted paper.

There are modifications of multiple-cylinder drying. One is
the **yankee** dryer, which is a single, large-diameter dryer
having a polished, smooth drying surface. As paper dries
against this polished surface, it acquires a high finish on one
side, which is called **machine-glazed.** Tissue and creped
papers are also dried on a single, large-diameter dryer and
are removed from it by a doctor that produces creping and
softness.

High-grade bond and writing papers are **air-dried.** Air
drying is done with little or no stress placed on the drying
web. Paper is taken from the paper machine in a damp state
and passed through high-temperature air in a festoon manner. Since it is allowed to shrink without restraint in all
directions, it acquires the familiar air-dried or **cockle** finish.

Most printing and writing papers, as well as other types of
paper, are **surface-sized** at the size press, which is usually
located before the last drying section. The size press consists
of two rubber-covered rolls that apply sizing solution to the
partially dried web as it enters their nip. Some of the sizing is
forced to penetrate below the paper's surface. The sizing press
is used to apply starch, the material most often used for surface sizing, along with other additives, including pigments for
coating. Sizing solution is dried in the last drying section.

The final step that controls the characteristics of paper before it leaves the paper machine is **calendering.** The machine calender has all-steel rolls in running contact. As the dried web is sent through the nips of these rolls, it acquires a smooth, denser surface, and its differences in thickness are evened out. The degree of calendering may be heavy, moderate, light, or none at all, depending on the finish desired. In some cases, the steel-to-steel nip of the all-steel-roll calender is replaced by an elastic or soft-nip of mating steel and soft, covered, resilient rolls. This recent advancement in soft-nip calendering at the paper machine or off-machine coater improves the printability of paper.

After drying and, if applicable, sizing and calendering, paper is usually reeled into a full-width machine roll, then taken to rewinders for winding into the desired roll diameters and widths. Off-quality paper is generally removed at the rewinder.

The quality of paper produced by the conventional, single-wire fourdrinier is limited because the forming paper web is disturbed by air at its top side and water drainage entirely through its bottom or wire side. It has long been known that the one-sided drainage on the fourdrinier wire produces a "two-sided" paper. To overcome this problem, papermakers have evolved various configurations of **twin-wire forming** or "two-sided drainage" paper machines.

Twin-wire former (Bel Baie).

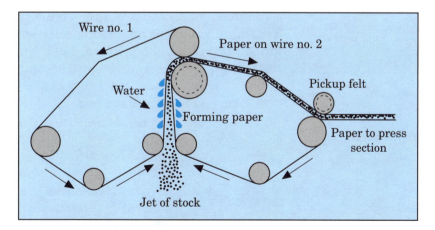

Twin-wire formers use two converging paper machine wires between which the sheet is formed and through which water is drained from both sides of the sheet during its forming. They operate at much higher speeds than the single-wire fourdrinier and make paper with two wire sides. In another

Beloit Bel Baie IV
twin-wire former.
*Courtesy Beloit
Corporation.*

configuration, known as a **top-wire** former, the paper is first
formed on a conventional fourdrinier wire. After being
formed through a short, forward movement, the top side of
the formed web is contacted by a second or top wire. A combination of wire tension, centrifugal force as the wires pass
over a curved forming shoe or roll, and vacuum suction boxes

Top-wire forming.

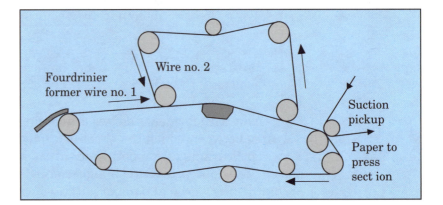

cause upward drainage from the top side of the paper web as it is sandwiched between the converged wires. Many other modifications of these basic twin-wire-forming/two-sided-drainage configurations have continued to evolve since their revolutionary inception in the 1960s.

Another type of paper machine, the **cylinder machine,** forms paper on a wire-covered cylinder rotating in a vat of water and suspended fibers. Water drains by gravity from the outside of the cylinder to its inside. Drainage deposits fibers on the outer surface of the wire. When the deposited fiber mat reaches the highest elevation of the rotating cylinder, it contacts a felt and transfers to it. The traveling felt, with the paper web clinging to its underside, receives one or more additional fiber mats produced similarly by successive forming cylinders.

An advantage of the cylinder-type paper machine is its ability to make thick, heavyweight papers whose composition can differ among their various individually formed plies. For example, cylinder machines are used to produce white-lined boards with a less costly dark fiber middle construction consisting of recycled wastepaper. Large quantities of wastepapers are recycled into paperboard via cylinder machines. Very little printing paper, however, is made on cylinder machines. Cylinder machines are limited by their slow speed and highly directional grain, and they are being replaced by twin-wire forming machines for the higher productivity of multi-ply paperboard.

Process Control

Process control, used to continually monitor and control the many time-varying disturbances that can affect paper quality, has become increasingly important for several reasons. As paper machines run faster and become larger, a continuous on-line measurement of critical paper properties becomes necessary to keep them within specification limits. Samples have long been, and still are, taken from each turned-up machine reel and tested off-line to determine if paper conforms to specifications. By itself, however, this procedure is inadequate for controlling the output of many high-production paper machines and meeting the performance requirements of today's printing equipment. During the time lapse between sampling and testing, tons of paper might be made out of specification. To avoid this possibility, papermakers needed to devise a method for instantaneously testing for adjustment of process variables and control of paper uniformity.

Maintaining a uniform profile of basis weight at the slice. Basis weight profile is thereby automatically and continually maintained within prescribed limits by closed-loop control.

In addition, the shift to more rollfed paper has placed greater responsibility on the papermaker for ensuring that paper constantly conforms to specifications as it is being made. The close human inspection and removal of off-quality paper that is done during paper sheeting is not possible when making rolls.

Process control is further necessary to reduce costly change-off time during grade changes on high-production machines. Measuring the paper properties of a wide, high-speed, traveling paper web without contacting it or disturbing its surface or travel is a technological accomplishment. Sensing devices continuously scan the moving web and may traverse back and forth across its width. For quality control purposes, their output is read out as a graphic profile of properties or is fed to the computer for closed-loop on-line control of properties as the paper is being made. These sensing devices operate on such physical principles as the following: the passage of **beta rays**—streams of negatively charged particles—through a web to measure basis weight; the influence of a traveling paper web through a magnetic field to indicate thickness; infrared reflection from the web to determine moisture content; X-ray absorption by paper to analyze its ash; and light transmission through the web to monitor opacity. Among the paper properties controlled on-line are gloss, brightness, color or shade, and coating weight.

Mill-wide, on-line process control is a dynamic, fast evolving technology and a noteworthy achievement for making papers that must meet increasingly higher standards for printability and consistent performance on printing and converting equipment.

Fully automatic off-line paper testing laboratories are replacing conventional manually operated paper testing equipment. Their advantages include faster testing for many paper properties and quicker transformation of test data into useful quality control formats such as graphs and numeric reports that are printed out or displayed on a colored screen.

Quality Assurance

Paper, made from naturally produced raw materials, is not as uniformly structured as materials like glass, plastic, or metal. Its properties can vary from one area to another during a given run. Paper has grain direction and is two-sided. Its inherent variability must be taken into consideration in a testing and sampling program. This requires use of a prescribed sampling plan and frequent testing. Paper quality is assessed for its conformance to a predetermined standard or to a specification dictated by the end-use requirement. Clearly understood decision limits for acceptance or rejection must be established.

Tests of routine production are often plotted on charts that vividly indicate conformance or nonconformance to specifications. These daily quality control records are kept for future use. Many of these tests are made with specialized instruments, while others are of a subjective nature and include rating paper formation and checking for visual defects like dirt, torn sheets, and dimensional accuracy. Printing papers may also be inspected by actual printing press evaluation.

Statistical theory and analysis are used to determine the degree of long- or short-term conformance to specifications and to detect and correct undesirable deviations or trends in paper properties. Analysis of complaint history and feedback from the customer regarding a paper's performance can be used to great advantage by the quality control department.

Quality control, like paper machines, functions around the clock, advising the manufacturing department when it is not making paper that is up to standard. Quality control may also be responsible for auditing the quality of all incoming raw materials, the quality of the pulp being manufactured, and all operations that follow papermaking, which are finishing, coating, and converting. The responsibility of quality control may extend all the way from the wood to the finished paper product leaving the mill. The quality control department is recognized as an essential element for producing paper that consistently meets the increasingly higher performance standards demanded for its printing and converting.

Standard Methods for Testing Paper

Most paper testing is done with specialized instruments and under prescribed conditions. In the United States and in many other English-speaking countries, the technical standards and methods for testing paper are determined and published by the Technical Association of the Pulp and Paper Industry **(TAPPI).** Other countries have similar organizations that provide standards for paper testing. International standards (SI) are established by the International Standards Organization (ISO). Where corresponding test methods exist, TAPPI and ISO methods are usually similar.

A testing procedure must meet prescribed guidelines to become a **TAPPI Official Test Method.** It must provide test results that are accurate and sensitive to small differences in individual paper properties and reproducible results among various paper laboratories over a long term. Once adopted, a TAPPI test is recognized as the authoritative method. Without Official Test Methods, the results of testing among numerous paper laboratories would not be comparable. The issuance, revision, and withdrawal of test methods is an ongoing process through the efforts of TAPPI and its many professional members.

TAPPI publishes hundreds of testing methods, including methods for testing numerous individual paper properties, the calibration and standardization of testing instruments, and procedures for obtaining samples that are representative of the lot to be tested. The Official Test Method for each individual paper property is indicated as **TAPPI T,** followed by its identifying number.

Test methods that do not have the Official Test Method designation but have practical application are published as **TAPPI Useful Test Methods.** Where applicable for testing individual properties, they are indicated as **TAPPI UM,** followed by their identifying numbers.

Since the physical and mechanical properties of paper are very sensitive to its moisture content and to its surrounding relative humidity, testing must be done under a closely controlled environment. The standard testing atmosphere prescribed by TAPPI is 23.0±1.0°C (73.4±1.8°F) and 50±2%

relative humidity. Before testing, paper samples are conditioned to this atmosphere for a recommended minimum number of hours to bring the samples into equilibrium with the atmosphere.

When testing for properties like folding endurance, tear resistance, tensile strength, and stiffness, papermakers must consider the directionality characteristics of paper due to its grain. These values are individually reported for the machine and cross-machine directions. Felt- and wire-side tests are reported separately for such properties as smoothness and pick resistance.

Roll Building Technology

Sophisticated process control is required to meet the needs for wider and larger-diameter rolls, along with higher levels of printability on lighter-basis-weight coated and uncoated papers at ever increasing press speeds. Process control begins at the paper machine forming section and ends at the winder. To build rolls that will have the required level of printability and runnability, paper must first be made within narrowly controlled tolerances for cross-machine (CD) profile of basis weight. Ingenious ways are used to control the slice opening at various cross-machine locations to form a paper web that conforms to acceptable profile limits of basis weight variation. Sensors that scan in the cross-machine direction feed back information to control moisture profiles. Cross-machine caliper control, crucial to building good rolls, is maintained

The Vari-Top, a single-drum, individual station winder designed to produce jumbo rolls of high-density papers like lightweight coated and supercalendered printing paper.
Courtesy Jagenberg.

by sensors that scan the web prior to calendering and issue commands to increase or decrease nip loading at selected cross-direction segments of the machine calender to reduce and level out variations in web caliper profile.

As roll diameter and width are increased, abrupt CD variations in caliper and moisture become increasingly detrimental to winding an evenly structured roll. With a nonuniform caliper profile, high-caliper areas will wind into hard areas and produce more winding tension in these areas in relation to adjacent softer areas. Differential tension between hard- and soft-wound areas will produce ropes, corrugations, and paper that unwinds with uneven draws. The printer wants rolls that unwind with even tension across the roll throughout the roll. Winding tensions that are too great may lead to paper being stretched beyond its ability to return to its original dimensions. Too soft a winding near the core with tight outer winding can cause telescoping and starring when the roll is subjected to shock. Ideally, a roll should be wound to a uniform tension that is no greater than that necessary to maintain its integrity throughout shipment and handling.

High-speed roll winding has become an increasingly complex operation with the use of larger-diameter and wider rolls and the growing demand for lighter-weight, high-density coated papers. Control of the numerous variables of paper rolls and their complex interplay during winding is no longer adequate by mechanical arrangement alone. Advancements in roll winding technology include electric drives and electronic controls and, more recently, computerization, which constantly governs and optimizes the winding process for specific grades and types of paper. A further advancement is winding equipment specifically designed for certain grades of paper.

Finishing Operations

Finishing begins at the paper machine reel and ends when the paper is packaged for shipment from the mill. It represents the final preparation of paper and may involve further converting operations such as rewinding, sheeting, trimming, altering the finish by embossing or supercalendering, sorting, inspection, and packaging.

At the paper machine winder, rolls may be slit to widths required by customers and packaged for shipment, or they may be sent to the finishing department for further processing. **Rewinders** are used for further processes such as rewinding, slitting to smaller widths and specific diameters, winding on cores of specific construction, and operations not feasible on the paper machine winder. For good runnability on web presses, careful rewinding is of utmost importance. **Salvage rewinders** are used to rewind rolls; to remove defective paper, splicing, and other defects; and to salvage quality paper. Rolls are packaged by efficient automatic handling, transporting, and wrapping equipment—often without human assistance.

Rolls are converted to sheets on the **sheeter,** which consists of a single- or multiple-roll backstand, a rotary cutting unit, and a layboy, where sheets are piled and jogged. There are two types of rotary cutters. The **single rotary cutter** has a fixed-position bedknife with a second knife mounted in a rotating cylinder. As the rotary knife contacts the bedknife, it cuts the paper web with a shearing action. The **double rotary cutter** has two knives, each mounted on cylinders that rotate in synchronization with the web only at the time of cutting. As the two rotating knives contact, they are made to move at the web speed, and their shearing action cuts the web. The cutoff dimension, or sheet length, is determined by the speed of the rotary knife relative to web speed. Sheet width is determined by the spacing between the web slitters. Cut sheets are transported to the layboy by traveling belts.

Paper is trimmed on the **guillotine trimmer.** The trend is to eliminate guillotine trimming by **precision sheeting.** Precision sheeters cut accurately controlled sheet dimensions so that trimming becomes unnecessary. While the edges of

Sheeter and sorter (Synchro-Fly). The peripheral speed of two rotating knife drums is synchronized to the web speed. Sheets are automatically sorted for defects. *Courtesy Jagenberg.*

precision-sheeted paper do not have the "block of ice" appearance of guillotine-trimmed paper, precision-cut paper has more uniform sheet dimensions throughout a load than guillotine-trimmed paper. Precision sheeting to the final sheet size has expanded into the larger sheet sizes.

Sheet sorting and inspection for defects like dirt, wrinkles, sheet distortion, torn and folded sheets, and holes may follow cutting and trimming, or may be done automatically as the paper is being cut. Automated systems based on optical, mechanical, and electronic principles have been devised to replace human inspection during or after sheet cutting. Packaging on skids or in cartons is the final operation for sheet paper.

Supercalendering is a distinct finishing operation. Unlike the paper machine calender, whose rolls are all made of metal, the supercalender has alternating metal and soft, resilient ("filled") rolls. The resilient rolls consist of highly compressed fabrics or paper ground to a smooth surface. Under pressure, the hard metal rolls press into the resilient rolls at the nip and cause them to push out on each side of the nip. As the rolls rotate in contact, the material of the resilient rolls flows, or creeps, in attempting to return to its normal, full diameter. Much like a flatiron on an ironing board, this relative motion of the soft roll on the metal roll surface produces a polishing action on the paper as it passes through the nip. The degree of polishing, smoothness, and gloss imparted to paper depends on its resiliency, its forma-

A supercalender. Paper enters at the top, passes between the nips of steel and soft (filled) rolls, and emerges with an enamel finish at the bottom.

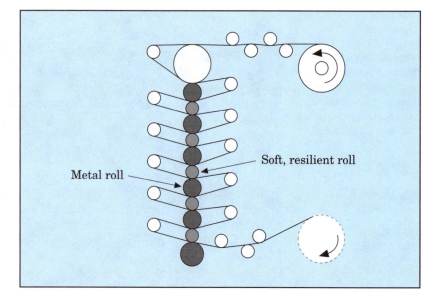

Soft, resilient roll

Metal roll

tion and papermaking furnish, its moisture, and, for coated paper, its coating composition.

Papers are given a pattern finish by **embossing.** An embosser is similar to a supercalender. It has a metal roll engraved with the desired pattern that rotates above a soft cotton-filled backing roll. The backing roll has been patterned by running in direct contact with the engraving roll. As paper passes through the nip of these two rolls, it receives the embossed pattern.

The Coating of Paper

Coatings are used to modify the surface of paper for particular requirements. The two principal types of coating are **pigments** and **adhesives,** or **binders.** Pigments are used to cover the fibers and to obtain a smoother surface. Adhesives bind the pigment particles to each other and to the paper substrate. They also control final coating properties such as ink absorptivity, water resistance, gloss, and pick resistance.

Pigment coatings are applied to paper for an improved printing surface. The coated paper surface has a much denser and more uniform structure than the fibrous network of uncoated papers. Because printing inks do not cover or wet fibers evenly but tend to concentrate in the numerous voids existing among the fibers, a pigment coating that fills the voids and covers the fibers produces a smoother surface, and one that is more uniformly wetted by printing inks. The degree of ink absorptivity and ink holdout of a coated surface for specific printing needs is controlled by coating formulation. Coated papers thereby enhance the brilliance of printing and quality of reproduction. Coating also increases the whiteness and opacity of paper and makes it possible to obtain high or low paper surface gloss with superior ink holdout.

The most commonly used pigment for coating is highly refined clay. **Coating clays** consist of tiny, naturally occurring platelet-shaped particles that shingle or slip over each other during coating and calendering to produce good coating coverage, gloss, and ink holdout. A delaminating treatment of clay causes its larger aggregates of platelets to separate into many more and thinner platelets. This results in coating with a better fiber coverage and an improved printing surface, particularly for lightweight coated papers. Calcium carbonate has a different particle shape and is used to increase brightness and ink absorptivity. It may also be used to produce lower gloss coating. Titanium dioxide imparts high brightness and opacity when used in a coating pigment.

Synthetic plastic pigments are sometimes used to achieve enhanced gloss and high ink holdout in higher-grade-level coated papers.

Coating binders may be either natural or synthetic. Binders derived from natural sources are starch, casein, and soya protein. Starch originating from corn, wheat, potatoes, or tapioca is by far the principal coating binder. Since it does not produce a water-resistant coating, it is modified or blended with other binders to provide water resistance. The principal synthetic binders are **styrene-butadiene** and **vinyl acrylic lattices.** Synthetic binders are widely used for high paper gloss, greater ink and varnish holdout, unexcelled coating flexibility without cracking during folding and binding, and improved coating wet-rub resistance.

Coating formulations may contain small amounts of different additives to control coating properties during application and end use. For example, dispersants are used to wet each pigment particle and make the coating flow properly, lubricants are added for gloss development during supercalendering, and waterproofing agents may be incorporated for water-resistant coatings.

Coating formulations, including their pigment and binder systems, must meet the combined requirements for proper application at the coater and for the level of printability needed by the printer.

To produce paper with the desired final properties, the coating must be compatible with its paper substrate, which is called **body stock, raw stock,** or **base stock.** Covering the base stock with coating does not necessarily eliminate its deficiencies. The base stock must have the best formation and uniformity of surface consistent with economics, along with the strength demanded for printing, binding, and other end uses. The **coat weight,** or amount of coating applied to the base stock, depends on the final basis weight and the grade level. As basis weight is lowered, coat weight is reduced to maintain a base stock of sufficient weight for meeting thickness, strength, opacity, and other requirements. The choice of coating pigments, binders, and base paper is dictated by economics and use requirements. Lower-cost coatings and groundwood base stocks are used for publication coated grades, whereas the more expensive coating materials and brighter all-chemical wood-based stocks are required for higher grade levels.

Various systems are used to apply coating to paper. The print-type roller system applies a premetered film of coating to the paper web in a manner similar to ink distribution from the fountain to the plate on a printing press. Because this system leaves a pattern in the applied coating, it is now little used. The paper machine size press is sometimes used for light coating applications or for precoating base stock.

These and other earlier coating methods have largely been replaced by **blade coaters.** Blade coating produces an unexcelled leveling of the coating and a flat, dense, smooth-coated surface without undesirable patterns. Because of its ability to produce superior printing surfaces and to coat lighter-basis-weight papers at much higher speeds than previously used methods, blade coating is the most widely used method.

Blade coaters differ in design, but they operate on two basic principles: (1) applying an excess coating to a paper web and (2) metering the coating to a final film thickness by a doctoring or trailing device. In one basic blade coating

Blade coating with a trailing-blade coater. An applicator roll applies a surplus of coating to the paper web. A flexible steel blade evens off ("doctors") the excess coating, producing a very level coated surface.

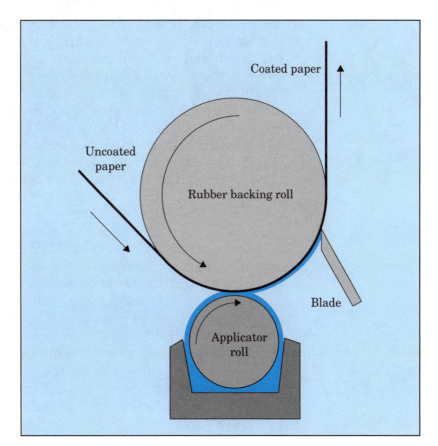

A flooded-nip coater (two coating stations). *Courtesy Potlatch Corporation.*

design, coating is applied to the web by an applicator roll that carries coating from a coating pan to a flooded open nip or gap between itself and the paper web. Coating is transferred to the paper at the flooded nip. A flexible steel blade that bears against the web then doctors off excess coating, meters a fixed amount on the paper, and produces a very level coated surface. The **short-dwell** type of coater is preferred for the high-speed production of lightweight coated papers. The elapsed time and distance of web travel between coating application and its metering is substantially reduced for improved printability of coated surfaces. Coating under pressure is forced through a slice or orifice directly onto the nearby web, followed almost immediately by a metering blade or bar that levels out the applied coating film. As coating is drawn under the blade or metering device, it fills in the "valleys" and is metered to the peaks of the "hills." Blade coating without supercalendering is used to produce matte coated papers for offset printing, while blade coating combined with supercalendering is employed in making very smooth, dense enamel papers for offset and gravure printing.

The **air knife coater,** like the blade coater, applies an excess coating, then removes the surplus by impinging a knifelike air jet upon the wet fluid coating. This leaves a metered, smooth coating film on the base paper.

An air knife coater. Surplus coating applied to the web is removed by an air knife jet, leaving a metered, smooth coating.

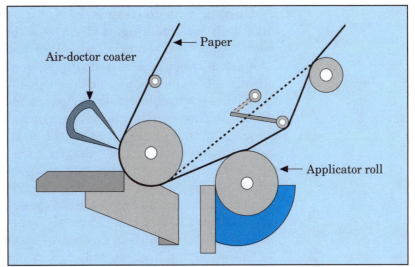

Cast coating is a distinctly different coating method. A wet coating is applied to the paper web before it contacts a casting drum, which is a heated drum having a highly polished drying surface. The moist coating is pressed firmly against the drum surface for finishing and drying. During drying, the coating is cast into a direct image of the highly polished drum. After drying, the coating is released from the drum surface, resulting in an extremely smooth, mirrorlike glossy paper, having high bulk and ink absorptivity. Supercalendering is not required.

Cast coater. A wet coating is applied to the paper web before it contacts a casting drum, which is a heated drum having a highly polished drying surface.

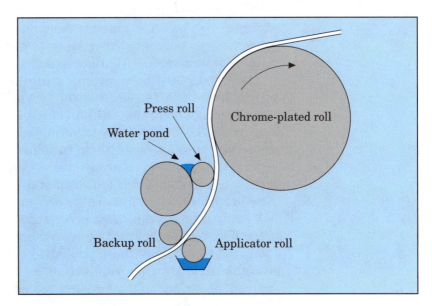

On-machine coating is done at the paper machine, in line with papermaking. It eliminates the operation of reeling, storing, and transporting base stock to the coater. This type of coating is not practical for all paper grades and has the disadvantage of shutting down production when operating problems occur with either the paper machine or the coater. **Off-machine coating** is an operation separate from and subsequent to that of the paper machine. It requires the reeling, storage, and transport of base stock and has the following advantages: a much higher operating speed than the paper machine; the capacity of coating the output of more than one paper machine; and the potential for operating a paper machine and coater independently, without the downtime on either machine shutting down production on the other.

Premium and higher-grade coated papers have high brightness and gloss with the greatest uniformity of ink absorption. They may be double-coated per side for a superior printing surface. Low-gloss or dull-finish enamels are made with lower glossing coating formulations or with modifications of the supercalender for suppression of gloss development. Coated papers are embossed for a textured surface having high, uniform ink holdout.

Alkaline Papers   Alkaline papers are papers that have a pH of at least 7.0, while acid papers are those with a pH below 7. Paper pH is determined by the acidity or alkalinity of the internal sizing used. **Internal sizing,** achieved by adding a material to the paper furnish before it reaches the paper machine, gives paper varying degrees of resistance to penetration by liquids (usually water-based). Alkaline papers are internal-sized by an alkaline-compatible synthetic material, most often alkyl ketene dimer or alkyl succinic anhydride. Acid papers receive internal sizing from the addition of rosin and aluminum sulfate, or alum. While rosin and alum make papers less water-receptive, they also cause them to yellow and become weak and brittle—sometimes after a very short time. Alkaline papers, which do not contain rosin and alum, can maintain their brightness and strength for centuries.

A study conducted in 1955 predicted that books published in the first half of this century would not last until the year 2000, and that 75% of those published before 1940 would be unusable 25 years after publication. As a result of such predictions, librarians and others interested in archival materials have become interested in alkaline papers. Many alkaline papers are both permanent and durable, which means that they can withstand both time and a certain amount of handling without being compromised. Alkaline papers are making inroads on the acid paper market, and some speculate that acid papers will eventually become unavailable.

Both alkaline and acid papers contain mineral pigment fillers that give paper optical characteristics (such as brightness and opacity) and surface characteristics (such as smoothness and ink receptivity). Three fillers are clay, titanium dioxide (TiO_2), and calcium carbonate ($CaCO_3$). Clay is the most abundant and least expensive of the three; however, it is also the least bright and has the lowest refractive index (light scattering capability). Titanium dioxide has the highest brightness and the highest refractive index, but is much more expensive than the other two. Calcium carbonate has high brightness and a refractive index that is greater than clay's, but lower than titanium dioxide's. It is as inexpensive as clay, but cannot be used in acid papers because it dissolves and causes foaming in acid papermaking conditions. Calcium carbonate is compatible with the alkaline papermaking process, although alkaline papers containing calcium carbonate were originally very abrasive because of the filler's grittiness.

Abrasiveness is still a concern with calcium carbonate, particularly at high filler levels. The size of the particle and its shape and source determine its abrasiveness. As the filler particle's size decreases, it becomes less abrasive and has a greater index of refraction, which means that the resultant paper will have greater opacity. This paper, however, will also be less strong. Currently, alkaline papers are partially filled with a precipitated calcium carbonate that is relatively soft.

While alkaline papers have many advantages over acid papers, the presence of calcium carbonate has the potential to cause printing problems in the offset lithographic process. Acidic dampening solutions are used in lithography to keep the nonimage areas of the plate water-receptive. If the dampening solution reacts with the calcium carbonate in the paper, it can neutralize the acid in the dampening solution and reduce its effectiveness. The dissolved calcium can also react with the materials in the dampening solution, the plate, and/or the inks. In some cases, this type of reaction has resulted in the blinding of certain aqueous plates. When used with calcium-carbonate–filled sheets, some paper plates have been subject to toning. An accumulation of filler material in the image areas of the blanket can cause piling, which deteriorates image quality and causes plate wear. Buildup in the nonimage areas of the blanket can weaken the water-receptive layer and cause toning and scumming.

Printers have a few options available to counteract problems caused by alkaline papers. These options range from treating the rollers to using the least amount of fountain etch recommended. Printers can avoid problems altogether by testing their stock with a litmus pen before running it, and monitoring the solution with a pH strip or an electronic pH meter during the pressrun.

Recycled Papers   Recyclable wastepapers are classified into five major groups according to their reuse as fibrous sources by the paper industry. About half of all U.S. recycled wastepaper consists of discarded fiber and corrugated containers, which are recycled into linerboard, corrugated containers, and other paperboards. Mixed papers unsuitable for recycling into white papers are used to manufacture paperboard and construction paper and board. Old newspapers and over-issue news represent a significant percentage of the total wastepaper recycled. While in past years this source was recycled mainly into paperboard, since 1970 it has been used increasingly to manufacture deinked newsprint, and its use continues to grow in various U.S. regions. Pulp substitutes—as generated by printing and paper converting plants and consisting primarily of non-printed, white uncoated paper—are recycled into fine printing and writing papers, as well as into sanitary and tissue paper products. Tabulating cards, coated papers, and printed white papers are another source of recyclable paper for high-grade deinking.

Approximately 80% of the paper recycled in the United States is used to manufacture paperboard. Much of this comes from sources like old corrugated containers, mixed wastepaper, and old newspapers, catalogs, and directories. Wastepaper recycled into paperboard is generally not deinked.

The recycling symbol. The three arrows of the recycling symbol represent the three phases of any recycling program—collection, processing, and the manufacture of recovered materials into new products. There are two versions of the symbol: one in which the arrows appear in outline form and another in which the arrows appear in a solid black circle.

Recycling symbols.

The outline symbol indicates that the product is recyclable. The symbol in the solid black circle indicates that the product has been recycled. Since both symbols are only recommendations created by the American Forest and Paper Association, manufacturers should include a sentence or two telling the consumer about the product's origin and the fact that it was recycled and/or can be recycled. Some states mandate that paper must contain a certain percentage of recycled fiber before the recycling symbols can be used.

History of recycling. Recycling in the paper industry began in the United States in the 17th century. Initially, cotton and linen rags were recycled into paper. Deinking of recovered paper for recycling began commercially in the mid 1800s and grew tremendously during the early 1900s.

Paper recycling grew rapidly during the Second World War as part of an effort to conserve natural resources, but declined afterward. In the early 1970s, the recycling of recovered paper began to grow again in response to concern over tree harvesting techniques such as clear cutting and the reported decline in the number of forests. Most recently, as the threat of filling the nation's landfills to capacity has become a reality, paper recycling is again receiving attention. Paper and paper products account for nearly 40% of all landfilled materials.

Currently, the use of recovered paper fiber by domestic manufacturers is growing more than twice as fast as the use of virgin wood fiber. This recycling boom is driven mainly by government edict, not economics. The United States Environmental Protection Agency (USEPA) states that printing and writing paper purchased by the federal government is required to contain 50% total recycled fiber. Of this 50%, the EPA has not yet specified a particular percentage to be post-consumer fiber. In October 1993, however, an Executive Order was passed stipulating that, beginning in 1995, paper purchased by the federal government must contain at least 20% post-consumer fiber in order to be labeled recycled. This requirement will increase to 30% by 1999.

Recovered paper. Recovered paper can be classified as either postconsumer—loosely defined as paper that is disposed of at the end of the product's lifespan, such as old magazines and newspapers; old corrugated containers, boxes, and cartons; food packaging; and office waste—or preconsumer, which includes paper and paperboard waste generated after completion of the papermaking process, such as envelope cuttings, binding trimmings, butt rolls, and obsolete stock.

Bales of old newspapers, magazines, and catalogs being transferred to a pulping tank.
Courtesy International Paper.

Currently, tissue, board, and newsprint are the largest applications for recovered fiber or recycled paper. Printing and writing paper, which accounts for more than half of all paper produced in the United States, uses less recycled fiber because "recycling up" ("up cycling"), or producing a higher quality product from lower-quality materials, is generally cost-prohibitive. Extensive recycling procedures must be performed on recovered paper (especially postconsumer grades) to produce the aesthetic and physical properties that printing and writing papers demand. The comparatively lower cost to utilize recovered fiber in tissue, cardboard, and newsprint is the reason why they contain significantly higher percentages of recycled fiber than do printing and writing papers. Historically, recycling coated "offset" paper was not economically feasible because coated paper nets less reusable fiber than uncoated. However, uncoated fine grade paper and coated fine grade paper can be mixed and recycled into fine grade papers. In fact, with the advent of flotation, a deinking process described in later paragraphs, at least 15% of the furnish must be coated stock because the clay provides the surface area that enables the process to work.

The process of recycling. Prior to the actual mechanical and chemical process of recycling, recovered paper must be separated from other waste, and then sorted into various waste grades. There are more than 70 grades of recovered paper. Depending on the intended end use, some waste grades can be grouped together.

Recycling itself consists primarily of repulping, deinking, contaminant removal, and often bleaching. The "deinking pulp mill" process starts with repulping, which is an operation similar to a kitchen blending process. Alkali, detergent, and dispersing agents are normally used to repulp recovered paper. The form and particular combination are determined by the type of furnish that will be deinked and the quality of deinked pulp desired.

Alkali, generally in the form of sodium hydroxide, reacts with oil-based ink vehicles to release the pigment. In this reaction, *saponification*—the forming of soap and alcohol—occurs. Saponification is important because in some cases the soap that it produces provides the wetting that a pigment needs in order to be more easily dispersed without the addition of detergent.

Some inks, however, such as metallic inks, cannot be removed by alkali alone and require the addition of a detergent. As mentioned above, the pigment must be wet so that it can be more easily dispersed once it has been released from the fiber. Pigment can be made hydrophilic, or water loving, by **detergent.** Detergents must be added to unsized papers or papers that do not have oil-based vehicles that saponify with the addition of alkali.

Dispersing agents are used in repulping to prevent re-agglomeration, which is reclustering and redeposition of the dispersed pigment onto the fibers. Polyphosphates of sodium and hydrophilic polymers are suitable dispersing agents.

Deinking. The recycling of wastepaper to make fine white printing and writing paper requires **deinking,** the removal of ink and other unwanted materials, or contaminants. Higher grades of wastepapers with fewer contaminants are required for deinking. Examples are tabulating and card stocks and waste such as milk cartons, envelope cuttings, and printing wastes generated directly by converting operations.

In general, deinking involves cooking and coarse screening, after which the pulped wastepaper is usually completely defibered. Cleaning, including centrifugal cleaning to remove unwanted material, and fine screening follow. Washing and bleaching are the final steps. The individual steps of deinking vary, depending on the type of wastepapers used and the intended end products.

The popular techniques for ink removal are **washing** and **flotation.** Screens are used to remove large ink particles and synthetic contaminants via particle size separation, and centrifugal cleaners remove inks and other contaminants via density separation principles. Washing removes small ink particles and fillers, and flotation removes particles that tend to float. Both washing and flotation are chemi-mechanical processes.

In wash deinking, dispersants such as silicate anions, along with physical shear and impact, remove the inks from the paper fibers and disperse the inks into tiny particles that can be rinsed away. Once the inks are separated from the fibers, they are chemically altered with nonionic surfactants to hold them in the water phase of the slurry. When the fibers are strained from the water, the inks stay with the water and the fiber is "washed" clean. Wash deinking also removes fines and ash, the absence of which causes the pulp to be brighter and stronger. Wash deinking is very effective for certain types of inks and is used to remove water-based inks from wastepaper. This process is expensive, however, because it requires a lot of water that must be handled and treated. Some deinked pulp manufacturers have reported that they do not recover as much paper from wash deinking as they do from flotation deinking because some of the filler is washed away with the ink and other contaminants in the rewashing process.

In flotation deinking, the inks are first treated with collector chemicals to make them hydrophobic. Calcium soaps of fatty acids are commonly used as collector chemicals. Once the inks are free-floating, they are collected on air bubbles injected into the pulp slurry and floated to the flotation cell surface where the inky foam is removed and separated from the remaining fiber slurry. Some clay in the fiber slurry tends to improve flotation efficiency, although the exact mechanism is not completely understood.

Flotation deinking normally uses less water than wash deinking. To adequately deink many postconsumer wastepaper furnishes and produce deinked pulp suitable for printing and writing papers, pulpmakers use a combination of the two systems. Because the action of the chemicals used in wash deinking and flotation deinking can run counter to each other, the combination requires proper chemicals and water separation.

Deinking xerographic- and laser-printed papers. Xerographic- and laser-printed papers require different deinking treatments than papers printed by conventional processes. The size of xerographic ink (toner) particles cannot be reduced by chemicals. These inks will soften and agglomerate during conventional washing, but only because of the high temperature involved. Some treatments therefore employ pulping to help break xerographic inks into particles. Other treatments, successful but expensive, combine washing, flotation, and dispersion. Still other treatments are under development or are proprietary formulations.

As nonimpact printing grows, deinked pulp producers that supply printing and writing mills will have to develop ways to deink papers printed by these processes to prevent the papers from being recycled into less demanding products (tissue, liner, medium newsprint, etc.). If the cost to "up cycle" these nonimpact grades is prohibitive, consumers will have to subsidize the extra cost of "up cycling" by paying more for printing and writing paper.

Properties of recycled papers. For some, recycled papers bring to mind paper with a rough texture and an obviously speckled or mottled appearance. This "recycled look" is, in fact, manufactured and often even printed on clean white paper. It is not the way most recycled papers turn out unless, of course, mistakes are made in their production. Generally,

Rolls of recycled paper. *Courtesy International Paper.*

recycled papers of a certain grade specification cannot easily be distinguished from virgin fiber papers of the same grade specification. A properly made recycled paper will be as stable, strong, and smooth as a comparable paper made from virgin fiber and contain the appropriate moisture content and pH balance for ink drying.

The major differences between recycled, deinked pulp and virgin pulp are brightness and strength. Generally, deinked pulp is stronger than hardwood kraft pulp, but weaker than softwood kraft pulp. Bleached deinked pulp is lower in brightness than bleached hardwood or softwood kraft pulps. Blending recycled fiber with virgin fiber ensures that the paper achieves the necessary physical and optical characteristics.

Recycling paper, particularly paper printed by nonimpact processes, is still an evolving technology. To keep abreast of developments and to be privy to information about experimental processes, refer to paper technology and/or graphic arts journals and paper technology associations.

Appendix

Formulas

Symbols

BWe	Basic Weight	RWi	Roll Width
BL	Basic Length	RWe	Roll Weight (net)
BWi	Basic Width	LP	Length of Paper in Roll
ReWe	Ream Weight	CD	Outside Diameter of Core
SL	Sheet Length	RF	Roll Factor*
SWi	Sheet Width	BT	Book Thickness
PT	Paper Thickness	NP	Number of Pages in Book
RD	Roll Diameter		

Sheets

1. Ream weight for a given sheet size and basis weight:

$$ReWe = \frac{SWi \times SL \times BWe}{BL \times BWi}$$

2. Basis weight for a given ream size and its given ream weight:

$$BWe = \frac{ReWe \times BL \times BWi}{SL \times SWi}$$

---

*LP in feet; RD, CD, BL, BWi, RWi, BT, and "length unit" in inches; PT in points (1 pt. = 0.001 in.); RWe and BWe in pounds; RF depending on basic size as follows:

17×22 in.: 0.00420	25½×30½ in.: 0.00202
20×26 in.: 0.00302	24×36 in.: 0.00182
22½×28½ in.: 0.00245	25×38 in.: 0.00165
23×35 in.: 0.00195	

†LP in meters; RD, CD, BL, BWi, and RWi in centimeters; BT and "length unit" in millimeters; PT in micrometers; RWe in kilograms; BWe in grams per square meter.

3. Equivalent weight in another basic size (denoted by the subscript 2) for a known basic size and weight (denoted by the subscript 1):

$$BWe_2 = \frac{BWe_1 \times BL_2 \times BWi_2}{BL_1 \times BWi_1}$$

Rolls

4. Length of paper in roll of known diameter and paper thickness:

$$LP* = \frac{65.45(RD^2 - CD^2)}{PT}$$

$$LP\dagger = \frac{78.54(RD^2 - CD^2)}{PT}$$

5. Length of paper in a roll of known width and net weight (not including wrapping and core):

$$LP* = \frac{41.67 \times RWe \times BL \times BWi}{RWi \times BWe}$$

$$LP\dagger = \frac{100,000 \times RWe}{RWi \times BWe}$$

6. Net roll weight for specified roll dimensions, paper thickness, and actual basis weight:

$$RWe* = \frac{RF \times (RD^2 - CD^2) \times RWi \times BWe}{PT}$$

$$RWe\dagger = \frac{0.0007854(RD^2 - CD^2) \times RWi \times BWe}{PT}$$

7. Fractional weight loss of a roll as its diameter is reduced from RD_1 to RD_2:

$$\frac{RWe_1 - RWe_2}{RWe_1} = \frac{RD_1{}^2 - RD_2{}^2}{RD_1{}^2 - CD^2}$$

---

*†See footnotes on first page of appendix.

8. Fractional weight remaining on a roll whose diameter has been reduced from RD_1 to RD_2:

$$RWe_2 = \frac{RD_2{}^2 - CD^2}{RD_1{}^2 - CD^2}$$

Books

9. Thickness of a book with a given number of pages and a measured thickness of four sheets of paper:

$$BT^{*\dagger} = \frac{NP \times 4(PT)}{8{,}000}$$

10. Number of pages per inch or centimeter for a measured thickness of four sheets of paper:

$$NP/\text{length unit}^{*\dagger} = \frac{8{,}000}{4(PT)}$$

Tables

Table 1: Weight (lb.) per 1,000 Sheets of Standard Sizes and Weights of Book Papers

Basis Weight (lb.)										
(25×38-in. ream)	30	35	40	45	50	60	70	80	100	120
g/m²	44	52	59	67	74	89	104	118	148	178
Size (in.)										
17½×22½	25	29	33	37	41	50	58	66	83	99
19×25	30	35	40	45	50	60	70	80	100	120
23×29	42	49	56	63	70	84	98	112	140	169
23×35	51	59	68	76	84	102	118	136	169	203
24×36	54	64	72	82	90	110	128	146	182	218
25×38	60	70	80	90	100	120	140	160	200	240
28×44	78	90	104	116	130	156	182	208	260	312
32×44	88	104	118	134	148	178	208	238	296	356
35×45	100	116	132	150	166	198	232	266	332	398
38×50	120	140	160	180	200	240	280	320	400	480
42×58	154	179	205	230	256	308	358	410	512	614

*†See footnotes on first page of appendix.

Table 2: Weight (lb.) per 1,000 Sheets of Standard Sizes and Weights of Bond and Related Grades (Duplicator, Mimeo, Onionskin, and Manifold)

Basis Weight (lb.) (17×22-in. ream)	8	9	13	16	20	24
g/m^2	30	34	49	60	75	90
Size (in.)						
8½×11	4	4.5	6.5	8	10	12
8½×13	4.7	5.3	7.7	9.5	11.8	14.2
8½×14	5.1	5.7	8.3	10.3	12.8	15.3
11×17	8	9	13	16	20	24
17×22	16	18	26	32	40	48
17×28	20.5	22.8	33	41	51	61
19×24	19.5	22	32	39	49	59
22×34	32	36	52	64	80	96
24×38	39	44	64	78	98	118
28×34	41	46	66	82	102	122
34×44	64	72	104	128	160	192

Table 3: Weight (lb.) per 1,000 Sheets of Standard Sizes and Weights of Ledger Paper

Basis Weight (lb.) (17×22-in. ream)	24	28	32	36
g/m^2	90	105	120	135
Size (in.)				
17×22	48	56	64	72
17×28	57	71	81	92
19×24	59	68	78	88
22×34	96	112	128	144
24×38	118	136	156	176
28×34	122	142	162	204

Table 4: Weight (lb.) per 1,000 Sheets of Standard Sizes and Weights of Cover Paper

Basis Weight (lb.) (20×26-in. ream)	50	60	65	80	100	130
g/m^2	135	162	175	216	270	351
Size (in.)						
20×26	100	120	130	160	200	260
23×35	155	186	201	248	310	402
26×40	200	240	260	320	400	520
35×46	310	392	402	496	620	804

Table 5: Weight (lb.) per 1,000 Sheets of Standard Sizes and Weights of Printing Bristols

Basis Weight (lb.) (22½×28½-in. ream)	67	80	90	100	120	140	160	180	200	220
g/m^2	147	175	197	219	263	307	351	395	438	483

Size (in.)										
22½×28½	134	165	180	200	240	280	320	360	400	440
23×35	168	201		252						
26×40	217	260		325						

Table 6: Weight (lb.) per 1,000 Sheets of Standard Sizes and Weights of Index Bristols

Basis Weight (lb.) (25½×30½-in. ream)	90	110	140	170	220
g/m^2	163	199	253	307	398

Size (in.)					
20½×24¾	117	144	182	222	288
22½×28½	148	182	230	280	364
22½×35	182	222	284	344	444
25½×30½	180	220	280	340	440

Table 7: Weight (lb.) per 1,000 Sheets of Standard Sizes and Weights of Tag

Basis Weight (lb.) (24×36-in. ream)	100	125	150	175	200
g/m^2	163	203	244	285	325

Size (in.)					
24×36	200	250	300	350	400
22½×28½	148	186	222	260	296
28½×45	296	372	444	520	592

Table 8:
Conversion Factors for Basis Weights and Grammage
(1 in. = 0.0254 m   1 lb. = 453.60 g   1 m = 39.37 in.   1 g = 0.002245 lb.)

Basic Ream Size (in.)	To convert from grammage to lb./ream multiply g/m² by:	To convert from lb. to g/m², multiply lb./ream by:
17×22	0.266	3.76
20×36	0.370	2.70
20×30	0.427	2.34
22×38	0.438	2.28
22½×28½	0.456	2.19
25½×30½	0.553	1.81
23×35	0.573	1.74
24×36	0.614	1.62
25×38	0.675	1.48
1,000 ft.² (paperboard)	0.205	4.88

Table 9: Weight Range of Various Papers in Grams per Square Meter

Type of Paper	g/m²
LW Uncoated Printing	25–60
Bond, Manifold, Copying	30–90
LW Coated	44–67
Newsprint	45–55
Printing Papers	59–178
Ledger	90–135
Cover	135–351
Tag	163–325
Index Bristol	163–398
Printing Bristol	147–483

Table 10: Equivalent Ream Weights for Different Types of Paper

Basic weights are in **bold** type.

Type of Paper	Book (25×38)	Bond (17×22)	Cover (20×26)	Bristol (22½×28½)	Index (25½×30½)	Tag (24×36)
Book	**30**	12	16	20	25	27
	40	16	22	27	33	36
	45	18	25	30	37	41
	50	20	27	34	41	45
	60	24	33	40	49	55
	70	28	38	47	57	64
	80	31	44	54	65	73
	90	35	49	60	74	82
	100	39	55	67	82	91
	120	47	66	80	98	109
Bond	33	**13**	18	22	27	30
	41	**16**	22	27	33	37
	51	**20**	28	34	42	46
	61	**24**	33	41	50	56
	71	**28**	39	48	58	64
	81	**32**	45	55	67	74
	91	**36**	50	62	75	83
	102	**40**	56	69	83	93
Cover	91	36	**50**	62	75	82
	110	43	**60**	74	90	100
	119	47	**65**	80	97	108
	146	58	**80**	99	120	134
	164	65	**90**	111	135	149
	183	72	**100**	124	150	166
Bristol	100	39	54	**67**	81	91
	120	47	65	**80**	98	109
	148	58	81	**100**	121	135
	176	70	97	**120**	146	162
	207	82	114	**140**	170	189
	237	93	130	**160**	194	216
Index	110	43	60	74	**90**	100
	135	53	74	91	**110**	122
	170	67	93	115	**140**	156
	208	82	114	140	**170**	189
Tag	110	43	60	74	90	**100**
	137	54	75	93	113	**125**
	165	65	90	111	135	**150**
	192	76	105	130	158	**175**
	220	87	120	148	180	**200**
	275	109	151	186	225	**250**

Table 11: U.S. Basis Weights Expressed as a Common Denominator in Grams per Square Meter

23×35	20×26	22½×28½	25½×30½	17×22	24×36	25×38	g/m²
				—	—	20	30
				9	—	—	34
				—	—	24	36
				11	—	—	41
				—	—	30	44
				13	30	33	49
				—	—	35	52
				15	—	—	56
				—	—	40	59
				16	—	—	60
				—	40	—	65
				—	—	45	67
				—	—	50	74
				20	—	—	75
				—	50	—	81
				—	—	60	89
				24	—	—	90
				—	60	—	98
				—	—	70	104
				28	—	—	105
	40			—	—	—	108
	—			—	70	—	114
	—			—	—	80	118
	—			32	—	—	120
	—			—	80	—	130
	—	—		—	—	90	133
	50	—		36	—	—	135
	—	67		—	90	—	146
	—	67		—	—	—	147
	—	—		—	—	100	148
—	—	—	—	40	—	—	150
—	60	—	—	—	—	—	162
—	—	—	90	—	100	—	163
100	—	80	—	—	—	—	175
—	65	—	—	—	—	—	176
—	—	—	—		—	120	178
—	70	—	—		—	—	189
—	—	90	—		—	—	197
—	—	—	110		—	—	199
—	—	—	—		125	—	203
—	80	—	—		—		216
125	—	—	—		—		218
—	—	100	—		—		219
—	—	—	—		150		244
—	—	—	140		—		253
150	—	—	—		—		262
—	—	120	—		—		263
—	100	—	—		—		270
—	—	—	—		175		285
175	—	—	—		—		306
—	—	140	170		—		307
—	—	—	—		200		325
200	—	—	—		—		349
—	—	160	—		—		351
—	130	—	—		—		352
		180	—		—		395
		—	220		—		398
		—	—		250		407
		200	—		—		438

"A" Paper Sizes

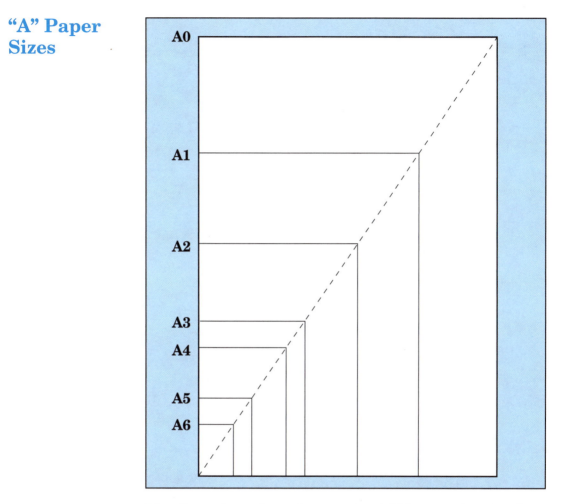

The above chart shows international "A" paper sizes. In this system, a full-stock trimmed-sheet size is designated "A0." It measures 841×1189 mm, or approximately 33⅛×46¾ in. Progressive divisions of the "A0" sheet are obtained by halving the sheet along its longest edge.

A#	Size (in.)	Size (mm)
A0	33.11×46.81	841×1189
A1	23.39×33.11	594×841
A2	16.54×23.39	420×594
A3	11.69×16.54	297×420
A4	8.27×11.69	210×297
A5	5.83×8.27	148×210
A6	4.13×5.83	105×148
A7	2.91×4.13	74×105
A8	2.05×2.91	52×74

Glossary

abrasion resistance The resistance of a paper or paperboard surface to being worn down, roughened, or disrupted by sliding frictional contact with other surfaces, as measured by the weight loss of a weighed test sample.

absolute humidity The total amount of water vapor in a unit volume of the atmosphere.

absorbency The ability of paper to take up contacting fluids.

accelerated aging A method of predicting the long-term aging characteristics of paper by exposing it to an elevated temperature and a controlled environment of dry or moist heat for a specified time, and then measuring its strength loss.

acid-free paper A paper having no acidity and no residual acid-producing chemicals. Acid-free papers may also be slightly alkaline to resist the harmful effects of an acidic environment and provide greater longevity.

actual basis weight The basis weight of paper as actually measured under its existing environmental condition. This weight may differ from a paper's nominal basis weight because of manufacturing variations and the influence of variable moisture content on the paper's weight. See *basis weight*.

adhesive binding Joining the pages of a book along one edge by the application of an adhesive (usually a hot-melt) to its roughened backbone. A cover may be applied directly on top of the tacky adhesive.

adhesive-coated paper

Paper coated on one side with an adhesive that is activated by moistening (for gummed papers) or by heat (for heat sealing) or that is permanently tacky (for pressure-sensitive applications).

air conditioning

The simultaneous control of the relative humidity, temperature, and purity of the air.

air-dried paper

A web taken from the paper machine and passed, freely supported, through an enclosed area with circulating hot air, so that the paper is free to dry without tension or restraint.

air knife coater

A device that applies an excess coating to paper and then removes the surplus by impinging a flat jet of air upon the fluid coating, leaving a smooth, metered film on the paper.

air shear burst

A type of burst in a roll caused by air entrapped during winding. See *burst*.

alkali resistance

Freedom of paper from a tendency to become stained or discolored or to undergo a color change when brought into contact with alkaline products like soap or adhesives.

alkaline sizing

Incorporation of synthetic internal sizing agents and alkaline fillers in papermaking furnish to produce papers that are slightly alkaline (whose pH is somewhat above 7).

American National Standards Institute (ANSI)

A nationally recognized coordinating body whose functions are to identify and fulfill needs for standards and to act as the interface, on matters of standards, between the government and the private sector and between the United States and international bodies.

American Paper Institute (API)

An organization that coordinates the many different needs of the broad-based paper and paperboard industry, including statistical information relating to the production, consumption, export, and import of paper and to raw materials, energy, governmental regulations, forecasts, environmental matters, and transportation.

apparent density

Weight per unit volume.

appearance properties

Paper properties, including its whiteness, brightness, color, gloss, and opacity.

archival paper   A paper that is made to be permanent and is used for long-lasting records.

artificial parchment   A paper, resembling genuine vegetable parchment, that is produced from a wildly formed fibrous structure.

ash content   The residue after complete combustion of paper at a high temperature, expressed as a percent weight of the original test sample, and representing the amount of filler in a paper.

back-edge curl   A curved shape that develops at the back edge of a press sheet during offset printing as a result of printing heavy solids close to the back edge.

back-trap mottle   Mottle that occurs while the paper is going through the press. It is distinguished from other mottle by its disappearance when the last one or two blankets are lifted off the print.

bagasse   Papermaking fiber derived from the fibrous residue remaining after sugarcane has been crushed and its juices have been extracted.

baggy paper   A web that unwinds with nonuniform draws and whose width does not uniformly support web tension.

bamboo   A woody plant of the grass family used for papermaking fiber in some countries.

basic size   The adopted sheet size used to define basis weight, differing for various papers. See *basis weight.*

basis weight   The weight in pounds per ream of paper cut to its basic size in inches.

beater   The original mechanical refiner, in which paper fibers suspended in water are circulated around an oval tub and passed between the refining surfaces of the rotating metal bars of the beater roll and the stationary metal bars of the bed plate.

beater-sized pulp   Papermaking furnish to which sizing is introduced during refining. *Alternative terms:* internal-sized pulp; engine-sized pulp. See *sizing.*

beater sizing	Sizing introduced to papermaking furnish during refining. Also called *internal sizing*.
Bekk smoothness	The smoothness of paper as measured by the Bekk instrument, expressed as the time required for a given volume of air to flow between the measuring surface and the paper surface.
belt press	A printing press that uses two continuous belts to print books in an in-line operation that transforms rolls of paper to delivered books, ready for binding at the end of the press.
blade coater	A device that first applies a surplus coating to a paper web and then evenly levels and distributes it by means of a flexible steel blade.
blade cut	A blade scratch that cuts deeply into or through the web. See *blade scratch*.
blade scratch	A very fine, hairlike indentation in a coated surface, running in the grain direction; blade scratches are caused by a particle of varied origin becoming lodged behind the blade during coating.
blade streak	A wider indentation than a blade scratch, caused by a large particle having become lodged behind the blade during coating.
blank	A thick type of paperboard, coated or uncoated, produced on a cylinder machine and designed for printing. Thickness ranges from 15 to 48 pt. (0.38 to 1.22 mm).
blanket contamination	Any material that becomes attached to the blanket and interferes with print quality.
bleaching	A chemical treatment and further purification of chemical pulps to bring them to a white state and to improve their chemical stability and permanence; and a chemical treatment of mechanical pulps to alter or remove some of their coloring substances and to improve their brightness.
blister	Oval, sharply defined, bubblelike formation that bulges out on both sides of the web. Such bubbles occur during the heat-set drying of coated papers.

blister cut   A web cut, usually diagonal to the machine direction, normally resulting from excess paper that accumulates as a blister at the entrance of a nip and cuts the paper as it passes through the nip. See *calender cut*.

blocking   The sticking together of printed sheets caused by wet ink that continues to hold them together after the ink dries.

body stock   The paper substrate to which coating is applied for the manufacture of coated printing papers.

bonding strength   Amount of resistance to the forces of picking, splitting, delamination, and splitting of ink films during printing.

bond paper   A writing paper, originally used for printing stocks and bonds, now used for letterheads, stationery, and forms.

book paper   A term used to describe a group of papers of a higher grade than newsprint, which are used primarily for book and publication printing and a wide variety of commercial printing applications. Book papers, as a class, include coated and uncoated papers in a wide variety of basis weights, colors, and finishes.

brightness   Percent of reflectance at a standard wavelength (in the standard test, 457 nm—a blue wavelength that most readily detects the yellowing of paper).

bristol   A heavyweight paper, usually 6 pt. or more in thickness, used for printing, filing, and index systems, and for mailing cards.

bulk   The thickness of a number of sheets of paper or of a number of pages.

bulking index   A paper's single-sheet thickness in inches divided by its basis weight, or its inches of thickness per pound of basis weight.

bulking number   The number of sheets that will bulk 1 in. (25.4 mm) under a specified applied pressure. Bulking number multiplied by 2 gives pages per inch.

burst   An irregular separation or rupture of the web from one of the following causes: entrapped air in the roll during winding;

nonuniform nip velocities between hard and soft sections of high and low caliper, respectively, during winding; an abrupt change in cross-machine sheet caliper; or a roll wound so tightly that its wound-in tension exceeds its ultimate tensile strength.

bursting strength
The resistance of paper or paperboard to rupture as measured by the hydrostatic pressure required to burst it when a uniformly distributed and increasing pressure is applied to one of its sides. *Alternative term:* Mullen test or "pop" test.

business forms bond
A bond paper manufactured for the specific requirements of web printing and converting and the end uses of continuous business forms.

calcium carbonate
A bright white pigment used as a filler in alkaline-sized papers and as a coating pigment.

calcium hypochlorite
A bleaching agent for paper.

calender cut
A diagonal cut in a web normally caused by a blister at the entrance of a nip in a machine calender or supercalender. See *blister cut.*

calendering
Passing the web between the nips of steel rolls at the end of the paper machine to impart the desired finish.

caliper
The thickness of a single sheet of paper or the perpendicular distance between two surfaces, as measured with a micrometer that applies a static load for a specified time; expressed as points, or thousandths of an inch, in traditional units and in micrometers in metric units.

caliper shear burst
A rupture of the web caused by nonuniform nip velocities between a high- and a low-caliper section of the roll during winding.

carbonless paper
Paper that uses a chemical reaction between two different contacting coatings to transfer images when pressure is applied.

carryover piling   Piling that occurs in the image area caused by first-down inks building tack and transferring back from paper to succeeding blankets with enough splitting force to cause the coating to pick.

case-bound book   A book bound with a stiff, hard cover.

cast coater   A device that applies a wet coating to a paper web; the web then contacts a heated drum having a highly polished surface, casting the coating into an image of the smooth, mirrorlike drum surface.

cellulose   A complex polymer structured by nature from carbon, oxygen, and hydrogen; the major component of the cell walls of wood fibers and other plants used in papermaking.

centrifugal cleaner   A device that uses centrifugal force and a cyclone action to remove dirt, metallic particles, and other unwanted material from papermaking fibers prior to papermaking.

chain marks   The larger widely spaced lines, approximately 1 in. (25 mm) apart, that appear in laid-finish papers.

chalking   The dusting off of ink that is not firmly bonded to the paper.

check paper   A strong, durable paper made for the manufacture of bank checks.

chemical ghosting   Gloss or dull ghosts of images that are printed on the reverse side of the sheet, caused by the chemical-activity influence that inks have on each other during their critical drying phases. *Alternative terms:* fuming ghosting; gloss ghosting. See *ghosting*.

chemical pulp   Pulp obtained from wood or other plant sources by chemical digestion, or cooking, that liberates the cellulose from the fibrous raw material.

chemical thermo-mechanical pulp (CTMP)   A mechanical pulp produced by treating wood chips with a mild chemical prior to refining them.

chipper   A device that reduces debarked wooden logs to chips.

chlorine dioxide   A chemically very reactive gas used in one or more of the stages of multiple-stage bleaching of chemical pulps.

CIELab L*a*b*   Scales adopted by the International Commission on Illumination (CIE) for the international use of color measurement.

clay   The material most commonly used as a papermaking filler and for the coating of paper. It is mined in its natural form, then refined for papermaking by crushing, washing, and fractionation.

coated-one-side label   A coated-one-side paper designed specifically for the requirements of label papers, including printing, varnishing, lacquering, bronzing, diecutting, and the labeling application.

coating binder   That part of a coating formulation whose purpose is to bind the pigment system to the body stock and to obtain many of the desired properties of the final coated paper, such as pick and water resistance, ink receptivity, flexibility, gloss, and blister resistance. Binders are obtained from natural sources like starch, casein, and soya protein, or are produced synthetically.

coat weight   The amount of coating applied to base stock, usually expressed as pounds of air-dried coating on the surface of a 25×38-in. (635×965-mm) ream.

Cobb size test   A method of measuring the degree of sizing of paper or paperboard by the weight of water absorbed under prescribed conditions during a specified time.

cockle   A finish produced by air drying, normally applied to bond and onionskin papers.

color   The visual sensation whose characteristics are affected by the wavelengths of the light that produces it. A paper appears colored when it selectively absorbs light of certain wavelengths and reflects light of other wavelengths to the observer.

compressibility   The extent to which a substance undergoes reduction of thickness under pressure, such as that applied by printing impression.

conditioning	The complete and equal exposure of all areas of paper to accurately controlled and specified atmospheric conditions so that its moisture content throughout reaches equilibrium with the surrounding atmosphere. Temperature conditioning refers to bringing the paper's temperature into equilibrium with the atmosphere without removing its wrapping and exposing it to the atmosphere.
conformability	The extent to which a paper's surface will change its contour under printing pressure to contact the ink on the printing plate more completely.
coniferous trees	Cone-bearing (softwood) trees.
contact angle method	A method of indicating the degree of paper sizing by measuring the contact angle that a water drop develops on the paper's surface.
continuous pulping	Production of pulp in a continuous digester as opposed to a batch digester.
contrast ratio opacity	Opacity of paper as measured by the TAPPI contrast ratio method: the ratio of diffuse reflectances of a single sheet of paper when backed by a black, light-absorbing surface to its reflectances when backed by a white, highly reflective surface. See *opacity; diffuse opacity.*
converting paper	A paper made to be altered, fabricated, or changed into a paper product through a conversion process or treatment; for example: envelope paper, carbonizing base paper, and business forms bond.
corrugations	Bands of relatively uniform width that extend around a paper roll parallel to the machine direction and contain diagonal markings resembling a rope or tire-like pattern.
cotton content papers	Papers whose fibrous content is all or partially cotton. Former term: *rag content papers.*
cotton linters	The short, seed-hair fibers that remain on cotton seeds after ginning; these fibers are used to make fine-textured, durable writing papers.

couch roll   A paper machine roll with a perforated shell through which a vacuum is applied for final water removal before transfer of the web to the press section.

cover paper   A heavy paper designed to serve as the outer layer and protective cover of a booklet or paper application.

cracked edge   A broken edge of the web that usually extends only a short distance inward from the edge.

cross-machine direction   A direction perpendicular to the direction of web travel through the paper machine. Abbreviated as CD.

cross-machine tension burst   A burst caused by an abrupt change in cross-machine paper caliper or by winding the roll too tightly.

cut-size paper   Paper cut in small sheets, generally up to and including 11×17 in. (279×432 mm), for use in printing, copying, or duplicating.

cylinder machine   A type of paper machine that forms a web of paper on a cylindrically shaped mold revolving in a vat of water-suspended fibers.

dandy roll   A hollow wire-covered roll that rides on the paper machine wire and compacts the wet, newly formed web to improve its formation and, if required, to impart a watermark or laid finish to the paper.

debarking   The removal of bark from wooden logs or pulpwood sticks by mechanical or hydraulic means prior to their conversion into mechanical or chemical pulps.

deciduous trees   Broadleaf (hardwood) trees, which lose their leaves annually.

deckle   A term sometimes used to refer to the width or trim of a paper machine.

deckle edge   The untrimmed feather edge of paper produced at the edges of the web on the paper machine. Deckle edges are sometimes artificially produced.

dehumidification   The removal of moisture from the air.

deinking

The process of recovering fibers from printed wastepaper by using heat, chemicals, and other means to remove ink and coatings, unwanted materials, and contaminants; a recycling step in the manufacture of white, printing, and writing papers.

delamination

A continuous splitting, or separation, of the paper's surface by the tack of the ink and rubber blanket.

densitometer

An instrument that measures the optical density of a small area of a graphic image or base material.

density (physical)

Mass (or weight) per unit volume. See *apparent density.*

densometer

An instrument that measures the air resistance of paper in terms of the time required for a given volume of air to pass through a given area of the paper under a constant pressure.

dew point

The temperature at which air of a given absolute humidity becomes saturated with water vapor.

diffuse opacity

Opacity determined with an opacimeter by comparing the ratio of light reflected by a single sheet of paper backed by a black body to the same sheet when backed by many thicknesses of itself. Previously known as *printing opacity.*

diffuse reflection

The scattering of light in all directions away from a surface.

digester

The vessel in which wood chips and other fibrous raw materials are cooked with chemicals to liberate cellulose fibers for the production of chemical pulp.

dimensional stability

The degree to which paper maintains its linear dimensions with changes in its moisture content or applied stresses.

dished roll

A roll having a progressive edge misalignment, either concave or convex, that can be observed immediately upon unwrapping.

disk refiner

A device having two vertical disks with refining surfaces of various ridged or serrated contours, in which one disk is rotated while the other is kept stationary, or both disks are rotated in opposite directions, causing pulp fibers to undergo rubbing, rolling, dispersing, and cutting.

dot slurring   Smearing or elongation at the trailing edges of halftone dots.

doubling   The appearance in the print of "ghost" or weaker dots whose positions are out of register with their full-strength, true dots.

doughnut hickey   A printing flaw consisting of a small, solid printed area surrounded by a white halo, or unprinted area.

dryback   The decrease in the gloss of an ink that occurs during the drying of sheetfed offset inks.

dry indicator size test   A method of measuring the water resistance of paper via a water-sensitive dry indicator powder that indicates the end point of the test.

drying oil   An oil that is changed to a solid by the action of oxygen.

dry picking resistance   The picking resistance of paper in the absence of water or moisture, as opposed to wet pick resistance, which involves the presence of moisture. See *picking*.

dull finish enamel   An enamel paper that is supercalendered to a low gloss level.

duplex paper   Paper that has different colors, finishes, or surfaces on its two sides.

duplicating paper   The copy paper used for spirit duplicating.

durability   The ability of paper to maintain its properties with continued use and handling.

dusting   The accumulation of visible-size particles from the paper on the nonimage areas of the blanket. *Alternative term:* powdering.

edge tear   A broken edge of the web that usually extends only a short distance inward from the edge, but can initiate a web break.

edge tearing resistance   The resistance of paper to tearing when the tear is started at its edge.

electronic manifest

A description of a manifest for a shipment of goods (paper) transmitted electronically from a manufacturer's computer to a recipient's computer system on the day of shipment.

electrostatic printing

Any of several nonimpact printing processes that rely on the attraction of a toner to a surface that bears an electrostatic image; examples are laser printing, xerography, electrophotography, and electrography.

embossed finish

A surface pattern given to paper by passing a web between the nip of an engraved metal roll and a mating soft backing roll. Rolls can be engraved to produce various surface patterns.

embossing

Raised, heavily printed areas in a press sheet due to a deformation of the paper from the tack of the ink film and blanket.

emulsification

The process of dispersing one liquid into another as droplets when the two liquids do not mix.

end leaf

A strong paper manufactured for the specific requirements of combining and securing the body of a book to its case.

English finish

The smoothest finish made on a paper machine and obtained through maximum calendering. English-finish book paper has a very uniform formation and high filler content and is calendered to a very smooth, level surface.

envelope paper

Paper made for the specific requirements of diecutting and folding envelopes on high-speed envelope machines.

equilibrium moisture content

The moisture content of paper having the same relative humidity as its surrounding atmosphere, under which condition the paper neither loses nor gains moisture when exposed to the atmosphere.

equilibrium relative humidity

The relative humidity of the atmosphere at which paper, when exposed to the atmosphere, will neither gain nor lose moisture: where the vapor pressure of water vapor in the atmosphere and the vapor pressure of moisture in the paper are equal. See *relative humidity*.

equivalent weight

The basis weight of paper expressed in terms of a different basic size.

esparto   A wild grass that grows in North Africa and Spain, long used as a source of papermaking fiber in European and North African countries.

eucalyptus   Any of numerous species of tall, fast-growing trees indigenous to Australia and grown increasingly in other world regions for pulpwood.

extensible paper   A paper that has a built-in ability to stretch and to withstand sudden shock without tearing.

fadeometer   An instrument used to measure the lightfastness of paper, inks, and other materials under controlled and reproducible conditions.

fanning-in of image   A condition in which the printed image and register marks become narrower at the trailing edge of a press sheet than at its gripper edge; caused by printing on a tight-edged sheet that stretches out during printing and then snaps back.

fanning-in of web   A decrease in web width or sidewise spread after printing a color, which causes succeeding colors to print longer than the preceding.

fanning-out of image   A condition in which a printed image and register marks becomes wider at the trailing edge of a press sheet than at its gripper edge; caused by printing on a long-grain, wavy-edged sheet that compresses toward its center during printing and then springs out again.

fanning-out of web   An increase in web width after printing a color, which causes succeeding colors to print shorter than the preceding.

fastness to light   The ability of paper or paperboard to resist yellowing or fading, or a change in color upon exposure to light.

FDA regulations   Regulations promulgated by the Food and Drug Administration (FDA) for the use of paper, paperboard, and inks for food and drug packaging.

feathering   The lateral spreading of ink over a paper's surface when written upon with a pen having a water-based ink; used as a test for sizing.

felt finish   A finish applied to paper at the wet press with felts having a weave different from that of normal paper machine felts.

felt side   The top side of a paper formed on the single-wire paper machine.

fiber cut   A short, straight, fairly smooth cutting of the web caused by a fiber bundle, or shive, as the paper passes through the calender.

fiber puffing   The roughening of a coated paper surface, primarily of a paper containing groundwood fibers, that occurs during heatset drying.

fibrilla   One of the threadlike elements of the cellulose fiber that is separated from its wall by the action of refining.

fill   Sizes that utilize the full width of papermaking equipment.

filler   Inorganic materials like clay, titanium dioxide, calcium carbonate, and other white pigments added to the papermaking furnish to improve opacity, brightness, and the printing surface. *Alternative term:* loading.

film coating   The application of a very lightweight mineral coating to paper, sometimes at the paper machine size press. *Alternative term:* wash coating.

finish   The surface characteristics of paper, often described by a single term such as vellum or wove.

finishing   The various steps required to prepare paper for shipping in the form requested by the customer, after it has been made on the paper machine or has been coated.

flame-resistant paper   A paper treated with flame-retardant chemicals to prevent the spread of flame if the paper is ignited.

flax tow   Source of linen fibers used for papermaking.

flexural stiffness   Resistance to an applied bending force.

flotation deinking	A method of removing ink and other contaminants from reclaimed paper by producing an ink-bearing froth that rises to the surface of flotation cells and is skimmed off.
fluff	Loosely bonded surface fibers. *Alternative term:* fuzz.
fluffing	The removal of fibrous materials from a paper's surface during printing. *Alternative term:* linting.
fluorescence	A physical process of converting high-frequency radiation (most commonly ultraviolet light) into visible light. Fluorescent materials—such as fluorescent pigment colors—absorb ultraviolet light and discharge it as bright visible light. Fluorescence in paper is made to occur by the use of fluorescent dyes or optical brighteners.
foils	Stationary, arc-shaped plastic surfaces that support the moving paper machine wire and help to remove water from its underside; used in place of table rolls.
folding endurance	The number of double folds a paper will withstand under tension and specified conditions before it breaks at the fold line.
formation	The structure and the degree of uniformity of a paper's fiber distribution, as judged by transmitted light.
fourdrinier	A paper machine, named after the brothers who first made it commercially successful, that forms a continuous web of paper on a horizontal, forward-moving, endless wire belt.
free sheet	A paper that does not contain groundwood or mechanical pulp.
friction	The resistance to movement that is created when one material slides or tends to slide over itself or another material. See *static friction; kinetic friction.*
frozen stresses	Stresses in paper caused by the web being dried under tension and remaining after the web has been dried.
fuming ghosting	See *chemical ghosting.*

furnish	The mixture of fibrous materials and nonfibrous additives such as fillers, sizing, and colorants in a water suspension from which paper or paperboard is made.
fuzz	Loosely bonded surface fibers. *Alternative term:* fluff.
galvanized	See *mottled.*
ghosting	The appearance of faint replicas of images in undesirable places, caused by chemical or mechanical processes other than setoff or show-through. See *chemical ghosting; mechanical ghosting.*
gloss	The attribute of paper that causes it to be shiny or lustrous.
gloss ghosting	See *chemical ghosting.*
glueability	The speed of bonding and the bonding strength that develops when the two surfaces of a paper or paperboard are joined with adhesive.
grain	The pronounced alignment of paper fibers in the direction of their flow on the paper machine.
grain direction	The direction of the predominant orientation of paper or paperboard fibers, parallel to the direction of flow of fibers on the paper machine.
graininess of halftones	Nonuniformity of tone in halftone dots, resulting in a sandpaper-like appearance.
grain-long	Having grain parallel to the longer dimension of the sheet.
grain-short	Having grain parallel to the shorter dimension of the sheet.
grainy edge	A surface roughness that sometimes develops at the outer extremities of the paper web during its drying.
grammage	The designation of paper or paperboard weight in the metric system as grams per square meter.
groundwood free	A paper that does not contain groundwood or mechanical pulp.

groundwood pulp	Pulp produced by grinding bark-free logs against a revolving stone in the presence of water at atmospheric pressure.
gummed paper	A paper coated on one side with an adhesive activated by water.
Gurley densometer	A device for measuring the resistance of paper to the passage of air, expressed as the time required for the passage of 100 cm^3 of air through 1 sq.in. of paper under specified conditions.
gusseting	A waviness and, in extreme cases, actual creases that form at the heads of the inner pages of a closed-head press signature.
hair cut	A smooth, curved cutting of the web that occurs as an imbedded hair in the web passes through the calender.
handling stiffness	The ability of a paper to support its own weight when being used, for example, during the reading of a newspaper.
hardbound book	See *case-bound book.*
hardness	The degree of a paper's resistance to indentation by some other material or object, such as type, a printing plate, or a stylus, pen, or pencil.
hard-sized	Having a high degree of internal sizing. See *sizing.*
hardwood trees	Deciduous or broadleaf trees, which lose their leaves annually.
headbox	The part of a paper machine that delivers a uniform dispersion of fibers in water at the proper velocity through the slice opening to the paper machine wire.
heat-resistance splice	A splice made with splicing materials that will not soften and cause splice failure when the paper web reaches elevated temperatures during heatset drying.
heat seal	Use of heat for sealing bags or containers made from thermoplastic materials.
heat-seal paper	A label paper coated on one side with an adhesive that is activated and becomes tacky with the application of heat.

heat-transfer paper   Paper used as the substrate for heat transfer printing. The paper is first printed with the desired pattern using inks containing sublimable dispersed dyes. When the printed paper is brought into contact with the fabric by the application of heat and pressure, the dyes transfer the design to the fabric by sublimation.

hemicellulose   A constituent of wood that is, like cellulose, a polysaccharide, but less complex and easily hydrolyzable.

hemp fiber   Papermaking fiber obtained from the hemp plant, which grows in Central America and the Philippines, or from rope or cordage made from hemp.

hickey   An imperfection in printing consisting of either a small, solid printed area surrounded by a white halo, sometimes described as a doughnut hickey, or an unprinted spot surrounded by printing, called a void hickey.

humidification   The addition of moisture to the air.

humidity   A term that describes the presence and quantity of water vapor existing as a gas along with other gases in the atmosphere.

Hunter L,a,b values   Scales, widely used to define and measure color, devised by Hunter Associates Laboratory, Inc.

hygro-expansivity   The percent elongation or shrinkage of a paper caused by a given change in its moisture content.

hygrometer   An instrument used to measure the relative humidity of air.

hygrometry   The measurement of humidity.

hygroscopic   Capable of absorbing moisture from the air.

hysteresis   The amount of change in moisture content of a paper indicated by its ascending and descending curves for relative humidity representing opposite starting points in its conditioning history. Due to hysteresis, the equilibrium moisture content of a paper, when conditioned to a specified relative humidity, will differ depending on its previous moisture history.

image area piling   A puttylike buildup of paper materials and inks on the image area of the blanket, which takes on the color of the ink.

impression tolerance   The relative ease with which paper receives letterpress images and its ability to produce acceptable print quality with impression pressures higher or lower than the optimum.

index bristol   A bristol paper designed for file cards and records, index systems, and ruled forms.

ink absorbency   The property of paper that determines the rate and the amount of ink penetration into its surface after ink is applied by the press plate or blanket.

ink chalking   A condition, believed to be caused by drier inactivation, in which a printed ink film can be easily rubbed off the paper (usually coated paper).

ink flotation sizing test   A method of measuring the degree of internal sizing by floating a test sample on a colored writing ink and measuring the time for ink penetration through the paper.

ink hickey   An imperfection in printing caused by a particle of dried ink or ink skin that prints as a dark spot surrounded by a white halo.

ink holdout   The extent to which paper retards the inward penetration of a freshly printed ink film.

ink-in-water emulsion   An emulsion of ink and water in which the ink is broken up into fine droplets surrounded by water. See *water-in-ink emulsion*.

ink jet printing   A nonimpact printing process that produces images on paper or a recording surface by electrically controlling the flow of a high-velocity stream of microscopic ink droplets from a pressurized ink jet system.

ink receptivity   The ability of a paper surface to accept ink uniformly and adequately from the plate or blanket during printing.

ink rub resistance   The resistance of an ink film to scuffing or rubbing on paper or paperboard, as measured using abrasion or rub testing devices.

ink setoff	The transfer of wet ink from the surface of a freshly printed sheet to the back of its succeeding sheet in the delivery pile.
ink setting	The penetration of an ink vehicle into a paper surface to the extent that pigment particles are compacted to a relatively solid layer whose surface is no longer fluid enough to transfer to adjacent sheets.
inkometer	An instrument that measures the tack of an ink.
internal bond strength	The transverse force required to delaminate a unit area of paper.
internal sizing	Sizing incorporated into the papermaking furnish and existing throughout the paper's structure. *Alternative term: beater sizing.* See *sizing*.
internal tear resistance	The amount of work required to tear paper through a fixed distance after the tear has been started.
International Standards Organization (ISO)	An organization that establishes and coordinates uniform, internationally accepted standards.
ISO paper sizes	A range of paper sizes that have a constant width-to-length ratio, or aspect ratio, of 1 to 1.414; when cut in half, papers in this size range produce sizes that retain that same width-to-length ratio.
jordan	A refiner consisting of a conical rotor with longitudinal bars surrounded by a shell, also fitted with longitudinal bars, so that fibers are brushed out and cut. Jordan refining follows refining by a disk or beater.
jute	Paper fibers obtained from cuttings of burlap or sacks made from the jute plant, which grows principally in India and Pakistan. Jute is used for exceptionally hard and durable papers such as tag.
K and N ink absorbency	A practical test for comparing the ink absorption rate of different papers. A thick film of a nondrying ink is applied to overlapped samples of different papers for a specified time; when the ink is removed and wiped clean; the depth of stain indicates relative ink absorbency.

Kamyr digester   A vertical digester for the continuous cooking of wood chips and the production of chemical pulp.

kaolin   A fine, white clay used as a filler or coating pigment in the manufacture of paper.

kenaf   An annual agricultural plant, native to India, that has a long fiber in its bark that is suitable for papermaking.

kinetic friction   Resistance to the continuing sliding of one material over the same or another material once movement has begun.

kraft paper   A strong paper made from sulfate pulp, used for paper products like wrapping, bags, and envelopes.

label paper   A paper, usually coated one side, made for the specific requirements of labeling applications, including printing, finishing, and performance with labeling equipment.

laid   A finish produced with a dandy roll having closely spaced wires.

laid antique   An antique finish paper made with a laid-type dandy roll simulating the finish of the handmade paper.

laid line   One of the fine, closely spaced lines of a laid finish paper, as contrasted to its widely spaced, perpendicular chain lines.

latex-treated paper   Paper whose fibrous network is impregnated with latex for durability, high edge-tear resistance, wet strength, and flexible, leatherlike properties. It may be coated for improved printability and resistance to oils, grease, and water.

ledger paper   A paper similar to bond, but made in heavier basis weights to provide the stiffness and durability needed for data entry, ruling, and record systems.

levelness   The evenness of macroscopic surface contour.

lignin   The complex constituent of wood that binds its cellulose fibers together.

lightfastness   The ability of paper to resist change in color, fading, and yellowing, upon exposure to light.

lightweight coated (LWC)   Coated paper whose basis weight, at a basic size of 25×38 in. (635×965 mm), is 40 lb./ream (59 g/m^2) or less, primarily the no. 5 groundwood grade level, which is printed in roll form only.

lightweight printing paper   Printing paper that has exceptionally high opacity for its weight and is designed for printing applications requiring lightweight paper. These papers, at a basic size of 25×38 in. (635×965 mm), have a basis weight range of 17–40 lb./ream (25–59 g/m^2).

linen finish   A finish imparted to paper originally by plating with linen cloth, now by embossing with a linen-cloth pattern.

lint   Loosely bonded surface fibers that become attached to a plate or blanket and interfere with print quality.

linting   The removal of fibrous material from paper during printing. *Alternative term:* fluffing.

loading   Inorganic materials like clay, titanium dioxide, calcium carbonate, or other white pigments added to the papermaking furnish to improve opacity, brightness, and the printing surface of paper. *Alternative term:* filler.

long-grain sheet   A sheet whose longer dimension parallels the grain direction.

machine direction   The direction in which fibers flow to the paper machine; the direction of web travel through the paper machine.

machine finish   A smooth finish obtained on the paper machine by calendering.

machine glazed   Having a highly polished finish applied to one side of the paper by drying it against the polished surface of the large-diameter cylinder of a Yankee-type paper machine.

making order   An order for items not stocked but made according to the specifications of the purchaser.

manifold paper   A lightweight bond paper used for making carbon or manifold copies or for airmail correspondence.

manila hemp   A fiber, obtained in the Philippines and Central and South America, used for manufacturing strong, tough papers.

matte surface	A surface having a very low gloss, reflecting most of the incident light in all directions.
mechanical ghosting	Ghosting caused by ink starvation or by a blanket with a swollen or depressed area. See *ghosting*.
mechanical pulp	Pulp produced from wood by mechanical treatment and without chemicals; for example, by grinding wooden logs or passing wood chips through a disk refiner.
MICR check paper	Paper suitable for checks whose characters are printed with magnetic ink in a special magnetic ink character recognition font that permits automatic sorting and processing by special equipment.
milking	A buildup and consequent softening of coating on the non-image areas of the blanket, usually resulting from the insufficient water resistance of the coating.
mimeograph paper	A copy paper made for the stencil duplicating process.
moisture-barrier wrapper	A wrapper designed to act as a barrier to the transmission of moisture, to prevent the harmful consequences of moisture loss or gain.
moisture content	The amount of moisture contained by paper, expressed as a percentage of its total weight.
moisture welts	Bands, raised welts, or soft wrinkles, appearing close to the outer part of the roll and running in the machine direction, caused by moisture absorption from the air. *Alternative term:* moisture wrinkles.
mottled	Visibly nonuniform density, gloss, or color of printed ink films. *Alternative term:* galvanized.
Mullen test	The test commonly used to measure bursting strength, and named for the machine that performs the test. *Alternative terms:* burst and "pop."
multistage bleaching	Bleaching in successive steps to obtain white fibers without chemical damage.

nanometer   The unit for measuring light wavelengths. Equal to 10^{-9} meter.

NASTA   The acronym for the National Association of State Textbook Administrators, an organization that establishes specifications for all materials used to manufacture elementary and high school textbooks.

newsprint   A paper manufactured mostly from groundwood or mechanical pulp, specifically for the printing of newspapers.

nip   The line of contact between two rolls in a papermaking or printing operation, particularly those through which the paper passes (such as a calender, supercalender, or offset printing press).

nominal weight   The basis weight for ordering and specifying paper and the basis weight to which paper is made, allowing for manufacturing tolerances.

nonreturnable core   A fiber or paper roll core that is used only once.

nonwood fibers   Papermaking fibers derived from plants other than trees such as cotton, flax tow, bagasse, hemp, jute, bamboo, grasses, and cereal straw.

nonwoven   Fabric-like materials, made from fibers longer than those normally used for papermaking and bonded together by chemical, mechanical, heat, or solvent treatment.

OCR paper   Paper made for the specific needs of optical character recognition equipment.

off-machine coating   Application of coating to paper after it has been removed from the paper machine, or as a separate operation to papermaking.

offset paper   A printing paper, coated or uncoated, made for the specific requirements of offset printing.

onionskin   A lightweight, air-dried, cockle finish bond paper used for file copies of correspondence and for airmail stationery.

on-machine coating	Application of coating to the paper at the paper machine or in-line as it is being made.
opacimeter	An instrument used to measure the opacity of paper.
opacity	The property of paper that obstructs its light transmission and prevents the show-through of printing.
optical brightener	A colorless dye that has the ability to absorb ultraviolet radiation and to emit it as visible radiation. The visual brightness of paper is increased by using an optical brightener.
optical density	The ability of an image area to absorb some portion of incident light, expressed as the logarithm of the image opacity.
out-of-roundness	A roll shape irregularity caused by storing a roll on its side, using excessive roll clamp pressure, or dropping or bumping the roll.
outturn sample	A representative sample taken from a run of paper or from a delivery.
oxidation	Combining oxygen with the drying oil in a printing ink to promote a slow chemical reaction that produces a dry ink film.
page pull test	A test that measures the force required to pull a page from the backbone of an adhesive-bound book.
paperboard	A paperlike product having greater basis weight, thickness, and rigidity than paper. With a few exceptions, paperboard has a thickness of 12 points (0.3 mm) or more.
papeterie	A heavily filled, uncoated paper with a smooth, vellum, or embossed finish, used for the manufacture of greeting cards and social correspondence.
papyrus	A tall plant native to the Nile region, whose pith was sliced and pressed into matted sheets by the early Egyptians to produce the first writing material exhibiting many of the properties of paper. The word "paper" originated from papyrus.

perfect white surface   A theoretical surface that reflects light diffusely in all directions, reflects light of all wavelengths uniformly, and absorbs no light component of the spectrum.

permanence   The ability of a paper to resist change in one or more of its properties during storage and with aging.

pH   The potential of the hydrogen ion, a measure of the degree of acidity or alkalinity, expressed as the negative logarithm of the concentration of hydrogen ions in moles per liter.

picking   A disturbance of the paper's surface that occurs during ink transfer when the forces required to split an ink film are greater than those required to break away portions of the surface.

pigment   A finely divided solid organic or inorganic white or colored material that is insoluble in substances such as water and oils, in contrast to a dye, which is soluble. White pigments like clay, titanium dioxide, and calcium carbonate are used in papermaking. Colored pigments are commonly used in printing inks.

piling   Materials from paper, ink, or paper and ink that accumulate on a blanket in sufficient quantity to affect print quality. Piling may occur in the image or nonimage areas.

plate finish   A high finish, produced by supercalendering, originally achieved by placing paper between polished metal plates and subjecting it to a repeated rolling pressure.

plucking   A disruption of a paper surface strong enough to overcome the internal bonding of the fibers or of the coating to the base paper. Plucking is caused by tack forces of the ink and rubber blanket. *Alternative term:* surface picking.

ply   (1) A designation of thickness for blanks and other paperboards. (2) The number of individual sheets of paper that make up a set of business forms.

polymerization   A chemical reaction — usually carried out with a catalyst, heat, or water, and often under high pressure — in which a large number of relatively simple molecules combine to form a chain-like macro-molecule. Some printing inks dry by polymerization (a chemical reaction between the binder and solvent leaves a tough and hard ink deposit on the substrate).

"pop" test   An expression used to describe the Mullen or bursting strength test.

porosity   The ease with which air passes through paper, which may be expressed as the rate at which air flows through a given area under stated conditions.

powdering   The accumulation of visible-size particles from paper on the nonimage areas of the blanket. *Alternative term:* dusting.

precision sheeting   Sheeting produced to accurately controlled dimensions and tolerances so that guillotine trimming becomes unnecessary.

prekissing   A premature contact of paper and rubber blanket as the paper approaches the printing nip, which results in doubling.

pressurized groundwood (PGW)   A mechanical pulp produced by grinding wood under pressure at temperatures over 212°F (100°C).

printability   The extent to which the properties of paper lend themselves to the true reproduction of copy by the printing process used.

printing opacity   See *diffuse opacity*.

printing smoothness   The degree of contact, under printing pressure, between a paper's surface and the ink film on the printing plate.

print quality   The degree to which the appearance and other properties of a print approach the desired result.

pulp   Fibrous material for papermaking produced either mechanically or chemically from cellulose raw material.

pulpwood   Wood in various forms, such as round wood, logs, chips, sawdust, shavings, slabs, and edgings, used for the manufacture of wood pulp.

quality control   The testing and evaluation of products against an established standard during manufacture and the rejection of products that do not meet specifications.

raw stock
The paper to which coating is applied.

recovered fibers
Fibers recovered from wastepaper, from printing and converting operations wastes, and from forest and lumber mill residues for the manufacture of paper or paperboard.

recycled fibers
Fibers utilized from wastepaper for making paper or paperboard.

reel
The untrimmed roll of paper that is wound on the full-width shaft at the paper machine dry end.

refiner mechanical pulp (RMP)
A mechanical pulp produced by passing wood chips through a disk refiner with water instead of grinding the chips against a stone.

refining
The use of a mechanical device to break down papermaking fibers in preparation for papermaking.

refraction
The bending of light rays as they pass from one medium into another having a different refractive index.

register bond
See *business forms bond.*

relative humidity
The percent ratio of the pressure of water vapor in the air to the pressure of the saturated water vapor in air at the same temperature; the percent ratio of the amount of water vapor in the air to the maximum amount the air can hold at the same temperature.

resiliency
The ability of paper to recover its original thickness and surface contour after a printing impression.

ridge
A convex ring extending around a paper roll circumference caused by the buildup of a thicker-caliper strip parallel to the grain direction.

rigidity
Resistance to bending or flexing.

roll coating
The application, by rollers, of a premetered film of coating to a paper web.

roll-set curl
Curl resulting from paper having been kept in roll form so long that its curved condition becomes permanently set and

causes a cross-grain curl after sheeting. Can also result if reel-set curl is not sufficiently broken by decurling during sheeting. *Alternative term:* wrap curl.

rope mark   See *corrugation*.

rosin sizing   A chemically dispersed sizing material derived from rosin and commonly added to a papermaking furnish for imparting water resistance to paper. See *sizing*.

runnability   The ability of a paper to be printed without causing problems in the mechanics of the printing operation.

safety paper   Paper made to expose the forgery or alteration of documents by mechanical or chemical means and to meet the physical requirements of handling checks and other negotiable documents.

saturated air   Air that contains the maximum amount of water vapor it can hold at its existing temperature; air whose relative humidity is 100%.

secondary fibers   Fibers derived from wastepaper for reuse in papermaking.

semichemical pulp   Pulp produced by first giving wood chips a mild chemical cooking to partially remove and soften their lignin binder, then fiberizing the chips in a disk refiner; a high-yield pulp used for corrugated board, cores, and containers.

setoff   The undesirable transfer of wet ink to the succeeding sheet in the delivery pile.

shaded watermark   A watermark whose image-area paper is somewhat more opaque than the rest of the paper and has a darker appearance when viewed with transmitted light, as compared to a conventional watermark, which is visible because of its greater transparency. See *watermark*.

shake   The oscillation of the paper machine wire in a direction perpendicular to its forward travel, for improved fiber distribution and formation. Shake is not used on high-speed machines.

Sheffield porosity	The porosity of paper as measured by the Sheffield porosimeter, expressed as the rate of airflow through a specified area under stated conditions.
Sheffield smoothness	The smoothness of paper as measured by the Sheffield paper smoothness gauge, expressed as the rate of airflow between the measuring surface and the paper surface under specified conditions.
shive	An undefibered fiber bundle removed from wood during grinding, or one of a group of undigested fiber bundles remaining after the cooking of chemical pulp.
short-grain sheet	A sheet whose shorter dimension parallels the grain direction.
show-through	Visibility of printing on the reverse side of the paper.
side roll	A roll run side by side with other rolls to give a paper machine fill.
size press	That part of the paper machine at which surface sizing is applied to the web by passing it through the nip of two rollers.
sizing	The treatment of paper with materials or chemicals to impart resistance to water, oils, and other fluids, to seal down its surface fibers, and to improve its surface strength.
skips	Missing dots in gravure printing caused by lack of ink transfer from the individual cells of the gravure cylinder to the paper during printing impression. *Alternative terms:* snow; speckle.
slack-sized paper	A paper having a low degree of internal sizing.
slice	The adjustable rectangular orifice at the front of the paper machine headbox whose purpose is to deliver a continuous stream of water-suspended fibers having a uniform thickness, consistency, and velocity across the paper machine close to the wire speed.
slime spot	A fragile spot or hole in the paper resulting from a bacterial growth or slime that originated in the papermaking system and was formed into the paper.

sling psychrometer   A device having wet- and dry-bulb thermometers that are whirled vertically in the atmosphere to provide readings from which, in conjunction with psychrometric tables, the percent relative humidity is determined.

slurring   The smearing or elongation of halftone dots or type and line images at their trailing edges.

smashed bulk   The bulk of a number of sheets or pages of paper under a suddenly applied pressure and compression, as applied during the casing-in operation of book manufacturing.

smoothness   The evenness of microscopic surface contour.

snow   See *skips*.

snowflaking   Fine white specks that appear in offset printing, caused by water droplets remaining in the printing nip during impression.

soda pulp   A soft-fibered pulp produced by cooking hardwood chips with caustic soda.

softness   The comparative lack of resistance to indentation by a material or object such as type, a printing plate, or a stylus, pen, or pencil.

soft-nip calendering   A calendering process by which paper is passed through the elastic or soft nip of mating steel and soft-covered, resilient rolls, as opposed to the hard nip of all-steel-roll calendering.

softwood   Wood from the long-fibered coniferous trees.

speckle   See *skips*.

spectral reflectance curve   A curve that measures the reflection of light from objects as a function of wavelength throughout the visible spectrum.

spectro-photometer   An instrument that measures the color of paper as a wavelength analysis of its reflected light.

specular reflection   The reflection of light rays at an angle equal to the angle of incidence; for example, the reflection from a mirror.

spine	The back, or bound, edge of a book.
spirit duplication	A duplication process that involves moistening an alcohol-soluble dye image on a coated master and transferring it to a copy paper.
splitting	The tearing of large paper surface areas from a press sheet, usually starting in solid printed areas and continuing to the trailing edge of the sheet, sometimes forming a V-shaped tear.
standard testing conditions	Officially recognized environmental conditions under which paper is conditioned and tested for many of its properties; the TAPPI standard atmosphere for paper testing — 50% relative humidity and 73°F (23°C).
starred roll	A paper roll whose end has a star pattern resulting from a buckling of its too-loosely-wound inner layers caused by the force of tightly wound outer layers.
static electricity	The accumulation of electrons on materials such as paper whenever they are subjected to friction, pressure, or a sudden separation from various surfaces; static electricity causes interference with sheet separation and movement through a printing press.
static friction	The resisting force of friction before one surface begins to slide over another.
stencil duplication	See *mimeograph*.
stiffness	The ability of paper or paperboard to resist an applied bending force; especially, its ability to support its own weight when handled.
stock preparation	The treatment and modification of fibers to make them suitable for papermaking, including the beating, refining, and blending of fibrous and nonfibrous materials in the desired proportions for the papermaking furnish.
stress	The state of an object or material when it is resisting some applied force. Fibers in paper are usually under stress because of their shrinkage during drying.

strike-through   Excessive penetration of ink into or through paper.

structural curl   Curl resulting from structural differences between the two sides of paper, or from causes otherwise related to its structure.

styrene-butadiene   A synthetic latex commonly used as a coating binder because of the improved properties it imparts to coated paper.

substance   The basis weight of papers whose basic size is 17×22 in. (432×559 mm). *Alternative term:* substance number.

subway test   An adhesive-binding durability test that consists of evaluating the damage done to an adhesive-bound book after its pages have been separated in its middle and it has been bent completely backward, cover to cover, thereby subjecting the page joints at the backbone to maximum bending strain.

sulfate pulp   Chemical pulp produced by cooking wood chips in a solution of sodium hydroxide and sodium sulfide.

sulfite pulp   Chemical pulp produced by cooking wood chips with sulfurous acid and one of its base salts, which may be calcium, sodium, magnesium, or ammonia.

supercalender   A calender consisting of alternate hard steel rolls and soft filled rolls, giving a high-gloss finish to paper passing through the nips because of the slippage that occurs between a hard and a soft roll. A supercalender is operated separately from a paper machine or coater.

surface picking   See *picking*.

surface sizing   Sizing added to the paper's surface at the paper machine size press for increased ink holdout, higher pick resistance, greater surface hardness, and a cementing down of fibers to prevent fuzz and linting on an offset press.

surface strength   The ability of a paper to resist a perpendicularly applied force to its surface, such as that in the splitting of an ink film, before picking or rupturing occurs.

synthetic papers   Paperlike materials made by extruding a continuous plastic film; by the spinning, interweaving, and bonding of synthetic fibers; or by a papermaking process whereby cellulose fibers are replaced in part or completely by synthetic fibers.

tack
The resistance of an ink film to being split between two surfaces, as between rollers, plate and blanket, or blanket and paper.

tag
A strong, dense, hard, heavily calendered paper made from sulfate pulp and used for heavy-duty applications.

tail-end hook
A curl that develops at the back edge of press sheets as a result of printing heavy solids close to their back edge.

TAPPI brightness
The reflecting power of a pad of paper as measured with blue light (457 nm) under prescribed optical and geometrical conditions, as described in the TAPPI Official Test Method T 452.

Technical Association of the Pulp and Paper Industry (TAPPI)
A professional organization having international membership among the paper and allied industries, whose purpose is to further scientific advancement, research, and technical manpower needs, and to establish recognized technical standards (TAPPI Standards) and testing procedures pertaining to the manufacture and use of pulp and paper.

tear-at-the-fold
Paper coming apart at the fold because most of the fibers break during the folding process. Tear-at-the-fold (TAF) occurs mostly with heatset web printing because of the moisture loss in the dryer. Since moisture acts as a plasticizer for the fibers, the drier the fibers become, the more likely they will break when the paper is folded.

telescoped roll
A roll with progressive edge misalignment, concave or convex, due to slippage of its inner layers in the direction of its axis as a result of a thrust force on or within its body after being wound.

temperature conditioning
Bringing paper to pressroom temperature before it is unwrapped and printed.

tensile-at-the-fold
A test for predicting the extent to which coated papers will withstand heat degradation and folding without cracking or splitting at the fold line following heatset drying on web presses.

tensile breaking strength

The maximum tensile stress paper will withstand before breaking, when tested under prescribed conditions.

tensile energy absorption (TEA)

The energy-absorbing capacity of paper; its ability to withstand shock.

text paper

Fine-quality printing paper available in many finishes and textured surfaces, in white and colors, and with plain or deckle edges. Text is designed for deluxe printed booklets, programs, announcements, and advertising, and may be watermarked.

thermo-mechanical pulp (TMP)

Pulp produced by passing steam-preheated wood chips or sawdust through a disk refiner.

tight edges

Paper edges that have lost moisture and have shrunk because of their exposure to an atmosphere having a lower relative humidity than that of the paper.

tinting

A light scum that appears on unprinted areas of the plate and paper during offset printing, differing from ordinary plate scumming in that it can be removed from the plate with water when it first appears. Tinting, however, quickly returns when printing is resumed.

titanium dioxide

The oxide of the metal titanium, a very bright filler pigment used for its unexcelled efficiency in increasing paper brightness and opacity; a coating pigment used for the same purposes.

top-wire former

A machine that first forms paper by a short movement of a horizontal wire after which the topside of the paper is contacted by a second or top-wire, allowing water drainage to occur upward and downward from the web.

trapping

The acceptance by a previously printed ink of a succeeding overprinting ink film.

trim

(1) The widest web of paper, after allowance for trimmed edges, that can be made on a paper machine. (2) The paper trimmed off the edges of a web or sheet during finishing.

tub sizing Sizing added to the surface of paper by passing a web through a tub or bath of sizing, removing the excess, and drying. See *sizing*.

turnover A cracked edge or a slight tear in the edge of the web that has been folded over during slitting, winding, or printing.

twin-wire former A type of paper machine that uses two converging paper machine wires between which the sheet of paper is formed and through which water is drained from both sides of the sheet as it is being formed.

underrun A production and delivery of paper in less than the quantity ordered.

vegetable parchment A greaseproof paper with high wet strength, made by passing a paper web through a sulfuric acid bath that fuses its fibers into a homogenous mass.

vehicle The liquid part of an ink that gives it the flow properties that enable it to be applied to a surface.

vellum finish A fine-grained paper finish, smoother than antique.

virgin fiber A fiber derived from the original wood or plant source and used for the first time in papermaking.

viscoelastic Having the ability to be stretched up to a point and return to original size upon release of the applied stress.

viscosity The resistance offered to flow.

void hickey An imperfection in a printed image that appears as a white spot of missing image surrounded by printing. See *hickey*.

waffling Bands of embossing that occur where repetitious heavily printed image areas stretch and deform the paper because of the tack forces of the ink and blanket.

water finish A high, glossy finish obtained by moistening the paper web as it passes through the calender or by applying water to the calender rolls.

water immersion size test
A test of sizing made by measuring the weight of water absorbed by a sized paper or paperboard sample after it has been immersed in water for a given time and under specified conditions. See *sizing*.

water-in-ink emulsion
An emulsion of ink and water in which the water is broken up into droplets surrounded by ink.

waterleaf
A paper that absorbs water instantly. An unsized paper.

waterlogged ink
An ink that contains enough emulsified water to reduce its flow and its workability.

watermark
A localized modification in a sheet of paper, usually consisting of a visible reduction in the opacity of the paper, resulting in a translucent image. A watermark is produced by a dandy roll or watermarking bands while the paper still contains a large amount of water. See *shaded watermark*.

water vapor transmission rate
The weight of water (in grams) transmitted from one side of a 1-m^2 area of paper or paperboard to the other side in a one-day period under prescribed conditions; used to determine the effectiveness of a packaging paper as a moisture barrier.

wavy edges
Edges of paper that have become wavy and distorted by moisture absorption and fiber expansion due to exposure to a higher relative humidity than that of the paper or from cold paper being unwrapped and exposed to warmer air.

wax test
A pick test method using a series of graded adhesive stick waxes to measure the surface strength of paper.

wedding paper
A paper having a very uniform, closed formation and a refined surface without glare, used for printed and engraved wedding stationery, announcements, and executive correspondence.

wet end
The forming section of the paper machine; the section between the headbox and the dryer.

wet pick resistance
The resistance paper offers to picking after it has absorbed moisture.

wet strength
The strength of paper after it has been saturated with water for a specified time, determined by its wet tensile strength or its wet bursting strength.

wet tensile breaking strength
The tensile breaking strength of paper after it has been saturated with water.

wetting agent
A material capable of lowering the surface tension of water and water solutions and increasing their wetting power.

whiteness
The extent to which paper diffusely reflects light of all wavelengths throughout the visible spectrum. The assigned ideal white standard totally reflects all light throughout the spectrum. Departure of a preferred or observed whiteness from the assigned whiteness standard can be determined by comparing their spectral reflectance curves.

whitening
The accumulation of fine white material on the nonimage areas of the blanket.

whole-tree utilization
Cutting a tree at its base or ground level and converting its entire foliage, branches, and trunk into chips at the harvesting site.

wire mark
The impression of the paper formed by contact with the paper machine wire.

wire side
The side of the paper formed by contact with the paper machine wire.

wood free
A paper that does not contain groundwood or mechanical pulp. *Alternative term:* groundwood free.

wood pulp
Papermaking pulp obtained from wood.

work-and-tumble imposition
An imposition that uses the same guide edge of the press sheet and press guide but a different gripper edge of the sheet for printing its second side. *Alternative term:* work-and-flop imposition.

work-and-turn imposition
An imposition that uses the same gripper edge of the press sheet but the opposite press guide for printing its second side. *Alternative term:* print-and-turn imposition.

wove   Having the normal or regular finish of paper, as produced
                      with a plain-woven wire covering on the dandy roll.

xerography   A process of producing copies of an original by electrostatic
                      means.

yankee dryer   A single large steam-heated drying cylinder that produces a
                      glazed finish on the side of the paper that dries against it.

Z-direction   The tensile strength of paper measured perpendicularly to
tensile strength its surface.

Index

About the Author

Larry Wilson is president of Wilson's Consulting Service, Arrowsic, Maine. A graduate of the Rochester Institute of Technology with degrees in printing and chemistry, he started his career in graphic arts as superintendent of W.B. Saunders Publishing Company's offset printing plant, where he worked for six years. For the next 30 years Wilson worked for S.D Warren Company, a major paper manufacturer, where he handled customer complaints and directed the company's graphic arts research efforts. He spent the last ten years of his career with S.D. Warren as a leader for total quality management (TQM) and as human resource director.

Wilson also headed the Graphic Communications Association (GCA) Print Properties Committee. This committee, under his leadership, tested all phases of the printing process affecting image reproduction and quality.

About GATF

The Graphic Arts Technical Foundation is a nonprofit, scientific, technical, and educational organization dedicated to the advancement of the graphic communications industries worldwide. Its mission is to serve the field as the leading resource for technical information and services through research and education. GATF is a partner of the Printing Industries of America (PIA), the world's largest graphic arts trade association.

For 76 years the Foundation has developed leading edge technologies and practices for printing. GATF's staff of researchers, educators, and technical specialists partner with nearly 14,000 corporate members in over 80 countries to help them maintain their competitive edge by increasing productivity, print quality, process control, and environmental compliance, and by implementing new techniques and technologies. Through conferences, satellite symposia, workshops, consulting, technical support, laboratory services, and publications, GATF strives to advance a global graphic communications community.

The GATFPress publishes books on nearly every aspect of the field; learning modules (step-by-step instruction booklets); audio-visuals (CD-ROMs and videotapes); and research and technology reports. It also publishes *GATFWorld,* a bimonthly magazine of technical articles, industry news, and reviews of specific products.

For more detailed information on GATF products and services, please visit our website *http://www.gatf.org* or write to us at 200 Deer Run Road, Sewickley, PA 15143-2600 (phone: 412/741-6860).

Orders to:
GATF Orders
P.O. Box 1020
Sewickley, PA 15143-1020
Phone (U.S. and Canada only): 800/662-3916
Phone (all other countries): 412/741-5733
Fax: 412/741-0609
Email: gatforders@abdintl.com

GATF*Press:* Selected Titles

Colophon

What the Printer Should Know about Paper was edited, designed, and printed at the Graphic Arts Technical Foundation, headquartered in Sewickley, Pennsyvlania. The manuscript was edited in Microsoft Word and then imported into QuarkXPress for page layout. Line drawings were created in Adobe Illustrator, and photographs were scaled and cropped in Adobe Photoshop. Page proofs for author approval were produced on a Xerox Regal color copier with Splash RIP.

After the editorial/page layout process was completed, the images were transmitted to GATF's Center for Imaging Excellence, where all images were adjusted for the printing parameters of GATF's in-house printing department and proofed.

Next, the entire book was preflighted, digitally imposed using DK&A INposition, and then output to a Creo Trendsetter 3244 platesetter. The cover was printed two-up on a 19×25-in., six-color Komori Lithrone 28 sheetfed press with aqueous coater. The interior was printed on a 23×35-in., four-color Heidelberg Speedmaster Model 102-4P sheetfed press. Finally, the book was sent to a trade bindery for case binding.